MW01077734

BARRON'S BUSINESS LIBRARY

Credit and Collections

BARRON'S BUSINESS LIBRARY

Credit
and
Collections

James John Jurinski

BARRON'S

All inquiries should be addressed to:
Barron's Educational Series, Inc.
250 Wireless Boulevard
Hauppauge, New York 11788

Library of Congress Catalog Card Number 94-8919

International Standard Book Number 0-8120-4877-6

Library of Congress Cataloging in Publication Data

Jurinski, James.
      Credit and collections / James Jurinski.
         p. cm. — (Barron's business library)
      Includes index.
      ISBN 0–8120–4877–6
      1. Credit. 2. Collecting of accounts. 3. Debt. I. Title.
II. Series.
HG3701.J8   1994   94–8919
650'.0285"5369—dc20   CIP

PRINTED IN ITALY
4567   9929   987654321

Contents

Preface

The importance of credit in our society can hardly be over-stated. Credit allows consumers to enjoy a higher standard of living and permits businesses to expand and provide growth for the economy. It is hard to imagine how our economy could function if we were all limited to making cash purchases.

Businesses and individuals rely on credit for their daily purchases, yet many consumers and businesspeople take the availability of credit for granted. The credit and collections function, however, is the foundation of any successful business. To achieve success, business owners not only must be experts in delivering their goods or services, they also must know how to get paid.

This book is written to provide an introduction to both credit and collections: how businesses extend credit to their customers and how they ensure that the money gets collected.

Credit is so pervasive that an entire industry has developed around it. Credit bureaus, factors, and debt collectors all contribute to make the credit and collection system function efficiently. During the last twenty years, the government has passed a number of laws regulating the extension and availability of credit: for example, the Truth in Lending Act governs the disclosure of credit terms, while the Equal Credit Opportunity Act requires sellers and lenders to evaluate credit without regard to race, color, sex, religion, or national origin. These laws apply to nearly all businesses that sell to consumers.

Credit and collections does not fit neatly into one field. An effective credit and collections professional must be knowledgeable in accounting and business law and must also know at least a little psychology. Credit and collections is more an art than a science. This book will attempt to provide some practical insights to help business owners deal with credit and collections problems.

Although this book discusses many legal issues, those discussions should not be regarded as legal advice and should not be substituted for legal advice. The discussions in the text are, of necessity, generalized, and a slight change in facts or local law might change an answer. Additionally, although every effort has been made to ensure that all material is accurate at the time of this writing, law is constantly changing. If you have a question regarding a material matter, it would be wise to seek legal advice from an attorney in your area.

Finally, I would like to thank Paul Royster, my editor at Barron's, for his encouragement and helpful suggestions in completing this book.

James John Jurinski
Portland, Oregon

BARRON'S BUSINESS LIBRARY

Credit and Collections

Introduction: How Credit Works in the Economy

INTRODUCTION AND MAIN POINTS

This chapter examines how credit works in the economy, with emphasis on the distinction between consumer and commercial credit. Also explored are the advantages and disadvantages of credit, as well as privacy issues for businesses who offer credit to their customers. Finally, the chapter explains the credit management function and the role of the credit manager in a business. The role of revolving credit and bank cards is also discussed.

This chapter will describe

- The role of credit in the economy
- How the government regulates credit
- The distinction between consumer and commercial credit
- The advantages of credit to debtors
- The advantages of credit to sellers

ROLE OF CREDIT IN THE U.S. ECONOMY

Credit is an increasingly important part of the U.S. economy. In fact, consumer borrowing is at an all-time high, and there is no national policy to constrain the growth of credit. Indeed, the availability of credit is the lifeblood of the U.S. economy. From the U.S. government, to IBM and General Motors, to the corner grocery store, to individual families, the availability of credit keeps the wheels of the economy turning. It is hard to imagine our economy without the availability of credit.

GOVERNMENT REGULATION OF CREDIT

The importance of credit to the national economy has led the federal government to take an increasingly active role in the regulation of credit. During World War II the federal government regulated credit by restricting it. Since that time, the federal government's role has been to police abuses rather than to restrict the availability of credit. The government has enacted numerous laws governing the relations between lenders and borrowers. Many of these laws will be discussed in the course of this work.

Although the government's regulation of consumer credit is the most visible, the government also indirectly regulates the availability of general credit. For example, the Federal Reserve Board indirectly regulates credit through its regulation of the discount rate it charges to member banks. These banks adjust their interest rates—including the "prime rate"—accordingly. When the Federal Reserve Board drops its discount rates to encourage economic growth, the banks typically drop their lending rates; this has a ripple effect throughout the economy. The federal government also influences the availability of credit in other ways. For example, it is involved in the credit markets through *Fannie Mae* (the Federal National Mortgage Association), *Ginnie Mae* (Government National Mortgage Association), and *Freddie Mac* (the Federal Home Loan Mortgage Corporation); these all make markets in mortgage securities. The availability of tax deductions on home mortgage interest encourages individuals to borrow to purchase homes. In 1986 Congress repealed the tax deduction for consumer interest; this makes the use of credit cards relatively less attractive. Although the government's involvement in credit and collections is not always obvious, it is pervasive.

TYPES OF CREDIT: CONSUMER AND COMMERCIAL CREDIT

Generally, credit may be divided into two categories: consumer credit and commercial credit. Consumer credit is advanced to individuals for the purchase of goods and services for personal, family, or household use. Commercial credit is provided to businesses. This distinction will be used often in this book. Generally, consumer credit transactions are more closely regulated than commercial credit transactions.

ADVANTAGES OF CREDIT TO INDIVIDUALS

Credit allows individuals to acquire and enjoy items without having to save for their purchase. Although misuse of credit can cause problems, careful use can enrich consumers' lives. Without access to credit, most individuals would have to save for years before they could afford a car, a home, or college educations for their children. In countries such as Japan, where individuals save far more of their incomes than do Americans, such saving is necessary because credit is tightly restricted. If you want a home in Japan, you have to save to buy it. Obviously, this restricts home ownership to the wealthy and to those who have saved for a long time. In America, the availability of credit allows more people to enjoy homes, cars, and other products, even if they weren't born into a wealthy family. Restriction of credit by lenders or governments reduces the number of people who can buy homes, cars, or college education.

Criticisms of Credit

Some individuals criticize any use of credit. There is some validity to the criticism that the availability of credit hampers capital formation. Americans typically save less than their counterparts in other industrialized nations. This low savings rate decreases the available pool of capital for U.S. businesses and may raise their costs of doing business. To this extent, the easy availability of credit may be hurting U.S. competitiveness.

Other individuals criticize the use of credit on moral grounds. Indeed, some religions have at times prohibited money lending as immoral. These critics point out that the easy availability of credit diminishes initiative, thrift, and hard work.

Although some borrowers get over their heads with purchases, the vast majority of borrowers use credit intelligently. The use of credit can make sense when an item will be used over a period of time. A family home, for example, is owned on average for seven years. As a national policy, the federal government assists the operation of the mortgage markets to help Americans own their own homes. Without the availability of mortgages many families with children could not own their own homes.

ADVANTAGES OF CREDIT TO BUSINESSES

Businesses not only offer consumer credit to their customers; they are also major users of credit. The availability of *commercial credit* allows businesses to raise funds to buy equipment and inventory and to hire employees. The cost of this credit—which is tax deductible—can be recouped through profits from the sale of goods or services.

For example, to buy inventory a business borrows $100,000 with an interest rate of 10 percent and has a 15 percent net profit. Initially it appears that the business will be borrowing at 10 percent and reducing its profit margin to 5 percent. However, this transaction is potentially more profitable. The interest on the loan is tax deductible. If the corporation has an effective tax rate of 25 percent, the effective interest rate is only 7.5 percent (75 percent of 10 percent). Accordingly, the 15 percent profit is actually twice the effective after-tax cost of the interest.

Reliance on Credit

Although a few businesses operate on a cash basis, most rely heavily on credit. Many businesses offer credit terms to their customers and they also borrow funds themselves to operate the business. Most automobile dealerships, for example, are operated as private businesses. The car dealer has a franchise from one or more car manufacturers to sell certain makes of car. The auto dealer needs to purchase the cars for inventory available for sale to the public.

Consider the cost of an automobile dealer's inventory. If the average cost of a car is $10,000, and the dealer has 75 new cars in inventory, this inventory costs the dealer $750,000! Very few small businesses can afford to buy three quarters of a million dollars of inventory without borrowing money. Car dealers typically do borrow this money, a transaction known as "flooring" the inventory.

In fact, most businesses need to buy goods and services on credit. Although this incurs interest expense, a well-run business will still turn a profit. For example, the car dealer who has interest expense associated with flooring the inventory of new cars plans to be able to pay this interest and still sell the inventory at a profit. Keep in mind that for a business, interest is a tax-deductible expense (only certain types of interest are tax deductible for individuals).

ADVANTAGES OF CREDIT TO SELLERS

The availability of credit expands the economy because it makes more sales possible and puts resources into the most productive hands. In fact, the availability of ready credit is a great boon to sellers, who, if they were limited to cash sales, would find their sales volume and profits significantly lower.

It may seem that selling for cash would be preferable because there are fewer transaction costs involved, and no possibility of bad debts, since you receive payment at the point of sale. However, experience has demonstrated that a business that limits itself to cash sales will not be as profitable as a business that offers credit. Credit terms such as N30 (net due in 30 days) or N60 (net due in 60 days) or terms that allow a discount for prompt payment provide a form of short-term financing, improving the purchaser's cash flow position. The seller *must* offer credit terms to be competitive. With the credit incentive, a seller can increase volume and actually charge lower prices while improving profitability.

Profiting from Interest Income

The strictly-for-cash seller misses another profit opportunity— the interest income inherent in consumer credit sales. After all, banks' primary revenue sources are generally interest and fees. By refusing to offer credit, a seller relinquishes a potentially lucrative source of income. For example, a seller who offers credit terms of 1.5 percent per month (18 percent per year) might realize a better return than the company could make by just buying and selling inventory. Many large retailers have found that they make a better profit from their financing operations than from their retailing operations.

DISADVANTAGES OF CREDIT

Credit sales can have disadvantages. The primary disadvantage is the substantial cost of default by buyers. When a sale is made on credit and the buyer defaults, the seller has lost not only the profit but the cost of the goods. For a seller of services, the chance to sell the time to another client has been lost forever. Accordingly, it is a primary goal to minimize bad debt losses.

Additionally, the availability of credit does add to transaction costs. Sellers who wish to run their own credit operations will have to invest time and skill to the design of the credit system. Once designed, the system will require staffing and also management participation. If a seller decides not to create a system, but decides to rely on bank cards like VISA and Mastercard, some of these costs are eliminated. However, the seller will still be charged for the use of the cards.

PRIVACY ISSUES

The protection of privacy in credit transactions has taken on added importance in the last few years. Sellers must use care to protect the privacy of both customers and credit applicants. Data on an individual's credit application could be of value to other businesses. For example, an insurance company might want to know how much your customers earn to determine if they would be sales prospects for insurance. An automobile company might want to know the make, model, and age of your customers' cars to find prospects for new car purchase.

By applying for credit, individuals do forfeit certain rights to privacy. However, this information may not be misused, and privacy rights are protected at least in part by the Federal Fair Credit Reporting Act. This law, as well as other federal laws affecting credit, are detailed in Chapter 6, "Legal Requirements in Granting Credit."

The protection of individuals' privacy in general, and the protection of an individual's sensitive financial information in particular, will be strengthened by both the state and federal governments in the future. Businesses must be sensitive to preserve the confidentiality of all credit information from the application stage onward.

THE CREDIT MANAGEMENT FUNCTION

Managers should not view credit management as a mere afterthought. Rather, credit management is vital for almost all businesses no matter what their size. A business's success or failure in managing credit will directly contribute to the firm's profitability. While larger firms have entire departments delegated to managing credit, small businesses do not have the luxury of unlimited staff and financial resources for such specialization.

Some smaller firms will be able to have a credit manager, but others will have to give credit control to a manager with other responsibilities. Yet with careful planning and intelligent implementation, smaller businesses can also effectively manage the credit function and can profit from the effort. However, small firms must be aware that credit management will not happen by itself; this area requires knowledge, planning, and perseverance.

Managing credit consists of four basic tasks: establishing a credit policy, organizing responsibility for running the system, monitoring results, and reevaluating and improving the credit policy.

Management is needed to design an appropriate credit policy that enhances the firm's operations and profitability. Even the best credit policy will not be self-implementing. Management must also design procedures and delegate responsibility for running the system.

Smaller businesses face a number of constraints in implementing a credit system, because both financial and human resources may be limited. The budget may simply not permit hiring a full-time credit manager. Even in a small firm, however, responsibility for managing the credit system should be clear. A manager in charge of either sales or finances would be an appropriate supervisor of the firm's credit operations if a full-time manager cannot be hired.

Once a credit system is in place it must be closely monitored. Even good decisions can be undermined as business conditions change. No business, large or small, is immune from outside events. For example, suppose your firm has established a credit policy that allows workers from a nearby industrial plant credit limits between $1,000 and $1,500, and your collection policy has traditionally been liberal or even lax. If you learn that the plant will be closing or that large numbers of workers will be laid off, your credit and collections policies should be reevaluated and possibly changed to meet the new economic conditions of your customers. Monitoring the credit policy should be ongoing, with quarterly reviews by management.

ROLE OF THE CREDIT MANAGER

Large firms often have multiple credit managers. However, even small firms need a manager with general responsibility for overseeing the credit function, and although titles differ, we'll refer to this person as the credit manager. The credit manager must see that the firm's credit system is functioning efficiently on a day-to-day basis. The prime goal of a credit system is to increase both sales volume and profits. Accordingly, the operation of the credit system is of vital importance.

Generally the credit manager will work with other managers to establish a credit policy and will be responsible for designing and implementing specific procedures to carry out this policy. Unless the credit manager is working alone in a very small firm, the credit manager also has the responsibility for seeing that the staff who implement the credit system are complying with the credit policies and procedures established by management.

The credit manager typically has the responsibility to monitor overdue accounts and determine when to write off "bad debts." Finally, the credit manager, who monitors the credit system from day to day, will often prepare reports to management for cash flow planning and for regular reevaluation and improvement in the firm's credit policies.

CONSUMER VERSUS COMMERCIAL CREDIT MANAGEMENT

While some firms' customers are individual consumers, other businesses sell goods or services either primarily or exclusively to other businesses. Wholesalers, for example, typically act as agents who purchase goods from manufacturers and sell them to retailers, who in turn sell the products to individual consumers. When a business extends credit to an individual we call it *consumer credit*. When credit is extended to another business the transaction is referred to as *commercial credit*.

In a larger business different individuals and even different departments will be responsible for consumer and commercial credit transactions. Although the essential elements of consumer and commercial credit are similar, it is worth noting that the seller has different concerns depending on the type of customer involved.

RETAILING: REVOLVING CREDIT AND BANK CARDS

Retail credit should be viewed as a special subset of consumer credit because it presents a number of special challenges to the small business. Because of the often intense competition from larger retailers and discounters, the small retailer's credit policy takes on added significance as a means of generating sales volume and promoting customer loyalty. Promotions offering extended payment terms and low payments can help to generate retail credit sales. Small retailers can also use their credit customers for promotional mailings about new merchandise, sales, and special discount terms.

Smaller retailers have the option of adopting various types of retail credit plans. "Open-account" credit, sometimes referred to as a "regular" charge account, allows a purchase without a down payment and payment is expected within a set period, for example 30 days after the purchase or more typically 30 days after the bill is mailed. Interest is not typically charged on open accounts although a service fee may be imposed for late payment and as an incentive to insure prompt payment.

In an "installment credit plan" the customer pays the purchase price of the goods in installments. For example, a customer may be required to pay 25 percent of the price as a down payment, and 25 percent at the end of each of the following three months. Sellers offering an installment plan normally impose an interest charge that is calculated into the amount of the installments.

Revolving Credit Plans

A more sophisticated form of the installment plan is a "revolving credit plan." Under a revolving plan a customer is given a specific dollar limit. All of the customer's credit purchases are added up, and the customer will be contractually obligated to pay a certain percentage of the unpaid balance each month. The customer has the option of paying the minimum amount, the full amount due, or some amount in between. The retailer will impose a service charge, representing interest, on the unpaid amount.

For example, suppose a customer is given a credit limit of $1,000 and makes a $200 purchase and then a $400 purchase during May. At the end of May the revolving charge account will have an aggregate balance of $600. The plan may require the customer to pay 1/12 of the unpaid balance per month. The customer is obligated to repay $50 at the end of May ($600 × 1/12 = $50). If the customer decides to pay the minimum amount, $50, then the retailer will impose a service fee—typically 1 1/2 percent—on the unpaid balance of $550 ($600 balance less the $50 payment). This service fee represents interest income to the retailer and can be an important source of revenue. Consult Figure 1-1 for a description of this example.

May purchases:

> $200 May 3rd
> $400 May 23rd
> ———
> $600 End-of-Month Balance

Plan requires:

1)	1/12 of the unpaid balance per month:	$600 × 1/12	=	$50.00
2)	service fee of 1 1/2 percent of unpaid balance	$550 × 1 1/2 percent	=	$8.25

Minimum payment: $ 58.25

Remaining unpaid balance: $550.00

FIGURE 1-1 *Operation of Revolving Charge Accounts*

Advantages of Bank Cards

A large number of smaller retail businesses have made the decision to discontinue their own credit operations and rely solely on bank credit cards such as the VISA, MasterCard, and Discover cards issued by many financial institutions.

By relying solely on bank cards, the small business has effectively turned over its credit and collections business to VISA or

MasterCard. On the positive side, this eliminates the need for a credit manager, the need to screen potential credit customers, and the need to monitor and try to collect delinquent accounts. If customers fail to pay for their purchases, the card issuer, not the business, bears the loss. In a small business with few managers, eliminating your own credit operation will release manager's time for other management tasks. This provides risk-free cash flow and the company can accurately project revenue and expenses. Significant bad debts can jeopardize a small company's solvency.

Disadvantages of Bank Cards

There are a number of distinct disadvantages to eliminating your own credit operation. Accepting only a generic card will not necessarily build customer loyalty in the same manner as offering individualized credit accounts. The most significant disadvantage, however, is cost. By turning over your credit operation the business will forgo any interest income that can be earned on the accounts. That income will go to the financial institutions that issue the cards.

Disadvantages to eliminating your own credit operation:
1. Less opportunity to build customer loyalty
2. Loss of any interest income that can be earned on the credit accounts

Additionally, although the banks will promptly deposit cash in the seller's bank account after receipt of the credit charge slips, the bank will also charge a fee for its services. Credit card fees typically range between 1/2 percent of sales to 5 percent of sales depending on the volume of sales. Although a 5 percent fee may not sound high, profit margins on sales might not exceed 10 percent after deducting all of your expenses, and indeed may be even less. If your normal profit margin is 10 percent, a 5 percent credit card fee represents one half of your potential profit.

CHAPTER PERSPECTIVE

This chapter presented an overview of the importance of credit to both the economy as a whole and to individual consumers and businesses.

The availability of credit expands the economy because it makes more sales possible. In this way it puts resources into the most productive hands. However, credit sales can have disadvantages. The primary disadvantage is selling to buyers who default. Additionally, the availability of credit adds to the cost of transactions. The protection of privacy in credit transactions has taken on added importance in the last few years. Sellers must use care to protect the privacy of both customers and credit applicants.

The credit manager is responsible for designing and implementing procedures to carry out the firm's credit policy. Managers need to make decisions about credit availability, credit limits, and billing and collections policies, as well as the availability of cash discounts.

Credit management has traditionally been divided into consumer credit and commercial credit management. Consumer credit is given to individuals for personal, family, or household purposes. Commercial credit is given to businesses for commercial use. Many of the federal statutes regulating the use of credit apply primarily to consumer credit transactions.

Retail credit is a subcategory of consumer credit. Today, many smaller retailers rely exclusively on bank cards rather than establishing their own credit and collections systems. There are both advantages and disadvantages to this approach.

Establishing a Credit Policy

INTRODUCTION AND MAIN POINTS

The first chapter introduced the role of credit in the economy and how credit operations are classified as consumer or commercial credit. This chapter details the steps you need to take in establishing a credit policy for your business. First, consider if you want to offer credit directly or rely on bank credit cards. If you decide to run your own credit operation there are a number of decisions you must make. First, determine which of your customers will be eligible for credit and in what amounts. Although you can improvise your approach, experience suggests that it is more efficient to establish consistent credit procedures. These will also help you make rational decisions that will decrease your losses through credit operations.

After studying the material in this chapter, you will know the following

- The steps in establishing a credit policy
- The advantages of having the policy in writing
- The role of the credit manager in setting the credit policy
- How decisions are made about who should get credit
- How credit limits are set
- The differences between tight and loose credit policies
- How credit scoring can be used in making credit decisions
- How cash and trade discounts operate
- The need for periodic revision of the credit policy

ESTABLISHING A CREDIT POLICY

Because the availability of credit has a direct relation to the firm's sales and profits, establishment of a credit policy is a central concern in business planning. Although some businesses operate without formal credit policies, formalization is useful because it clarifies for management the link between credit and profits. Additionally, a clear credit policy helps the credit manager devise procedures that can carry out management's business plan.

A credit policy essentially establishes three criteria:

1. Credit availability: Will credit be freely available or will it be restricted?
2. Credit limits: How much credit will customers be granted?
3. Repayment terms: When is repayment required? What are the interest rates? When and how will collection efforts be handled?

POSITIVE EFFECTS OF CREDIT

The availability of credit will directly affect the firm's sales volume. Since credit makes it easier for potential purchasers to buy goods or services, sales volume will increase. Although you could rely on bank cards, some customers—especially younger or elderly ones—may not normally use bank credit cards.

The availability of credit also builds customer loyalty, because customers tend to return for follow-up purchases. The availability of credit also decreases price resistance, which also adds up to more sales and higher profits. Customers may not be reluctant to pay full price for an item or a service, but they may be temporarily short of cash.

For example, assume that a furniture store sells baby furniture. A young couple visits the store in January in anticipation of having a new baby in a few months. The couple finds a crib, dresser, and baby carriage that they like, but they don't have enough cash because they've just paid their Christmas bills. Also assume that this young couple does not have a bank credit card. If you have a credit plan, this couple may be perfectly willing to buy the items. They may not be price-sensitive if they plan on more children, because they may be looking for higher quality furniture that will last. Even if the couple has a bank credit card, you may be able to arrange a credit purchase that will be more advantageous for them. They may save interest expense and you will earn profit above the sales profit from the interest on the account.

If credit is too freely available, however, too many *marginal risks* may be accepted. A *marginal risk* is a credit customer who may not have the ability to repay. Acceptance of too many marginal risks will, in turn, depress profits despite the added sales volume. Some retailers advertise "We offer credit to anyone the law allows." Obviously these sellers are accepting some marginal risks that will probably default. To cover these losses sellers charge higher prices, accept a lower profit margin, or increase their sales volume to offset their credit losses.

MANAGEMENT'S ROLE IN SETTING THE CREDIT POLICY

Establishing a credit policy requires management to analyze its market and to design a policy that will enhance the firm's operations and profitability. Management should estimate the degree of credit availability that will generate the most sales and profits while minimizing problem accounts. Chapter 9, "Bad Debts," explains why a credit policy that results in virtually no customer defaults is not normally the best policy, and in fact, is usually a sign that the availability of credit is unduly restrictive.

Marketing Factors

Managers must consider other factors in establishing credit availability. The availability of credit also contributes to a firm's marketing efforts. For example, if a retailer's attraction is based at least in part on exclusivity, the firm's credit policy should reflect the marketing decision to aim for the top of the market by reserving credit accounts to only select customers.

Credit Limits

A business's credit policy should also determine appropriate credit limits. Management must consider not only the ability of individual customers to repay their debts, but also the aggregate of unpaid accounts. The firm will need to raise cash, if only to meet payroll and tax deadlines, so the dollar credit limits as well as the availability of credit should be planned carefully. Credit limits will be explored more fully later in this chapter.

Coordination with Collections Policy

Finally, the credit policy should also address the company's billing and collection procedures, which affect the timing of cash receipts and the business's ability to pay its own debts. Businesses should coordinate their billing and collection plans with their credit planning to ensure that income will meet anticipated cash needs. If this type of planning is not possible, or sales projections are speculative, management should anticipate the need for cash by establishing a line of credit with a bank. This will make periods of cash shortages easier to weather.

WHY HAVE A WRITTEN POLICY?

Although it is possible to operate without a written credit policy, there are distinct advantages to having your policy set down in writing. Some businesses may not even realize that they have a policy. Yet even if decisions are improvised as customers ask for credit, the sum of those decisions does amount to a policy. If customers have been treated similarly, then the implicit policy needs only to be formalized in writing. On the other hand, if these ad hoc decisions are inconsistent and sometimes illogical, a written policy will help introduce order into a chaotic process. This will communicate policy and procedures to staff, and management can then evaluate its credit department, guide its credit manager, and establish goals and the means to accomplish them.

Advantages of a Written Credit Policy

There are at least four major advantages of having a written credit policy:
1. assures consistency in granting credit
2. provides uniformity of treatment to customers
3. allows better decisions by having predetermined criteria
4. speeds decision making.

Value of Consistency

A written policy and usable guidelines will assure your making consistent decisions. This helps eliminate costly mistakes and unacceptable risks. A written credit policy also assures uniform treatment for your customers. A customer may be justly annoyed to learn that you have been providing more favorable credit terms to its competitors. For example, suppose a paint store granted some smaller contractors a $5,000 credit line and allowed them to pay their bills without interest within 60 days. Yet the store also sold paint to similar painting contractors on terms that demanded payment in 15 days and provided only a $1,000 line of credit. The more liberal terms would provide a real competitive advantage for a contractor, and this lack of uniform treatment could harm your reputation.

Of course not all customers will be treated alike. Having a written policy will help you to differentiate between customers. For example, a long-established customer with a good payment history would merit a high credit limit, while a new customer with no credit history should be given a much smaller line of credit. Setting credit limits is discussed later in this chapter.

Speeding the Decision-Making Process

Having a written credit policy can speed the credit decision, because once you have established guidelines you can refer to them each time you need to make a credit decision.

For larger firms, the written guidelines will allow much of the work to be performed by a staff person other than a manager. The staff person will make a credit recommendation based on the written guideline. The manager can then either confirm the decision, ask the applicant for additional information, or decide differently based on additional information. A policy is helpful, but a good manager will sometimes depart from the guidelines for valid reasons.

ESTABLISHING THE POLICY

A written credit policy can be long or short. It may provide specific guidance for granting credit and setting limits or it can just state general goals. Any credit policy should, however, address the following eight questions:

1. Who is responsible for deciding who gets credit?
2. Who is responsible for establishing credit limits?
3. What factors control the initial decision to grant credit?
4. What factors determine the applicant's credit limit?
5. What are normal payment terms (how soon is payment due)?
6. What are normal interest terms?
7. What discount terms are available?
8. How will delinquent customers be dealt with?

In smaller firms one person—usually a manager with responsibility over financial matters—will determine who gets credit and will also set the credit limit. In larger firms, this responsibility may be divided among several employees. For example, a sales rep may be able to give "instant credit" up to $100. Larger amounts would have to be approved by the credit manager or in some cases even the treasurer or owner of the business.

ROLE OF THE CREDIT MANAGER

Large firms often have multiple—regional or district—credit managers. However, even small firms need a manager responsible for overseeing the credit function. Although titles differ, we'll refer to this person as the credit manager. The *credit manager* has responsibility to see that the firm's credit system is functioning efficiently on a day-to-day and a year-to-date basis. As we discussed in Chapter 1, the prime goal of a credit system is to increase sales volume and net profit. Accordingly, the operation of the credit system is of vital importance.

Generally the credit manager works with other managers to establish a credit policy and designs and implements specific procedures to carry out the policy. Unless he or she is working alone in a very small firm, the credit manager also has the responsibility for seeing that the staff that implements the system complies with the credit policies and procedures established by management.

The credit manager typically monitors overdue accounts and, as determined by the controller or company management, writes off "bad debts." Finally, the credit manager monitors the credit system on a day-to-day basis and prepares formal or informal reports to management for cash flow planning and for regular reevaluation and possible improvements in the firm's credit policies.

WHO SHOULD GET CREDIT? TIGHT VERSUS LOOSE CREDIT

Credit policies can be either conservative or liberal. When a firm adopts a conservative policy, credit will be extended only to customers who are deemed very likely to repay their debts. At the extreme, a firm might require a prompt payment record, verifiable evidence of a specific annual income, and even financial statements showing considerable net worth. Although such precautions do not guarantee payment, they would reduce bad debt risk.

At the opposite extreme are sellers with liberal credit policies who extend credit to literally anyone. Businesses with loose credit policies are characterized by large sales volume and heavy bad debt losses caused by customers who are poor credit risks. Obviously, most sellers position themselves between these two extremes.

Which Approach?

At first glance it may appear that a tight credit policy will best enhance profits. By restricting credit only to those most likely to pay, you are virtually eliminating the possibility of nonpayment. When a firm is not paid for goods, it not only loses the anticipated profit from the sale, but also the cost of the goods if they cannot be reclaimed.

For example, if an item costs a firm $80 and a customer buys the item on credit for $100, the firm will make a $20 profit when the customer pays the bill. The seller may also make a small profit from interest, depending on the credit terms. If the sale becomes a bad debt, the seller has not only lost the opportunity to earn the $20 profit but also the $80 invested in the cost of the inventory. The seller will have to sell five additional units, each with a $20 profit, to make up the loss (5 units × $20 profit each = $100).

Despite these grim figures, in most cases a liberal credit policy produces greater profits than a conservative policy, depending, of course, on market conditions. The key here is volume. By restricting credit to the most creditworthy only, a seller greatly restricts sales volume and profits. The better goal is to increase sales volume so that the profit generated by the volume more than offsets the expected bad debt losses. As Figure 2-1 suggests, your credit policy should aim at a position somewhere between tight and loose. Additionally, this policy must be routinely reviewed to determine if it is meeting the company's profit goals.

Tight Credit	Loose Credit
|————————————|————————————|	
lower profits	unacceptable write-offs

FIGURE 2-1

For example, assume that the credit manager has proposed loosening credit with the estimated anticipation of thirty additional sales, two of which will result in bad debts. Using our same $100 item with a $20 profit, we see that we can anticipate suffering a $200 loss from the two bad debts but an increase in profits of $600 from the increased sales volume, for a net gain of $400.

$20 profit per unit × 30 units   = $600 profit
$100 item × 2 anticipated bad debts   =   − 200 loss
Net Result: $400 increase in profits

Net profit would be increased even higher if the seller can reclaim the goods from the defaulting customer.

Calculating the optimum credit policy is almost an art. Many firms tighten their credit policies during economic downturns. The credit manager must be aware of both national and local economic conditions in designing a credit policy that will maximize profits while minimizing bad debt losses.

SETTING CREDIT LIMITS

Once the decision has been made to grant credit to an applicant, the business must determine how much credit. This amount is typically referred to as the *credit limit* or credit line. Not all customers should get the same limit, which should be based on the relative financial strength and credit rating of the applicant. The approach would be the same whether the applicant is a business or an individual. If the applicant is in a strong financial position, and reports from credit bureaus and other references indicate that the applicant pays bills promptly, then the applicant could be given a fairly generous credit line, but still limited to one or two months' expected payment.

After six or twelve months of business without any problems this credit line could be increased. On the other hand, if the applicant has trouble paying bills, the credit line might even be reduced or withdrawn. Applicants with less financial strength or for whom there is little or no credit history should get a modest initial credit line. Their credit lines could also be increased over time, but at a slower pace than a customer with a long credit history.

Setting the credit limit is a matter of using professional judgment after weighing the evidence. Normally the decision maker will be looking at the customer's credit application and supporting documents, along with reports furnished by commercial credit bureaus. Analyzing credit applications is discussed in Chapters 4 and 5. One means of implementing the credit policy is to use "credit scoring," a systematic approach to granting credit and setting credit limits.

CREDIT SCORING

Once a business has established a basic credit policy, management must formulate and implement procedures to answer four questions:

1. Which customers will receive credit?
2. How much credit will they receive?
3. When will payment be made?
4. What will be payment terms?

A business that has dozens, hundreds, or thousands of customers can use credit scoring, a commonly used method that systematically rates potential credit customers based on various attributes. The customer's rating helps determine whether to extend credit, and can also determine a credit limit and special payment terms. (See Figure 2-2, which illustrates a credit scoring grading form.)

Art or Science?

At the outset managers should realize that determining credit-worthiness is subjective. In extending credit the credit manager is predicting future behavior of the customer based on past events. Also, while the credit manager may have much relevant information in making the decision, all relevant information will not be at hand.

This quantification process can create a false impression of precision. Credit scoring should be used only as an aid and not as a substitute for human analysis and common sense. Credit scoring can overlook significant positive or negative evidence of creditworthiness, which can produce a costly bad decision or a missed opportunity for profits. Finally, managers should keep in mind that predicting a customer's future financial ability is inherently uncertain.

A credit scoring system seeks relevant evidence of the applicant's likelihood of paying bills. Usually firms look at an individual applicant's income, assets, past payment record, length of employment, home ownership, and general reputation. The business will request the credit applicant to submit evidence or indicate where the information can be verified. Once verified, the applicant's attributes are graded and a total score is derived.

For example, a firm might use a scoring system using only income, assets, and past payment history and might assign a grade to each attribute from 1–10, with 10 points the highest score. Assume that an individual applicant has a good job, has average assets, but a spotty repayment record. The firm's credit scoring system might give the applicant a grade of 10 for income, 5 for assets, and 2 for payment history for a total score of 17. The firm might have a policy of always granting credit to applicants with scores over 20 while denying credit to those with scores under 10. Applicants with scores between 10 and 20 would be individually evaluated by the credit manager. In this example, the score of 17 would not automatically qualify or disqualify the applicant. The credit manager could well decide that although the applicant has a strong financial record the applicant's payment history makes him a poor risk. Again, credit scoring should

CREDIT SCORING FORM

Attributes   **Verification / Score (1–10)**

Income

Liquid Net Assets

Other Assets

Past Payment History

Community References

Total Score:

40 points or more:	accept application
20 points or less:	reject application
20–40 points:	refer application to credit manager

FIGURE 2-2

be used as an aid in making decisions rather than as a substitute for thoughtful analysis.

CASH AND TRADE DISCOUNTS

When a seller of large items like equipment sells on credit, the terms of sale often include a cash discount. Commercial credit managers often use cash discounts to encourage prompt payment of an account. For example, if a small manufacturer makes a credit sale of equipment worth $100,000 to a larger company, the seller may offer a 2 percent cash discount if the account is paid in 10 days. In other words, the buyer will be able to purchase the equipment for $98,000, not $100,000.

Sales price: $100,000
Terms: 2/10 net 30 (2% discount if cash paid in 10 days,
         net due in 30 days)

$100,000   purchase price
×   2%   discount terms
$2,000   cash discount

$100,000   purchase price
− $2,000   discount
$98,000   net price after discount

FIGURE 2-3 *Computation of Cash Discount*

Although this discount may look advantageous only to the buyer, it actually benefits both parties. The buyer obviously gets a good bargain by promptly paying the bill and receiving a $2,000 price reduction. The seller is able to convert the $100,000 unpaid purchase price (*account receivable*) into cash in a short period of time. This is especially important for small firms and start-up businesses that may have trouble meeting payroll, tax, and loan obligations. The need for a steady and predictable cash flow for a small business cannot be overemphasized.

Advantages of Discounts over a Credit Line

Even if a seller has a line of credit with a bank that lets the company borrow funds on short notice, a line of credit may not be as efficient in raising cash as the cash discount. Continuing with our example, assume that our seller does not offer a cash discount on the sale of the $100,000 of equipment but has arranged a line of credit with a bank and must pay 12 percent simple interest on any borrowing.

Also assume the seller is short of cash and borrows $100,000 on the line of credit to pay back a loan. Although the seller has requested prompt payment it believes that the buyer will take three months to pay. The seller plans to repay the $100,000 loan in three months when the buyer pays for the equipment. The bank will charge an interest fee of $3,000 for the three months ($100,000 × 12% × 3/12 = $3,000). By offering the 2 percent cash discount to the buyer, the seller would have forgone only $2,000. Even though the bank interest is tax deductible, the seller in this example would still be dollars ahead by offering the cash discount instead of relying on the line of credit.

NEED TO REEVALUATE CREDIT POLICIES

Once a credit system is in place it must be closely monitored to serve two purposes: first, to observe if the system is functioning efficiently, and second, to determine if the firm's credit policy is sound. It is possible that a credit policy is unsound from the start. For example, a small retailer just starting business may grant quite liberal credit terms to encourage sales, only to discover an unexpectedly high customer default rate from the very outset of business.

On the other hand, a credit policy that has functioned well for years may need to be reevaluated and amended. For example, if a furniture store with a tight credit policy notes a marked decrease in credit sales, the reason for the decline may be that the store's client base has changed with the neighborhood, and the old credit policy is no longer functioning effectively to build sales volume. A more liberal credit policy may be able to raise both sales volume and profits.

A key indicator of the success of the credit policy is the size and age of your accounts receivable. *Accounts receivable* are amounts owed to the business from credit sales. We will see in later chapters that the absolute size and also the age of accounts receivable provide managers with valuable information about the functioning of the firm's credit policy. Similarly, both the number and dollar amount of bad debt write-offs are critical in determining if the current credit policy is realistic. Armed with this information managers can carefully evaluate the current credit policy and implement changes that will enhance profitability. We will look at accounts receivable analysis in more detail in later chapters.

CHAPTER PERSPECTIVE

Establishing a credit policy is an essential step in operating a successful credit system. The credit policy will set goals and will suggest strategies and techniques for achieving those goals. Although many businesses operate with unwritten policies, a formal written credit policy has a number of distinct advantages.

In larger firms, the credit manager plays a critical role in establishing and maintaining the credit policy. Even in firms too small for a credit manager, other management personnel will make decisions affecting the policy. Two of the most important decisions are who will get credit and what limits will be set. Although in smaller firms this can be handled case by case, in larger firms with hundreds or thousands of customers and many times more applicants, this task must be delegated. This requires a well-designed procedure to ensure both uniformity and compliance with management's goals. The use of a standardized credit scoring system will also professionalize the credit function within the firm.

Although large and small firms differ in how they manage the credit operation, all firms can benefit from the skillful use of credit and cash discounts to encourage prompt payment.

In the next chapter you will learn about consumer credit and the operation of credit bureaus.

Consumer Credit and Credit Bureaus

INTRODUCTION AND MAIN POINTS

The quality of your credit customers and any difficulty you may have making collections result from decisions that you make in granting credit. If you make poor judgments and grant credit to untrustworthy businesses or individuals, you may have trouble collecting or may never collect at all. Accordingly this initial decision about the creditworthiness of potential credit customers is vital.

The decision about whether or not to extend credit to an individual customer is normally made after review of a credit application. This chapter will examine how to design and use a credit application for individuals. The next chapter will continue this discussion with additional techniques when selling to a business.

This chapter covers these topics
- The function of a credit application
- The design of an appropriate credit application
- How to investigate credit customers
- How to evaluate bank references
- The importance of checking trade references
- How to check references with credit bureaus
- The need to protect your customer's privacy
- The provisions of the Fair Credit Reporting Act
- How to avoid Fair Credit Reporting Act liability

FUNCTION OF A CREDIT APPLICATION

The most obvious function of a credit application is to provide information that will help a seller to determine first, if a buyer is creditworthy, and then how much credit to extend, and on what terms. For this purpose the applicant is asked to supply certain financial and nonfinancial information.

Using the Application to Educate Customers

Additionally, however, the information on the credit application can be used for other purposes, and the application itself can be tailored to educate the buyer in the proper use of credit. For example, the credit application may ask what a consumer would do about an overdue balance.

Using the Application as a Marketing Tool

Although some consumers make their buying decisions solely on price, many consumers value service and personal attention even more highly. Customers of a service business may not be aware of what competitors charge or the quality of the service. Customers, however, can tell if the service provider is sympathetic and courteous. Often, therefore, consumers make their buying decisions based on personal service rather than either quality or price. Successful businesses keep in contact with customers and alert them to useful new services or products.

The material in the credit application can be a tool for your business to maintain contact with your customers. A business can often use some of the information in advertising and promotional material for customers. This is more easily done if this information is transferred into a computer data base.

For example, assume that a retailer offers credit accounts to selected customers. The retailer's credit application asks for financial information, but it also solicits lifestyle information. The applicant is asked to list any children along with their ages; the make and model of the applicant's autos and whether the autos are owned free and clear or are financed. This information is primarily used in making credit decisions. For example, all things being equal, a couple with four children will have less discretionary income than a childless couple with the same earnings. Likewise, an applicant who has to make big monthly car payments will have less discretionary income than someone who saved and bought a car for cash.

However, this information could also be used by the retailer for marketing purposes. If the retailer sends out a special catalog or promotion about children's clothes it makes sense to send it to customers with children. Similarly, if the retailer is selling tires, it makes sense to send the advertising to customers who own their own cars and are potential tire buyers. Many businesses pay dearly for mailing lists of potential customers. When customers apply for credit, this type of information is free.

When the demographic and lifestyle information is included in a computer data base, the material can be sorted and used in various ways. For example, you could obtain a list of your credit customers with incomes over $75,000. This could be a useful list if you wanted to run a special promotion for these well-to-do customers. You can also locate your customers by zip code. If you have one or more locations and you have a special promotion at only one of those locations, this type of information would help you target your mailings.

Again, although credit applications are primarily designed for making decisions about granting credit, the information can also be profitably used for other purposes.

DESIGN OF AN APPROPRIATE CREDIT APPLICATION

Generally, there are two views about credit applications. Some credit professionals feel that an application should be relatively short to give an aura of informality to the application process and to build goodwill with the customer. These credit professionals feel that sufficient information can be gained from outside sources such as credit bureaus without inconveniencing the applicant by requiring large volumes of information on the credit application.

Advantages of Short Applications

Additionally, if a seller requires a lengthy credit application, some buyers will not take the time to apply; some buyers might resent long forms and will simply not complete the application. This may eliminate perfectly good credit applicants merely because of the design of the form itself.

One other advantage of shorter application forms is cost saving. It takes time to process lengthy credit applications, and it is unclear if these longer forms are really more fruitful than shorter forms. It is uncertain that using a longer form will uncover the kind of information that will change a seller's mind about granting credit. Usually credit mistakes and risks are disclosed after a buyer has failed to pay for goods, unless the lack of financial strength is really obvious from the application. But long formal applications may be useful for applicants with little credit history at their local credit bureau.

The Argument for Detailed Applications

Many credit professionals prefer longer application forms for two reasons: 1) a longer application permits the seller to gather more relevant information about the applicant; 2) the longer application makes the process more formal, thus alerting the applicant that the seller takes a serious interest in the credit collection function.

Credit professionals who favor longer applications point out that the most efficient way to gather information is by having the applicants themselves supply it rather than getting it from third-party sources. Additionally, this will let the applicant demonstrate financial resources that may not be readily verifiable from credit bureaus or from other sources.

For example, a credit bureau may verify employment and credit history but may not know that the applicant has a valuable interest in a nonpublic family business or that the applicant has received an inheritance. This sort of information may be revealed on a credit application but not through a credit bureau. If any amounts are suspect, the seller can always request the applicant to provide verification from a reputable third party.

Advantages of Each Approach

Because of the two divergent views, there is no clear answer whether a credit application should be long or short. If a seller wants an aura of informality, it may be best to use a short form and rely on third parties for additional verification of financial information. On the other hand, if one of the primary goals of the business is to minimize credit losses, then using a long form with lots of information may be the best course.

Even companies in the same business often differ in the types of application they require. For example, some oil companies and department stores have very short credit applications for new credit cards. On the other hand, some other oil companies and department stores require quite lengthy applications before a card is given to new customers.

INVESTIGATING CREDIT CUSTOMERS: IN GENERAL

Regardless of disagreement on whether credit applications should be long or short, all credit professionals agree that the credit investigation should be as thorough as possible. The best way to eliminate credit losses and bad debts is to do a careful investigation of credit applicants before they are allowed access to credit.

Interviews

Some credit professionals suggest that credit interviews be used in addition to formal applications and third-party information.

A skillful interviewer can elicit information and clues to personality that formal written applications will never reveal. Although the credit interview will probably range over the same questions that the credit application would contain, the investigator may be able to make a decision based on extra comments that the applicant makes while the application is being filled out.

For example, an application may not ask much about repayment history, but the applicant may mention problems with billing disputes with former credit accounts. This should raise doubts in the mind of the interviewer. Note that this kind of information would probably not be elicited on a standard written credit application.

Time Well Spent

Because of the time involved, and the labor intensiveness of the interview, most retailers don't use interviewers when granting credit, but merely rely on written applications and reports supplied by credit bureaus. However, many businesses just don't spend sufficient time in actually having a member of the staff analyze the information provided on the credit application.

Although some companies review credit applications with the proverbial fine-toothed comb, many others do very little verification of information and spend little time trying to do more than spot obvious trouble signs in the credit application. Managers must remember that credit is a privilege, not a right, and credit should not be awarded without question. Many bad debts can be eliminated if managers merely take the time to ferret out the bad risks. Some people make a career of victimizing merchants and have no intention of paying their bills. At the very least you need enough verification to eliminate this type of customer.

Dealing with Businesses

Managers should keep in mind that the federal laws restricting the types of questions that can be asked in credit applications apply only to consumers and not to businesses (see Chapter 6, "Legal Requirements in Granting Credit"). Accordingly, if your buyers are going to be businesses rather than consumers, the questions on your credit application can be far more comprehensive.

How the Credit Application Helps Collections

Surprisingly, the credit application itself can help collect bad debts. For example, when a seller asks for a bank reference and requests account numbers and the location of the branch in which the account is located, this information is not only relevant to the creditworthiness of the buyer, but will also help if the seller needs to attach the bank account if the buyer defaults after a credit sale. The address of the bank in addition to the account number will ease the process of reaching those assets.

Similarly the value and location of other assets, such as real estate, should be detailed on the credit application. Certain types of workers can attach a *lien* (a legal claim) against property when a customer refuses to pay (see Chapter 17, "Understanding Liens and Garnishments"). Carpenters, plumbers, and other tradespeople and artisans can impose mechanic's liens if they are unpaid. Other unpaid sellers who sue customers in small claims court may also need to attach assets in order to be paid. Having these assets listed and detailed in a credit application can be a great help in this type of collections work.

Verification of Basic Data
At the very least, much of the basic information on a credit application should be verified. For example, if an individual consumer is applying for credit and lists an address and a phone number, the credit department should look in a phone book or a credit directory to verify that the information is current. Likewise if a business has applied for credit, and listed itself as a corporation, the credit department should check with the State Corporation Commissioner to see that the corporation is in good standing with the state. If it is not, there may be a problem if a bill is not paid later.

Checking Bank References
Banks will usually reply to requests about banking relationships, either by mail or by phone. For example, if an applicant has listed $2,000 in a certain bank account, a bank will usually verify whether or not the account exists and whether that balance is accurate within a certain dollar range.

Employment References
Similarly, employment history can be easily verified by making a call to the employer after asking the applicant for the name and telephone number of a supervisor. Because many employers have been sued by unhappy employees, employers will normally confirm only that a person either works or has worked at a particular firm. Generally employers will not give out precise

details about compensation and will almost never make any negative comments—at least over the phone.

Checking Trade References

When an applicant has been asked for and has supplied trade references, these certainly need to be checked. Some sellers assume that if an application has listed a credit reference, the reference must be favorable. This can be far from the truth.

First, these references could be false; there might be no credit relationship whatsoever. Second, it is possible that the transactions were very small or not very recent. Third, a reference could be quite negative when actually checked. In other words, there are four possibilities and three of them are bad. This area should not be overlooked, especially after the information has been listed on a credit application. If the information is there, it should be used.

CHECKING CREDIT BUREAUS

Checking credit references takes time. The credit application may have eight to twelve references; they may not all answer the phones at your first try, or they may not have the information you need on the first call. It could take several hours, if not the entire day, to verify the information in a typical credit application. For this reason, most credit sellers rely to some extent on credit bureaus to help verify information about credit applicants.

A credit bureau is simply a private business that collects information relevant to creditworthiness of both individuals and businesses. Computers have greatly changed the operation of credit bureaus. Cooperation among credit bureaus in different parts of the United States has made it possible to share information among them and there are few people who will not show up in one form or another in credit bureau information files.

How Credit Bureaus Operate

Generally, a credit bureau earns its profits from fees for providing credit reports to credit sellers. Obviously, this information can be sold to more than one creditor in a particular market. For example, if a person moves to a new city, say Atlanta, and applies for credit at four local businesses, the credit bureau may be able to sell reports on this one individual to all four businesses.

Although at one time most credit bureaus were nonprofit organizations, now most credit bureaus are for-profit operations in one of two categories: 1) local credit bureaus and 2) those owned by large national corporations. Credit bureaus get their information from data shared with one another, from verifying employment and bank records, and from open public records, such as court records and lien records.

For example, a credit bureau would check the public record to see if a certain individual or business had filed for bankruptcy. However, credit bureaus get lots of information from credit sellers themselves. The bureau will have information about not only where credit has been granted, but also the payment history of the applicant. For example, was the payment normally on time, was it slow but consistent, or was it erratic?

Credit Reports

Credit reports may be written or oral. Subscribers to credit bureau reports can call the credit bureau for an oral report by furnishing the name and social security number of the applicant. The credit bureau will then try to locate the applicant in its computer files. Typically this will be done in a very short time. The credit bureau will then read off the record of transactions. These are typically credit accounts with notation of the applicant's bill-paying history.

For example, the report may mention that the applicant was consistent and prompt, or consistent but slow. Alternately the report may list negative factors, including a recent bankruptcy. Credit bureaus don't normally assign a rating in an oral report. Subscribers need to listen and evaluate the report and make up their own minds.

Written reports normally provide a great deal more detail. The advantage of the written report is that the subscriber can more carefully read and evaluate both positive and negative data. On the other hand, credit bureaus impose a higher charge for written reports. So the utility of having extra time to examine the record must outweigh the cost.

Standardized Reports

Although many credit bureaus are independently owned, the associated credit bureaus, a membership association, has introduced some standardization into written credit reports. The standard format adopted by the associated credit bureaus (ACB) and incorporated in Form 2000 is presented in Figure 3-1.

Besides the national/local distinction, there is another way to distinguish credit bureaus: one kind of credit bureau gener-

NAME AND ADDRESS OF CREDIT BUREAU MAKING REPORT		☐ SINGLE REFERENCE	☐ IN FILE REPORT	☐ TRADE REPORT
		☐ FULL REPORT	☐ EMPLOY & TRADE REPORT	☐ PREVIOUS RESIDENCE REPORT
		☐ OTHER _____		

	Date Received	CONFIDENTIAL REPORT
⌐ ¬	Date Mailed	
FOR	In File Since	
L ⌡	Inquired As:	

REPORT ON: LAST NAME	FIRST NAME	INITIAL	SOCIAL SECURITY NUMBER	SPOUSE'S NAME
ADDRESS: CITY	STATE	ZIP CODE	SINCE:	SPOUSE'S SOCIAL SECURITY NO.

PRESENT EMPLOYER:	POSITION HELD:	SINCE:	DATE EMPLOY VERIFIED	EST. MONTHLY INCOME $

DATE OF BIRTH	NUMBER OF DEPENDENTS INCLUDING SELF:	☐ OWNS OR BUYING HOME	☐ RENTS HOME	OTHER: (EXPLAIN) ☐
FORMER ADDRESS:	CITY:		STATE: FROM:	TO:
FORMER EMPLOYER:	POSITION HELD:	FROM:	TO:	EST. MONTHLY INCOME $
SPOUSE'S EMPLOYER:	POSITION HELD:	SINCE:	DATE EMPLOY VERIFIED	EST. MONTHLY INCOME $

VENDOR	KIND OF BUSINESS AND CODE	DATE REPORTED AND METHOD OF REPORTING	DATE OPENED	DATE OF LAST PAYMENT	HIGHEST CREDIT OR LAST CONTRACT	PRESENT STATUS				HISTORICAL STATUS				TYPE AND TERMS (MANNER OF PAYMENT)	REMARKS
						BALANCE OWING	PAST DUE AMOUNT	NO. OF PAYMENTS	NO. MONTHS HISTORY REVIEWED	TIMES PAST DUE					
										30-60 DAYS ONLY	60-90 DAYS ONLY	90 DAYS AND OVER			

This information is furnished in response to an inquiry for the purpose of evaluating credit risks. It has been obtained from sources deemed reliable, the accuracy of which this organization does not guarantee. The inquirer has agreed to indemnify the reporting bureau for any damage arising from misuse of this information, and this report is furnished in reliance upon that indemnity. It must be held in strict confidence, and must not be revealed to the subject reported on, except as required by law.

FIGURE 3-1 *Form 2000 Credit Bureau Report*

ally specializes in individual consumers who buy from retail stores and also buy services; another kind of credit bureau scrutinizes businesses.

Pricing

Although credit reports are useful they are not free. Obviously small businesses need to conserve funds, so it is essential to understand credit bureau pricing before deciding if credit bureau reports are for you.

Generally, a small business can become a subscriber by paying an initial fee of approximately $100. The user is then charged for each credit report. In fact, this is a small price to pay for this information. Because of the annual fee, the average cost of each report actually drops as the business requests more reports. Experience has shown that the price of an individual report is a good investment even for a small business.

Although you may have been able to discover independently much of the information in the credit report, it may reveal much more than your own investigation. Applicants are unlikely to list trade references that they have not paid. For example, you may call three trade references who give glowing reports about an applicant. However, you and these references may not be aware that twenty other merchants have gone unpaid. The report from the credit bureau will reveal this type of behavior. Generally, if the applicant hasn't paid other bills, there is no reason to think yours will be paid. Keep the cash customer but deny the credit application.

How to Find a Credit Bureau

The names of both local and national credit bureaus can be found in the yellow pages. The major national organizations include:

1. TRW Information Services
2. Trans Union Credit Information Company
3. CSC/Equifax
4. Dun & Bradstreet

TRW Information Services has a nationwide computerized credit checking system. TRW, because of its size, is able to update the information in its file monthly. Trans Union Credit Information Company is another national computerized credit bureau that also offers a unique service called TRACE, which can locate a consumer by social security number. Equifax also provides consumer as well as commercial credit reports.

If you desire information about a business applicant, a credit seller could use any of the credit bureaus mentioned. In addition, Dun & Bradstreet also offers credit reports on businesses.

PROTECTING PRIVACY

Businesses should be sure to protect the privacy of customers and potential customers at every stage in the credit process. Credit information and financial information about prospective customers is sensitive, and those customers should be able to anticipate that the business will protect their privacy when possible.

Note that when buyers use credit, they surrender a certain amount of privacy, whether they know it or not. In a standard credit report, businesses will be able to see the exact amount of purchases made on credit and the repayment history of the buyer. Many consumers are unaware that this type of information is not only collected but also passed among various kinds of businesses. In fact, some credit bureaus routinely sell lists of individuals who are good credit risks. Banks, other financial institutions, and retailers are eager to buy such lists of potential customers they would like to court.

FAIR CREDIT REPORTING ACT PROVISIONS

Because of past abuses in credit reporting, Congress passed the Fair Credit Reporting Act in 1971. This Act creates basic operating rules for credit bureaus. The goal of this federal law is fair, accurate, and impartial credit reporting, with respect to consumers' right to privacy. Although the Fair Credit Reporting Act applies primarily to credit bureaus, portions of the Act apply to those selling on credit, so a basic understanding of the Act is essential for any business that offers credit to consumers.

Although the provisions of this Act are very broad, the coverage of the Act is limited. The Act is part of the Consumer Credit Protection Act, which applies only to individual consumer transactions. It does not generally apply when a buyer is a business.

The Fair Credit Reporting Act not only gives consumers access to files at credit bureaus, but it also gives them the opportunity to correct errors in those files. Generally, when a consumer is denied credit, the consumer has the right to ask the credit seller the reason for the rejection.

The credit seller must tell the consumer the name and address of the credit bureau that prepared the report on which a denial was based. The credit bureau itself must provide both the nature and substance of any information about the individuals in the file and must also provide the sources of the information. This information must be provided without fee within 30 days after a credit rejection. Additionally, the credit bureau must tell who has received the report during the last six months.

If the consumer believes that the material in the file is inaccurate, the consumer may ask to have it corrected. If the credit bureau has made a mistake, the record must be corrected. If the credit bureau investigates and feels that no error occurred, the consumer may insist that the consumer's version of the story also be included in any future reports. The Act also provides that any negative information over seven years old must be deleted from the credit report.

CHAPTER PERSPECTIVE

Although the primary function of a credit application is to collect information on which to base a credit decision, the information can also be used in other ways—for advertising and promotion purposes, as well as potential debt collection.

Businesses should carefully design an appropriate credit application. Credit professionals are split on the best format: some prefer a short informal application while others prefer a more detailed form. A short form encourages customers to apply, but requires the seller to base the credit decision on information from credit bureaus. A longer form provides more information and also alerts the applicant that the seller is serious about the credit function.

Generally, sellers must either rely on the information provided in the credit application or request additional information from credit bureaus. At the very least the seller should always verify bank, trade, and employment references. Sellers should not assume that these references will be positive. Credit reports issued for a fee by commercial credit bureaus are usually a cost-efficient means of verifying an applicant's creditworthiness.

Although there are both local and national credit bureaus, and credit bureaus that specialize in individual reports or business reports, all credit bureaus have the same essential function: accurate reporting. To assure fairness and accuracy, all credit bureaus must now comply with the requirements of the federal Fair Credit Reporting Act.

Analyzing Business Credit Applications

INTRODUCTION AND MAIN POINTS

This chapter focuses on the special techniques needed to evaluate business applicants for credit. Commercial customers buy in larger quantities than individuals, so credit sellers must be more careful in offering credit and setting credit limits for business customers.

Additionally, because a commercial customer's financial affairs are more complicated than an individual's, more care must be taken in evaluating the customer's creditworthiness. This chapter focuses on some of the problems and techniques for evaluating business applicants for credit.

This chapter will discuss these topics
- The importance of financial statement analysis in checking business credit applications
- Generally accepted accounting principles
- The function and format of the balance sheet
- How to analyze the balance sheet in making credit decisions
- The function and format of the income statement
- The income statement in making credit decisions
- The importance of the cash flow statement
- The importance of analyzing cash flow
- The most important earnings and solvency ratios

FINANCIAL STATEMENT ANALYSIS

When advancing credit to a business, it is important to read and to analyze financial statements from the business. At one time it was unusual for a creditor to ask for financial statements from a business; now financial statement analysis is a standard part of most business credit applications. A credit manager needs to know basic principles about financial statements before analyzing the data.

Financial Statement Formats

Financial statements come in a fairly standard format with three basic components:

1. the balance sheet
2. the income statement
3. the cash flow statement

Financial statements are not created equal. A financial statement will be no better than the party who compiled it. In other words, if an uninformed person compiled the data, it may be inaccurate. Some business owners have been known to "doctor" financial statements when applying for loans. Accordingly, statements submitted by a credit applicant must be used with care.

For example, assume that you are a wholesaler who offers credit terms to selected customers. A well-known local retailer applies for credit and presents financial statements prepared by the retailer's internal accountant. The financial statements show a strong balance sheet with lots of cash and working capital (cash and near cash). Additionally the income statement and the cash flow statement all point to a healthy and creditworthy customer. Based on these financial statements you set a high credit limit of $20,000. The new customer promptly submits two $10,000 orders.

Two weeks later the customer files for bankruptcy. In the course of fruitless collection efforts you learn that the financial statements were inaccurate. The applicant had booked fictitious income and assets and had failed to list many large debts. In fact the business was insolvent when it applied for credit.

Protecting Yourself

How can you protect yourself from such disasters and frauds? At the start, be cautious if financial statements are not verified by a certified public accountant. Such statements should be given less weight in making a credit determination. In fact, some credit professionals advise that statements submitted wholly by an applicant should be attested to with a statement such as "I verify that the financial statements are true and accurate."

Although it is a crime in many states to submit false financial statements to secure a loan or credit, this will be little comfort if you cannot get paid or retrieve your inventory. The best policy is to be careful at the outset. If the account is large you might require financial statements prepared by a CPA. Alternately you may want to insure the accounts using credit insurance (see Chapter 7, "How to Get Paid").

Compilations, Reviews, and Audits

Managers and business owners should also be aware that financial statements verified by certified public accountants are not all the same. In fact, CPAs verify financial statements that have the same format, but offer different levels of reliability. The three types of reports that CPAs provide are called:

1. Compilations
2. Reviews
3. Audited Financial Statements

The highest level of service is the audit, in which the CPA has independently verified many of the numbers on the financial statements. The CPA renders an opinion as to the fairness of the numbers. This is somewhat like the Good Housekeeping seal of approval, and certified financial statements are the most trustworthy.

On the other hand, a compilation is the mere assembly by the CPA of numbers prepared by the client. Users should give less weight to compilations. Reviews fall between audits and compilations.

Compilations and Reviews

In a compilation, the CPA merely compiles or arranges the figures supplied by the client, without any testing. In other words, the CPA merely rearranges the client's numbers without verifying that they are accurate or even reasonable. In a review, the CPA goes somewhat farther and performs some "analytical review" of the material in addition to rearranging it. Here the CPA looks at the numbers to see if they make internal sense. For example, if the client's profits look high compared to sales, the CPA would have to investigate the seeming contradiction.

Audits

In an audit, the CPA expresses an opinion about the reasonableness of the numbers and their presentation. The CPA doesn't guarantee or insure that the numbers are accurate. The CPA does give an informed professional opinion that the financial statements fairly present the financial picture of the business. Even a CPA can be fooled by a clever but dishonest client, but audited financial statements are your best assurance when analyzing a potential business credit customer.

In determining the reasonableness of these numbers, CPAs do not check all the underlying data. For example, if the CPA tried to check sales this way, the CPA would have to look at hundreds or even thousands of receipts. Instead, CPAs assume that the books are essentially accurate but they sample a number of transactions, just to make sure. If the transactions they sample are not properly recorded in the books, then they do additional work. If the numbers on the financial statement don't seem accurate, the CPA will either give an adverse opinion or will disclaim any opinion at all.

Note that the CPA merely verifies the amounts supplied by the client. In no case does the CPA guarantee the accuracy of the financial statement. In fact, CPAs do not search for fraud even in an audit, unless something that suggests fraud strikes their attention.

Obviously, a credit seller can place more reliance on audited financial statements than those that are reviewed or compiled. Likewise, a review should inspire more reliance than a compilation.

GENERALLY ACCEPTED ACCOUNTING PRINCIPLES

A basic knowledge of generally accepted accounting principles will help a manager or business owner to analyze financial statements submitted by a potential credit buyer. Generally accepted accounting principles (GAAP) are the rules, procedures, and conventions that define accepted accounting practices. A review of a basic accounting textbook can be helpful in analyzing specific accounts. A book such as Barron's *Keys to Reading an Annual Report* can be quite useful in interpreting financial statements. When in doubt, advice from an accountant can be helpful.

THE BALANCE SHEET

The most important financial statement is called the balance sheet—also called the "statement of financial position," because it reports the assets, liabilities, and equity of the business at a particular time, normally at year end. The balance sheet is a listing of properties, called assets on the balance sheet, and debts, called liabilities. The balance is the net worth of the business. The basic accounting equation for the balance sheet is:

ASSETS – LIABILITIES = EQUITY or NET WORTH

The "balance" refers to the fact that the assets on the left-hand (debit) side must equal the liabilities and equity listed on the right-hand (credit) side. An illustration of a balance sheet can be found in Figure 4-1.

Balance Sheet

Assets

Cash	10,000
Short-term investments (Marketable securities)	20,000
Accounts receivable	15,000
Prepaid insurance	5,000
Inventory	70,000
Land	30,000
Buildings and plant	750,000
TOTAL ASSETS	900,000

Liabilities and Equity

Accounts payable	25,000
Salaries payable	75,000
Long-term mortgage payable	250,000
TOTAL LIABILITIES	350,000
Common stock (10,000 shares)	450,000
Retained earnings	100,000
TOTAL EQUITY	550,000
TOTAL LIABILITIES AND EQUITY	900,000

FIGURE 4-1 *Sample Balance Sheet*

Analyzing the Balance Sheet

Having access to a few years' balance sheets can be a great advantage. A seller can then analyze comparative financial statements to see how the buyer's operations have changed from year to year. For example, what is the buyer's cash position compared to the last few years? How do accounts receivable (money owed on current accounts) compare to last year? What are liabilities (debts) this year compared to last year?

Even in the absence of comparative financial statements, a balance sheet can be analyzed to determine the creditworthiness of a potential credit customer. Much of the basic analysis can be done with the use of comparative ratios that will be discussed later.

The Critical Accounts

There are a number of sensitive accounts on the balance sheet. Generally, a balance sheet is a good indicator of solvency, that is, the ability to repay debt. As we discussed earlier, because income is recognized on the accrual basis rather than on the cash basis, income is recognized on the income statement when a sale is made rather than when cash is in the bank. A buyer's income statement, therefore, may look good, but cash to pay bills may be lacking. The balance sheet provides some keys to determine whether the buyer will have the financial resources to repay.

Look especially closely at the cash position of the buyer. Are there adequate cash reserves as compared to current debt? A more sophisticated analysis involves the use of so-called "current assets"—that is, cash, marketable securities, accounts receivable, and inventory. In financial analysis, experts pay close attention to the relationship of those current assets and so-called current liabilities—that is, debts that must be repaid within a year. A non-current asset is one that is not expected to be turned into cash within the year or operating cycle—for example, property, plant, and equipment. The difference between current assets and current liabilities is known as "working capital."

Current assets – Current liabilities = Working capital

Operating Cycle

In analyzing a potential business credit customer you need to understand the operating cycle of a business. An operating cycle is the time required for a business to turn cash into cash again. For example, a retailer takes cash, buys inventory, and sells the inventory, often on credit. The business must then collect its accounts receivable to turn the inventory back into cash. This is the operating cycle: the business takes cash and turns it into cash again.

For retailers, an operating cycle may last a few weeks or a few months, but for some types of business an operating cycle can last up to a year or even longer. The classic example is distillers of Scotch whisky, who have an operating cycle of approximately 8 to 12 years cash to cash. Before extending credit, it is important to understand the buyer's operating cycle and how fast inventory can be turned into cash.

The most important items on the balance sheet for solvency purposes are cash, marketable securities, accounts receivable, and inventory. Marketable securities are stocks held by the business for investment purposes. Many small businesses simply don't have any marketable securities. Accounts receivable, amounts owed to the firm, are discussed more fully in Chapter 8, "Understanding Accounts Receivable." You should use the material in that chapter to evaluate accounts receivable.

Inventory is simply goods held for resale. For example, a florist has an inventory of flowers. A furniture store has an inventory of furniture. Don't be misled by certain inventory accounts, such as janitorial supplies to be used in business that are not held for resale.

THE INCOME STATEMENT

The income statement, sometimes known as the profit and loss statement, records the operating result of the business for a particular year. In some cases, income statements for a number of periods will be included so that trends can be spotted and analyzed. Generally, the income statement follows a standard format, although it becomes more complicated for a retail firm. Refer to Figure 4-2, which includes an illustration of an income statement.

Income Statement

Gross sales	520,000
Returns	(20,000)
NET SALES	500,000
Cost of goods sold	(320,000)
GROSS PROFIT	180,000
Selling expenses	(40,000)
General and administrative expenses	(50,000)
NET INCOME	90,000

FIGURE 4-2 *Sample Income Statement*

ANALYZING THE INCOME STATEMENT

In most businesses the net income of the firm does not represent cash, but income figured on an accrual basis. In accrual accounting, income is generally recognized when a sale and account receivable are recognized, not when the cash payment is received. Although a positive figure suggests the company will be able to repay its debts, you will recall that a positive net income is no guarantee of either solvency or bill-paying ability. However, two or more net losses in a row may suggest that the company's prospects are poor and its ultimate bill-paying ability is questionable—depending, of course, on the percent of the net loss and the amount of the operational profit.

In analyzing the income statement, several points should be kept in mind. First, the income statement typically segregates "operating income" from "financial income." Operating income tells how much the business is making from its sales operation, while financial income tells how much it is making from interest and financing activities.

Although investments and interest income are good signs, if the operating income of the business is meager, the long-term profitability of the business is questionable.

Expenses

The expense section must be carefully analyzed as well. Expenses that should be included are payroll, advertising, interest expense, and various overhead expenses. Are all major expenses listed? Are expenses being handled consistently year to year?

If at least two years of financial statements are available, you should compare the company's profit margins and overhead expense. The gross margin (or gross profit) is the difference between:

Sales – Cost of goods sold = Gross margin (Gross Profit)

Using Percentage Analysis

Gross margin is the difference between the cost of inventory and the price at which it is sold. These numbers can be expressed as percentages. Profit margin is gross margin divided by sales. When profitability declines, the business may be in trouble and may not be a good credit risk.

For example, assume that a business had the following three year results:

	Year 1	Year 2	Year 3
Sales	$200,000	$240,000	$300,000
Cost of Goods Sold	(160,000)	(195,000)	$250,000
Gross Margin	$ 40,000	$ 45,000	$ 50,000

In this example, the business looks increasingly profitable. Sales are rising nicely, and profit margin is always rising gently from

$40,000, to $45,000, to $50,000. If we express these numbers as percentages of sales, however, the picture is far different.

	Year 1	Year 2	Year 3
Sales	100%	100%	100%
Cost of Goods Sold*	(80%)	(81%)	(83%)
Margin*	20%	19%	17%
(*as a percent of sales)			

Using percentages reveals that the company is in fact becoming progressively less profitable on its sales. During the three years the gross margin has decreased from 20 percent to 17 percent. This is a 15 percent drop in profitability (3 percent change/20 percent) and the company appears headed for trouble.

Income statement analysis must be done with care. What seems obvious may not be correct on closer inspection.

Predicting a Customer's Cash Flow

A customer will need cash to pay your bill. Accordingly, it's important to be able to predict a customer's cash flow because that is also a measure of ability to pay your bill. If there is a severe cash flow shortage you may not get paid.

Although you may have a customer's cash flow statement in front of you, remember that this represents the customer's results from last year. To predict if your bill will get paid you need to predict the customer's cash flow in the future. Although predicting the future is always unreliable, you can get a general idea by analyzing a current balance sheet. A current monthly balance sheet is preferable to the latest end-of-year balance sheet, because the numbers will be more current.

A credit seller typically expects accounts receivable will be turned into cash within 30 to 120 days. Therefore, the amount of accounts receivable is a key to knowing how much cash the business credit applicant may have during the next six months to one year.

Similarly, inventory is typically turned into either cash or accounts receivable. Accordingly, the amount of inventory listed on the balance sheet is a key to both cash and accounts receivable. There should be careful analysis of both accounts receivable and inventory, because these assets will be turned into cash, thus directly affecting the bill-paying ability of the credit buyer.

Trouble Spots

However, be especially careful in looking at accounts receivable and inventory, because these are accounts that are also susceptible to manipulation or overvaluation. For example, if a business does not write off its bad debts, the accounts receivable will be overstated, so the assets on the balance sheet will be far too high. This may lead a seller to the conclusion that the buyer will have ample accounts receivable and ample cash flow with which to repay debt in the year ahead. In fact, many of those delinquent accounts receivable may never be turned into cash.

Another large asset item that may be misstated is inventory. Many firms fail to report inventory at a realistic value. For example, a retail furniture store may have obsolete items in its inventory that will never be sold. However, they may be reluctant to report them at a realistic value. Unsalable inventory should simply be written off the books. The credit customer may continue, however, to list unsalable assets on the balance sheet.

A credit seller analyzing the balance sheet may speculate that this inventory will probably be sold within the next year and turn into accounts receivable or cash. This may be a serious mistake if the inventory is not in salable condition or is overvalued for one reason or another. This should illustrate that the value of unaudited financial statements should be questioned and should not be given as much weight as figures audited by a CPA. A CPA will look at the reasonableness of both the accounts receivable and inventory figures on the balance sheet and will not express an opinion if those values are materially overstated. In fact, creditors who have relied on inaccurate balance sheets have been known to successfully sue outside CPAs who have audited the financial statements and expressed an unwarranted favorable opinion on their fairness.

THE CASH FLOW STATEMENT

A relatively new financial statement is called the statement of cash flows. As the name suggests, this statement summarizes information about the flow of cash in and out of the company from one year to the next.

To a creditor, this can be constructive information for determining whether to extend credit to a buyer. This is especially true when the customer's business does not change very much from year to year, so last year's statement will be a good predicter of this year's results.

A sample cash flow statement is shown in Figure 4-3.

Statement of Cash Flows

Cash flows from operating activities	198,000
Cash flows from investing activities	(181,000)
Cash flows from financing activities	(15,000)
NET INCREASE IN CASH	2,000
Cash at beginning of year	8,000
Cash at end of year	10,000

FIGURE 4-3 *Sample Cash Flow Statement*

Format

The cash flow statement shows cash flows from operating activities, investment activities, and financing activities. For example, the statement of cash flows will separate the amount of cash received from customers from the amount paid out to employees or to suppliers. The amount paid for interest and the amount paid for income taxes will also be detailed. The figure "net cash provided by operating activity" is the result of subtracting outflow from inflow. This is an important figure because it shows whether the business has a positive cash flow from its normal business.

There will also be an investing section that will show cash flows from investing activities. If a piece of equipment is sold, the sale price will be listed as inflow. If new equipment is purchased, the cost will be shown as outflow. Notice how easy it would be to show a positive cash flow by merely taking operating assets like cars, trucks, or computers and selling them during the year to provide more cash flow. Although this provides cash, it also decreases long-range profitability by selling off useful assets. Accordingly, you need to keep in mind that the real source of cash flow is operations, not financing.

The cash flow statement also shows cash flows from financing activity such as the issue of stock in a corporation or cash raised from issuing bonds or promissory notes. Finally, the statement also details amounts such as dividends or draws paid to owners.

It is important for creditors to know if a business can generate positive cash flow from its operating activities or whether it needs to borrow money or sell assets to maintain that cash flow. While net income on the income statement is an important measure, the ability to generate cash to pay debts is of more immediate importance to a creditor who expects to be repaid within a year. Accordingly, the manager responsible for approving credit lines to business customers should be well aware of the cash flow statement and how to use it.

IMPORTANT EARNINGS AND SOLVENCY RATIOS

One of the traditional and most important ways of analyzing a set of financial statements is to prepare earnings and solvency ratios. These are calculated by taking amounts from the balance sheet, income statement, and cash flow statement and deriving certain ratios. For example, a well-known ratio is working capital, which is merely the current assets minus the current liabilities or debts of a company. This shows the cushion that the company will have between the assets that will probably turn into cash within the operating cycle and the debts that need to be paid during that period. The greater the cushion, the greater comfort the creditor will have that the buyer will have the ability to pay for the goods during the period. Some of the more useful ratios are illustrated in Figure 4-4 at the end of the chapter.

CHAPTER PERSPECTIVE

Commercial customers normally buy in larger quantities than individuals, so credit sellers must be more careful in offering credit and setting credit limits when business customers are involved. Because a commercial customer's financial affairs are normally more complicated than an individual's, more care must be taken in evaluating the customer's creditworthiness.

The primary tool in evaluating a credit application from a business is financial statement analysis. This analysis must be performed with some knowledge of accounting conventions known as generally accepted accounting principles. Financial statements consist of three main statements: the income statement, the balance sheet, and the cash flow statement. Because your bill will be paid with cash, it is especially important to be able to predict the customer's future cash flows. Another useful tool is traditional ratio analysis. A number of useful financial ratios were illustrated in the chapter.

Earnings Performance Ratios from the Income Statement

Rate of return $=$ $\dfrac{\text{Income before interest expense and taxes}}{\text{Average total assets}}$
on assets*

Rate of return $=$ $\dfrac{\text{Net income}}{\text{Net sales}}$
on sales*

Liquidity (bill-paying) Ratios from the Financial Statements

Current ratio* $=$ $\dfrac{\text{Current assets}}{\text{Current liabilities}}$

Quick ratio* $=$ $\dfrac{\text{Cash + mkt. securities + receivables}}{\text{Current liabilities}}$

Inventory $=$ $\dfrac{\text{Cost of goods sold}}{\text{Average inventory}}$
  turnover*

Average collection $=$ $\dfrac{\text{Accounts receivable}}{\text{Sales}} \times 365$
  period**

* the higher the better
** the lower the better

FIGURE 4-4 *Earnings and Solvency Ratios*

Consult Barron's *Accounting and Taxation* for a further discussion of ratio analysis.

Using Collateral

INTRODUCTION AND MAIN POINTS

This chapter presents an alternative means of reducing risk—the use of collateral.

This chapter discusses these topics

- How collateral reduces risk
- When to request collateral from a customer
- What happens to the collateral after default by a customer
- The various types of collateral
- How real estate can be used as collateral
- How goods themselves can often be collateral
- The basis of UCC Security Interests
- The basic filing requirements
- How the law treats competing interests in collateral

HOW COLLATERAL REDUCES RISK

Collateral—a tangible asset offered as security until a debt is repaid—is a classic way for a lender or a credit seller to reduce the risk of nonpayment by a buyer or borrower. While certain retail sellers such as car dealers demand collateral from their customers, other types of businesses seldom require collateral before selling to credit buyers. All credit sellers should consider using collateral either at the time of sale or when collection of the bill seems difficult.

A seller can repossess collateral in the event that a credit buyer fails to repay the amount owed. For example, a bank typically demands collateral from a borrower. In the event of nonpayment the bank will be able to sell the collateral to satisfy the debt.

WHO ASKS FOR COLLATERAL

According to industry custom, most retailers seldom ask for collateral when they extend credit to a customer. However, certain retailers—such as car dealers and equipment dealers, among others—typically require collateral. Certain kinds of service industries do not ask for collateral, while others have collateral by operation of state law in the form of liens.

For example, when a CPA performs accounting services for a business, the CPA performs the services first, then sends a bill. By custom CPAs and other professionals do not ask for collateral even if they expect to submit a large bill. In some states professionals such as CPAs have the legal right to seize the customer's books and records as a *lien* for the work performed (a lien is merely a legal claim against property). However, the use of such liens by professionals is generally considered unethical.

Liens versus Collateral

When a carpenter performs services for a homeowner, the carpenter will not demand collateral to reduce the risk of nonpayment. However, the law provides that carpenters and other artisans who go unpaid can attach a *mechanic's lien* on the improved property and force it to be sold to satisfy the unpaid bill. In effect, the lien gives the artisan the same thing as collateral—the right to attach property should a bill go unpaid (for more on liens, see Chapter 17, "Understanding Liens and Garnishments").

Industry Custom

The use of collateral seems to depend more on industry custom than either the riskiness of the credit transaction or the sheer dollar amount of the transaction. For example, a retailer who sells a $500 suit may not request that the suit become collateral in the event the buyer fails to pay. On the other hand, a retailer who sells a $500 washing machine on credit will probably require that the washer itself stand as collateral for the unpaid purchase price.

Similarly, many businesses will provide thousands of dollars of services to a customer without requiring collateral or other risk-reducing tactic. In the event of default or a bankruptcy, the service provider is left with little recourse when competing against other creditors for the buyer's inadequate assets. (For more on this topic, see Chapter 19, "Dealing with Debtors in Bankruptcy.")

Collateral should be requested whenever risk is high. For example, when a business is dealing with a first-time buyer and is unable to assess the creditworthiness of the buyer by conventional means, a demand for collateral would be appropriate. Also, when a longtime customer falls far behind in making payments on an open account, the seller should consider insisting on collateral. In both cases, collateral greatly reduces the risk of nonpayment.

For example, if the buyer is in dire financial straits and is forced to file for bankruptcy, the Federal Bankruptcy Code protects creditors who have collateral and generally provides more limited remedies to creditors without the foresight to demand collateral. These creditors will get a percentage of the debtor's assets after all the collateral is used up and after all the lawyers' bills and court costs have been paid. Many times such creditors get nothing at all. (See Chapter 19, "Dealing with Debtors in Bankruptcy.")

Selling Goods

Sellers of tangible goods are in a much better position to request collateral than providers of services. Typically, the seller of goods on credit can request that the purchased item—such as a home appliance—become collateral. For three reasons sellers of goods on credit have a natural advantage when they demand collateral. First, the seller knows the identity of the property; second, using the purchased goods as collateral seems to be a natural part of the transaction; third, buyers will put up collateral simply because it's customary for such sellers to demand collateral.

Service Providers

Demanding collateral becomes more cumbersome when the seller is providing a service. Traditionally, service providers seldom request collateral. People know that a bank will demand collateral before it loans money. People know car dealers will finance a car only when they can repossess the car for nonpayment. But people would be shocked if a service provider asked for collateral. However, the law protects many such service providers with special liens that relate to the property for which the service is provided. (See Chapter 17, "Understanding Liens and Garnishments.")

EFFECT OF COLLATERAL AFTER DEFAULT BY CUSTOMER

For the credit seller there are several procedural advantages of collateral.

1. It increases bargaining power against a nonpaying buyer.

2. It provides assets that may be claimed in the event of default.

3. It provides protection in bankruptcy proceedings.

Consequences of Having Collateral

Demanding collateral has both legal and practical consequences. Legally, the availability of collateral gives a credit seller enhanced legal protection in the event of a default by a customer. Outside bankruptcy, the credit seller may be able to repossess and sell the collateral after a customer's default. Assuming the collateral retains its value and the sale proceeds pay off the buyer's debt, this protection greatly reduces the default risk for the seller.

Practical Advantages of Collateral

Collateral gives the creditor increased bargaining power over the customer. Customers with unsecured debts—debts not backed up by collateral—normally face no immediate consequences after a default. In contrast, a buyer who stands to lose collateral will typically be far more eager to see that the debt is paid and the property retained.

TYPES OF COLLATERAL

In most cases, when a credit seller sells goods to a customer, the goods themselves will serve as collateral.

For example, when an appliance dealer sells a stereo on credit, the stereo itself is the collateral for the transaction. If the buyer fails to make installment payments as promised, the stereo dealer has the right to repossess the collateral and resell it to raise cash.

Although goods themselves are collateral, there are other alternatives more commonly used by businesses who are not retailers, or by retailers who find they need collateral after the initial sale. For example, suppose an office supply company has sold several thousand dollars of office supplies on credit to an old customer. Because of a business downturn the customer is in financial straits and fails to pay the bill for several months. At this point the seller should try to convince the customer to pledge collateral to secure the unpaid bill. As we'll see, almost anything of value can be used as collateral. In this case, resourcefulness can really pay off. Even if the customer seems to have already pledged all available assets as collateral, there may be something of value—like a potential tax refund—that can help reduce the seller's risk.

Collateral Categories

Actually, anything of value can be put up as collateral. From the seller's perspective, the collateral should have an ascertainable value or market value and should also be easy to sell. However, even difficult to evaluate and difficult to sell collateral is better than no collateral at all.

Collateral is classified into a number of categories.

1. Consumer goods
2. Farm products
3. Equipment of the buyer
4. Inventory of the buyer
5. Intangibles
6. Real estate

Collateral is classified by its use to the buyer. The same item could fall into different classifications. For example, a stove is in the category of consumer goods if the buyer is a homeowner. If the buyer is a restaurant that same stove would be classified as equipment. If a retailer has bought the stove from a manufacturer or wholesaler, the stove would be classified as inventory.

Consumer Goods

As the name suggests, consumer goods are used or bought primarily for personal, family, or household use. Examples are clothing, home appliances, furniture, musical instruments, and jewelry.

Farm Products

Farm products include crops, livestock, or supplies used or produced on a farm, including the products of crops and livestock. For example, maple syrup, milk, and eggs would all be classified as farm products.

Equipment

Equipment is an item for use primarily in a business (including a farm or a profession). Examples are machinery and tools. Generally, tangible collateral that will not fit into the consumer goods, farm products, or inventory categories will be classified as equipment.

Inventory

Inventory is goods held for resale in the ordinary course of business. This would include both finished goods and the raw materials held by a manufacturer. For example, a furniture manufacturer's inventory would consist not only of finished pieces of furniture, but also furniture under construction (often called "work in progress"), and the wood, hardware, and upholstery material to be used in the manufacture of furniture.

Intangibles

Intangibles are property without physical form. Intangibles are rights rather than property. In some cases intangibles are evidenced by a legal document such as a stock certificate, but in other cases, there may be no document. For example, a person's right to receive money in the future (called an account receivable) is not typically evidenced by a piece of paper. In either case, such intangibles can serve as collateral for a debt.

Various kinds of intangibles can serve as collateral. In addition to accounts receivable, promissory notes, stocks, bonds, and even installment obligations held by the buyer can be collateral.

For example, if you are a wholesaler and have sold a refrigerator to a retailer on credit, and the retailer has sold the refrigerator to a consumer on an installment contract, the installment contract itself could be taken as collateral by the wholesaler to secure repayment of the debt owed by the retailer to the wholesaler. The wholesaler could thus obtain payment directly from the consumer.

Other types of intangibles can also serve as collateral. For example, even the right to receive a tax refund in the future can serve as collateral because it will turn into cash in the future.

After-acquired Clauses

A creditor can claim specific property once the debtor signs a "security agreement" describing the collateral. In addition, in some cases, a creditor may insert a clause called an "after-acquired" clause into the agreement with the debtor. An "after-acquired" clause allows the creditor to attach not only existing collateral but also property that the borrower may acquire in the future. For example, assume that a supplier has sold kitchen equipment on credit to a customer who operates a cafe. The agreement between the two businesses specifies that the seller can attach both the buyer's current equipment and also its "after-acquired" equipment as collateral. If the buyer purchases additional equipment even for cash, this equipment becomes the collateral for the credit purchase.

Obviously, this type of arrangement greatly benefits the seller and is detrimental to the buyer. No one else will want to lend money or sell on credit to the debtor. There are some exceptions to the operation of this type of clause, however.

The debtor will still be able to borrow additional funds or buy additional goods or inventory on credit despite the after-acquired clause if the debtor takes precautions. Generally when the debtor is buying additional equipment on credit the new seller must file a new security agreement and notify the first seller within ten days after the equipment is delivered. In the case of inventory, the new seller must take these steps before the inventory is delivered to the buyer. If these steps are taken, the new credit seller can have the newly delivered goods as collateral despite the presence of the after-acquired clause in favor of an earlier seller or lender.

REAL ESTATE AS COLLATERAL

Real estate can also be used as collateral for a debt. In fact, mortgages create a collateral arrangement in real property. When you finance the purchase of your home and you default, the bank or other financial institution will repossess your home, sell it at a foreclosure sale, and use the proceeds to satisfy the unpaid debt.

Businesses can also use real estate as collateral for debts. In this case, the parties would use a mortgage, typically a second mortgage, that needs to be filed in the county in which the real estate is located. When a seller takes a mortgage on the buyer's property, the seller will be able to foreclose on the property if the buyer fails to pay the debt as promised.

Lines of Credit

Lines of credit are often established on the basis of a mortgage, either for businesses or for individuals. A bank, for example, might grant a borrower a $40,000 line of credit, taking back a mortgage on the borrower's real estate. If the borrower uses the line of credit and fails to repay, the bank may foreclose on the real estate to satisfy the unpaid debt.

The proceeds of a loan secured by real estate need not be used to purchase real estate. For example, a buyer might put up some vacation property as collateral for a debt, but use the proceeds to buy goods from the seller or may use the proceeds for something else.

Fixtures

A common type of financing involves fixtures. A fixture is simply an item that is permanently affixed to real property. For example, if a cafe purchases an oven from a retailer on credit and attaches the oven into the real estate by using bricks and mortar to make the oven part of a wall, the item has been transformed into a fixture.

The law treats fixtures as real property rather than personal property. In other words, once the oven was bricked into the wall, it became part of the building. Because of this problem, the law requires a special fixtures filing for those who wish to use fixtures as collateral. Fixtures filings are generally filed in the county in which the real estate is located.

UCC SECURITY INTERESTS

To designate goods as collateral, parties must abide by state law. When one party can attach specific property as collateral, that party is said to hold a "security interest" in the property. There are generally two ways to create a security interest in the property.

1. By physical possession of the property (also called a "pledge")
2. By creating a security agreement

The most common way to create a security interest in personal property that is not real estate is to execute a written "security agreement" between the parties. The security agreement might specify that the creditor may claim specific property owned by the buyer as security for repayment of a debt. For example, a retailer may require a credit buyer of a refrigerator to sign a security agreement in which the buyer agrees that the seller may claim the refrigerator as collateral if the buyer fails to pay the purchase price of the refrigerator as agreed. The seller's security agreement creates a "security interest" in the refrigerator, which is now the seller's collateral. Note carefully that the buyer retains legal title to the collateral despite the seller's security interest.

Alternately, a seller may gain a security interest in property by merely taking possession of it. For example, in a pawnshop, the store owner has physical possession of goods and has a security interest in those goods for repayment of the debts of the customers. Similarly, any seller who takes physical possession of collateral will have a security interest in that collateral. For example, if a buyer gives a seller stock certificates as collateral until a purchase price for goods is paid, the seller holding the securities has a security interest in those securities and may sell them if not paid as promised. Because the security interest is created by possession, no written security agreement is needed.

FILING REQUIREMENTS

Although a valid written security agreement creates a security interest in property of the buyer, a security agreement only establishes the interest in the property between the two parties, but does not preclude a third-party claim. In order to establish priority to collateral, a credit seller must take an additional step beyond obtaining a security agreement from the buyer. The seller must also "perfect" a security interest in order to protect the collateral against the claims of other parties.

How to Perfect

A security interest is normally "perfected" by filing a document with the state called a *Financing Statement*. This is sometimes called "UCC Form 2" and the security agreement is sometimes referred to as "UCC Form 1." Once the UCC Form 2 is filed with the state government—usually at the state capital—the seller will have priority to the collateral over competing claims by other creditors or the government.

For example, assume that a credit buyer has defaulted and appears to be insolvent. At the same time, the seller needs to claim the collateral. Further assume that the Internal Revenue Service has issued a tax lien on all of the debtor's property. If the security interest of the seller has not been perfected with a filed financing statement, the IRS or another creditor may have prior claim on collateral, leaving the credit seller with nothing.

Filing a financing statement is relatively simple, and provides good protection to the credit seller because it gives absolute priority to the first party to claim the property as collateral.

The Pledge

An alternative way to perfect a security interest is by taking possession of the collateral. When a creditor or credit seller takes physical possession of collateral, a security interest is created; that interest is considered a "perfected" security interest that takes priority over other parties and other competing interests.

Automatic Perfection

The law also recognizes "automatic perfection" of security interests in certain cases. When there is a valid security agreement in force, the law in most states recognizes automatic perfection if the collateral is consumer goods or a farm product under $2,500 in value.

For example, if a retailer sells a household appliance worth $800 to a consumer on credit and takes a security agreement which allows the seller to claim the appliance as collateral, there is not only a security interest, but a perfected security interest in the appliance that operates automatically by law. This automatic perfection allows the seller to have priority to the appliance should the buyer default. Retail sellers are allowed automatic perfection because it eliminates the need for hundreds of thousands of UCC filings to be made in state capitals each year for hundreds of thousands of small household appliances subject to retail installment contracts.

COMPETING INTERESTS IN COLLATERAL

After a default, there may be competing interests in collateral. As a rule, within a class, first in time, first in right. In other words, if two parties hold a security interest in a particular item of collateral, the first party to obtain the security interest will prevail. Similarly, if two parties have a perfected security interest, then the first party to have perfected the interest will prevail. In a foreclosure sale, after a repossession, if the sale realizes more than the debt owed to the creditor with priority, the excess would go to the competing junior creditors. A full discussion of foreclosure is found in Chapter 18, "Repossessing Collateral."

CHAPTER PERSPECTIVE

Businesses that sell on credit should understand how the use of collateral can reduce risk. By demanding collateral a seller will have specific property to attach should the customer's bill go unpaid. Typically businesses engaged in rendering services do not ask for collateral.

Industry custom dictates which credit sellers normally request collateral. Businesses selling durables—such as appliances and autos—typically require the purchased item to stand as collateral. Sellers of goods usually request collateral from a customer with whom they are dealing for the first time. Additionally, it is a good idea to request collateral when a customer falls behind in making payments on a big order.

After a default by a customer the seller can repossess the collateral and sell it to satisfy the debt. Generally the repossession must be carried out without a breach of the peace and the sale must be conducted in a reasonable commercial manner.

Almost anything of value can be used as collateral. It is preferable that the collateral have an easily ascertainable value and can also be easily sold should the need arise. Most collateral is comprised of goods—either consumer goods, farm products, equipment, or inventory. However, intangibles such as accounts receivable and stock are good but often overlooked choices.

Additionally, real estate can be used as collateral. In this case the credit seller will be taking a mortgage on the property. Foreclosing on real estate is much more complicated than foreclosing against a security interest in goods under the UCC. Fixtures can also serve as collateral, but a special fixtures filing is required.

Occasionally two creditors will accept the same item as collateral if it has enough value. In this case the law has special rules that resolve the competing interests in the collateral.

Legal Requirements in Granting Credit

INTRODUCTION AND MAIN POINTS

This chapter will provide an overview of some of the legal requirements in granting credit. Business owners and managers need to be aware that the granting of consumer credit is strictly regulated by the federal government. There are penalties for violating these laws and ignorance of these provisions is no excuse.

After studying the material in this chapter you will know the following

- How the government regulates consumer credit
- The provisions of the Equal Credit Opportunity Act (ECOA)
- The important ECOA classifications
- How to avoid ECOA liability
- The purpose and the operation of the Truth in Lending Act (TIL)
- How interest rate and finance charge calculations are performed under the TIL
- Problems that could lead to TIL liability

GOVERNMENT REGULATION OF CONSUMER CREDIT

The federal government has passed a number of consumer protection regulations concerning consumer credit. Any business selling goods or services to consumers on credit must comply with every one of these federal laws. Additionally, many of these acts also apply to commercial credit transactions even when no traditional retail consumers are involved. You cannot assume because you deal only with other businesses that these laws will not apply to you and your business. There are also a number of state laws governing credit.

Formerly the federal government was not at all involved in consumer credit transactions. Credit was considered a private contractual matter between a business and its customers or clients. If there was any regulation at all, it was left to the states.

Today, businesses must be extremely careful in managing their credit function because this is strictly regulated by the federal government. Failure to comply with these laws can spell trouble for your business. There are at least four major federal laws that cover the credit function.

1. Equal Credit Opportunity Act (ECOA)
2. Truth in Lending Act (TIL)
3. Fair Credit Reporting Act (FCRA)
4. Fair Debt Collection Practices Act (FDCPA)

Before looking at these laws in detail, it's helpful to know why the federal government requires businesses, large and small, to bear this regulatory burden.

Purpose of Government Involvement

Congress enacted the Equal Credit Opportunity Act (ECOA) because businesses and lenders were awarding credit on a discriminatory basis. Women and minority-group members were being discriminated against systematically in the granting of credit and loans. Because of the importance of consumer credit in most Americans' day-to-day life, Congress stepped in to ensure that all Americans would have equal access to credit regardless of sex, color, religion, or national origin.

Before the passage of this law, it was not unusual for lenders and businesses to routinely discriminate against members of certain groups because they were not considered creditworthy. For example, it was extremely hard for women to get credit of any kind. There was a general perception that women were only "casual" workers and not part of the regular work force. Some people assumed that even if a working woman was single and employed she might soon get married, have a baby, and quit her job. Because there was some possibility that this might happen, many businesses routinely denied credit to all women. This treatment was obviously unfair, and because of the importance of credit in our modern society, Congress stepped in to assure that the marketplace would make credit available without regard to the applicant's sex.

Expanding Access for Minority Groups

Similarly, in years past, members of minority groups were typically denied credit by lenders and businesses. There was a perception that people of color were less creditworthy than members of the general population. Instead of judging a minority-group applicant's credit application on its own merits, many lenders and businesses simply rejected all applications on the basis of color.

For example, it was not unusual for interviewers to include a "code word" or symbol when a minority-group member made an application for credit. This code word or symbol would tip off the person in the credit department who would make the ultimate decision about granting credit, that the application should be denied.

Although there is evidence that subtle discrimination is still practiced against people of color, this type of discrimination is illegal under federal law. The best policy is to arrange your credit function to comply fully with both the letter and the spirit of the law.

Correcting Other Abuses

While the federal government is interested in expanding the access to credit, it is also interested in policing many abuses in granting credit. The Truth in Lending Act (TIL), Fair Credit Billing Act (FCBA), and Fair Debt Collection Practices Act (FDCPA) were all enacted because some businesses, credit bureaus, and collection agencies were either sloppy or dishonest.

Although most businesses, credit bureaus, and collectors are honest, some unscrupulous operators took advantage of many consumers, for example, by misrepresenting credit terms. Similarly, some credit bureaus were notoriously sloppy about maintaining their records, and the results were disastrous for the affected individuals. For example, if a credit bureau is sloppy or inaccurate, it could give a poor credit rating to an individual who in fact has an excellent bill-paying history. As a result, that individual may not qualify for a home mortgage or a car loan and without the use of credit may never be able to purchase a home or a car. In the past, bill collectors and collection agencies also often resorted to strong-arm tactics in collecting bills. For some collectors, midnight calls and the use of threats and profanity were a normal part of their business.

What Areas Are Regulated

In response to literally thousands of consumer complaints, the federal government now regulates the entire credit function. Because these are federal laws they apply equally in all fifty states. Together these federal statutes cover ten specific areas:

1. Advertising of credit terms
2. The credit application process
3. Access to credit
4. Disclosure of credit terms
5. Maintenance of an individual's credit history
6. Correcting credit bureau mistakes
7. Billing disputes
8. Correcting billing errors
9. Debt collections
10. Garnishments

Garnishments are discussed in detail in Chapter 17, "Understanding Liens and Garnishments." Additionally, in the federal bankruptcy law there are special rules governing collections; this is discussed in Chapter 19, "Dealing with Debtors in Bankruptcy."

With these federal laws, the granting of credit is no longer a private matter between a business and its customer. Ignorance of these laws is no excuse, and failure to comply with these laws can lead to stiff penalties. Although the country has been in a deregulatory mood, many consumer groups and politicians have continually called for more, not less, regulation in this area.

State Requirements

Many states have legal requirements in addition to the basic federal statutes discussed in the text. Because these requirements vary state by state, detailed coverage is impossible in a book of this size. Many states have usury laws—laws that establish a maximum interest rate on credit and lending transactions. You should consult a local attorney or a U.S. Small Business Administration office to learn what local requirements governing credit may exist in your area.

EQUAL CREDIT OPPORTUNITY ACT

The Equal Credit Opportunity Act (ECOA) was passed in 1974 with the goal of broadening the availability of credit within the economy. Congress realized that the business community had systematically denied credit to women and members of minority groups. The *Equal Credit Opportunity Act* is also known as Regulation B, Title VII of the Consumer Credit Protection Act.

The Equal Credit Opportunity Act prohibits discrimination on account of
1. Sex
2. Marital status

3. Race
4. Color
5. Religion
6. National origin
7. Age
8. Receipt of welfare funds

Marital Status

Although you may feel that unmarried persons are inherently worse credit risks than married couples, this belief cannot be used in making a decision about granting credit to an individual. Also, you must take part-time income into account in making a credit decision. It is appropriate, however, to inquire about the potential length of the part-time employment. Although part-time work is often temporary, many full-time workers can also be laid off or fired.

A business cannot insist that a married person applying for an individual account get a joint account instead. For example, if a wife applies for retail credit, the retailer cannot insist that the wife establish a joint account with her husband. However, the wife's own creditworthiness should be used in deciding whether she will be granted credit.

Creditors generally may not ask questions about marital status. However in community property states such as Texas and California—where husbands and wives have a one-half interest in both spouses' earnings and debts—this inquiry would be proper because the question is relevant to the amount of the applicant's earnings that could be legally claimed by the other spouse. Similarly, existing credit customers cannot have their credit limited or eliminated merely because they get married.

Other Privacy Protection

Other areas of family privacy are also protected from inquiry. For example, a business cannot inquire whether applicants are using birth control devices or whether they plan to have children.

When one spouse applies for credit, the business cannot reject the application merely because the applicant's spouse has a bad credit history. For example, suppose a married woman has applied for credit. The business learns that the applicant's husband has a very poor payment history and has filed for bankruptcy within the previous two years. Although this may seem relevant if the parties are married, the business cannot use this information to turn down the applicant's credit application, which must be judged on its own merits.

Not surprisingly the same rule applies to the bad credit rating of an ex-spouse. A business cannot use an ex-spouse's bad credit history to turn down an applicant.

A business is allowed to ask applicants questions about alimony, maintenance, and child support if the applicant has been divorced. Alimony and maintenance are amounts paid to an ex-spouse after a divorce. Child support is an amount paid to the ex-spouse to provide for a child of the preceding marriage.

Generally, a business may ask applicants if they are receiving alimony, maintenance, or child support payments, and if these funds will be used to repay credit obligations. At the same time, applicants must be informed that they need not answer these questions if the alimony, maintenance, or child support will not be used to repay the obligation.

Similarly, a business may ask a payer of alimony, maintenance, or child support if those payments will hinder the payer in repaying credit obligations.

Failure to Follow the Law

The Equal Credit Opportunity Act generally applies to a business that regularly offers credit terms. Violations of the Act can lead to serious consequences. If a credit applicant brings a complaint alleging discrimination, the applicant can sue you. If the court is persuaded that there has been discrimination, awards can be adjudicated:

1. Actual damages, if there were any
2. Punitive damages up to $10,000
3. Court costs
4. Attorneys' fees

Punitive damages—sometimes called "exemplary damages"—are intended to punish wrongdoers. By awarding a large damage amount the court is making an example of them. In "class action lawsuits" brought on behalf of large numbers of persons, punitive damages of up to $100,000 are allowed. Although it may be difficult for rejected credit applicants to specify the amount that they have actually been damaged, they may still be awarded punitive damages. Punitive damages are especially costly to the loser because they are not tax deductible.

AVOIDING ECOA LIABILITY

Generally, the ECOA applies to various steps in the credit application process. A business needs to take care in dealing with credit applicants face to face and also when corresponding with them in writing. Even the design of the credit application may lead to problems.

Credit Applications
Businesses have to be careful in designing forms for credit application that elicit information on prohibited classifications. For example, a credit application that gathers information about the race, religion, or national origin of credit applicants may be considered a violation of the Act because the information can be used for prohibited purposes. Questions on the application should be limited to eliciting relevant financial information.

Interviews
The interviewer of a credit applicant should take great care to avoid asking questions about prohibited subjects. Even innocent discussions may be enough to establish liability under the Act. This area has proved troublesome for some businesses because employees can violate the Act without any intention to discriminate. What might seem like an innocent comment or line of conversation may later lead to a lawsuit if a prohibited topic was discussed.

For example, suppose an employee chitchats with a prospective credit applicant who is obviously pregnant. If the employee asks the applicant whether she expects to have more children after her child is born, this would constitute a prohibited question under the ECOA, which prohibits inquiries about child-bearing intentions, capability, or birth control practices. Even though the employee did not intend to use the information in making a credit decision, the mere asking of the question is considered improper regardless of intent.

Avoid problems in this area:
1. Train the credit interviewer to comply with the law.
2. Prepare a script to be used in credit interviews.

Training the Interviewer
The employee who will be interviewing credit applicants should have a good understanding of the ECOA's requirements. The interviewer should understand that if prohibited topics come up during the interview, this could cause serious problems for the employer and that the interviewer should immediately change the subject. The interviewer should be pleasant, but should stick

with the questions and subjects in the script. If the applicant brings up a prohibited subject, the interviewer should merely disregard the comment and move on to a relevant topic.

For example, if an applicant tries to explain that her part-time employment is not related to her seeking to have a child, the interviewer should ignore the comment and ask a question on a different topic to redirect the interview into safer territory.

Credit Scoring

A credit scoring system is a technique that awards a score to a credit applicant. The higher scores supposedly signify creditworthiness, while a low score suggests a poor credit risk. A scoring system typically would award points to an applicant who has held a particular job for a number of years, has owned a home for a number of years, has few other debts, and has a good payment history. (See Chapter 2, "Establishing a Credit Policy," which discusses the operation of a credit scoring system.)

A credit scoring system that intentionally or unintentionally discriminates against protected groups is illegal under federal law. For example, a retailer may not devise a credit scoring system that awards points because the applicant is male or if the applicant is married.

Similarly, credit scoring systems may not use the age of an elderly credit applicant as a reason to turn down a credit application.

Evaluating Income from Part-time Jobs

A creditor cannot disregard part-time income. In the past, women more often had part-time income and this income was regularly ignored in credit scoring systems. For example, if a young couple applied for a joint credit account, the credit application would request information about both spouses' earnings. If the wife was working only part-time outside the home, the business might disregard her income when deciding whether or not to grant credit and what the couple's credit limit would be.

In the past, businesses commonly assumed that the wife would probably leave her job to raise a family. Today, acting on this assumption would be a violation of the law. Businesses granting credit—either to single or married persons—must count earnings from current part-time employment just as they would count any other earnings.

Interestingly, creditors may ask an applicant about whether child support, alimony, or other payments to or from an ex-spouse are going to continue in the future. However, the applicant must be given the option of not listing these sources or drains on income on a credit application. Once they are listed, however, the businesses may make inquiries about such payments.

Applications must also contain the following notice:

"The Federal Equal Credit Opportunity Act prohibits creditors from discriminating against credit applicants on the basis of sex or marital status."

This statement must be followed by a reference to the agency that would help investigate any claims. The ECOA is enforced by the Federal Trade Commission as well as by the United States Attorney General.

Finally, businesses should ensure that all credit scoring procedures and all other credit evaluations conform to both the spirit and the letter of the ECOA. The regulations require that the credit scoring system be demonstrably and statistically sound. It would be easy to design a credit scoring system that appears outwardly objective but has the result of maintaining past patterns of discrimination. For this reason, credit scoring systems must be designed and used with care.

Elderly Applicants

The law also makes special provisions for the elderly. When a credit scoring system is used, age may be used as a factor only when the scoring system itself is "demonstrably and statistically sound." Government regulations spell out precisely what this means. However, the scoring system cannot give a negative score to applicants merely because they are elderly. Similarly a business cannot deny credit to elderly applicants merely because they are so old that the seller cannot secure credit insurance on their account (see Chapter 7, "How to Get Paid").

When a business is considering credit to an elderly applicant and the business does not employ a credit scoring system, the age of the applicant cannot be a reason for rejection. However, age can have a bearing on the applicant's earning power and probable length of employment. Accordingly, these factors can be considered in making the credit decision.

However, businesses should remember that ECOA does not require credit to be given to anyone. Standard factors such as past credit history, employment, and length of time on the job are all relevant factors in determining whether or not the person will be granted credit.

Procedures after a Rejection

When an applicant is turned down for credit, if an explanation is requested, it must be provided. The best policy is to provide this in writing to establish that the notice has been given. If the adverse decision was based on a credit report, that fact should probably be mentioned at this point. As will be discussed, credit applicants have a right to examine their credit reports and also have the right to correct mistakes on those reports.

TRUTH IN LENDING ACT

The Truth in Lending Act (TIL), also known as Title I of the Consumer Credit Protection Act, was enacted to assist consumers in shopping for credit. The law's stated goal is

> "... to assure a meaningful disclosure of credit terms so that the consumer will be able to compare more readily the various credit terms available ..."

In the past, it was not unusual for credit sellers to advertise misleading or varying credit terms that proved confusing to consumers.

Interest can be calculated in various ways. If one retailer computes simple interest while the other uses compound interest, then the former will charge less for the credit. Even compound interest can be calculated differently. Compounding can be done on a daily, weekly, or monthly basis. Additionally, the seller could use the highest, lowest, or average monthly balance in computing the interest.

Additionally, unscrupulous sellers could offer a "low ball" interest rate and earn back additional profit by tacking on additional "fees." For example, assume that two retailers offer credit terms. One retailer offers credit at 11 percent simple interest. The other retailer offers 10 percent simple interest, but unlike the first retailer, also charges certain loan fees to implement the credit transaction.

Suppose a buyer purchases $1,000 of goods from the second retailer, and repays the balance exactly one year later. In addition to interest the seller charges the buyer a loan origination fee of $25, and also bills for its standard credit check of $25. In fact the buyer will be paying back a total of $1,150 comprised of

$1,000 for the goods, $100 of interest at 10 percent, and $50 in fees. If the buyer had purchased the goods from the seller charging 11 percent interest and no fees, the buyer would have repaid only $1,100. The imposition of various processing charges and the confusing use of different credit terms can make it extremely difficult for even sophisticated business people to compare credit terms. To remedy this problem, Congress enacted the Truth in Lending Act. The law is implemented by the Federal Reserve Board and other government agencies under a set of rules called "Regulation Z."

Basic Truth in Lending Disclosure Requirements

The Truth in Lending Act does not set rates of interest. What the law requires is that sellers and lenders disclose credit terms and interest rates in an identical manner. The act generally applies to credit transactions under $25,000 that involve individuals (not corporations or partnerships) who buy goods or services primarily for personal (nonbusiness) or agricultural purposes, with a stated interest charge or repayment in at least four installments. The $25,000 limitation does not apply to real estate loans.

There are two types of credit under the act: open end credit and closed end. *Open end credit* is extended when the amount of the credit is not fixed—as in a charge account for a retail customer. On the other hand, *closed end credit* is characterized by a fixed amount—as in a bank loan. Generally, the Truth in Lending Act requires disclosure in an open end arrangement before the credit is actually used. In a closed end situation the disclosure must be made before the contract is entered into by a consumer.

Under the Act, a credit seller must disclose the total dollar amount of finance charges that will be paid over the life of the installment. Additionally, the credit seller must provide an annual percentage rate of interest calculated under a federal system. The goal here is to make the terms comparable among different sellers or financial institutions. (Refer to Figure 6-1 for an illustration of the required disclosures.)

Although the requirement of disclosing the finance charges and annual percentage rates is well known, there are a total of 16 different disclosures that must be made by a credit seller:

1. Annual percentage rate
2. Finance charge
3. Lender's identity
4. Payment schedule

5. Prepayment penalties, if any
6. Charges for late payments
7. Insurance required
8. Filing fees required
9. Collateral required
10. Deposits required
11. Prohibitions on assumption of the obligation
12. Demand features of the note
13. Total sales price (including interest)
14. Adjustable rate features
15. Itemization of the financed amount
16. Disclosure of items in the loan contract that are not noted on the disclosure statement

Cooling Off Period

The Truth in Lending Act creates a three-day period in which the consumer can cancel the transaction. This three-day cooling off period does not apply to the purchase of a family home.

Advertising Rules

The Act establishes strict rules about advertising credit terms. If an advertisement mentions particular topics—called *trigger terms*—the ad is required to include other types of information. These trigger terms include:

1. Down payment amount
2. Dollar amount of payments
3. Number of payments
4. Period of repayment
5. Dollar amount of the finance charge

If the advertisement mentions any of these five topics, the following five disclosures must be made:

1. Cash price (or amount of a loan)
2. The required down payment (if any)
3. Number, amount, and frequency of payments
4. Annual percentage rate of interest
5. The total payments required (the "deferred payment price")

For example, suppose an ad states that an item is available for a low installment price of $199 per month. The dollar amount of the monthly payments is a trigger term. Once this appears in the ad, the ad must go on to make the additional five disclosures listed above.

ABC Auto Company   *Alice Green*

ANNUAL PERCENTAGE RATE The cost of your credit as a yearly rate.	FINANCE CHARGE The dollar amount the credit will cost you.	AMOUNT FINANCED The amount of credit provided to you or on your behalf.	TOTAL OF PAYMENTS The amount you will have paid after you have made all payments as scheduled.	TOTAL SALE PRICE The total cost of your purchase on credit, including your downpayment of $ _1500 –_
14.84%	$1496.80	$6107.50	$7604.30	$9129.30

You have the right to receive at this time an itemization of the Amount Financed.

☐ I want an itemization. ☒ I do not want an itemization.

Your payment schedule will be:

Number of Payments	Amount of Payments	When Payments Are Due
36	$211.23	Monthly beginning 6-1-81

Insurance

Credit life insurance and credit disability insurance are not required to obtain credit, and will not be provided unless you sign and agree to pay the additional cost.

Type	Premium	Signature	
Credit Life	$120 –	I want credit life insurance.	*Alice Green* Signature
Credit Disability		I want credit disability insurance.	_____ Signature
Credit Life and Disability		I want credit life and disability insurance.	_____ Signature

Security: You are giving a security interest in:

☒ the goods being purchased.

☐ _____

Filing fees: $ **12.50**   Non-filing insurance $ _____

Late Charge: If a payment is late, you will be charged $10.

Prepayment: If you pay off early, you

☐ may ☐ will not   have to pay a penalty

☒ may ☐ will not   be entitled to a refund of part of the finance charge.

See your contract documents for any additional information about nonpayment, default, any required repayment in full before the scheduled date, and prepayment refunds and penalties.

I have received a copy of this statement.

Alice Green   5-1-81
Signature   Date

* means an estimate

FIGURE 6-1 *Truth in Lending Act Disclosure Form*

Failure to comply with these advertising rules can lead to trouble. Government agencies can order a business to change its advertising. Failure to comply with such an order can lead to a $10,000 fine.

CHAPTER PERSPECTIVE

During the first half of the twentieth century, credit transactions were largely a private matter between the buyer and the seller. However, this area is now tightly regulated by both the federal and state governments. Reacting to thousands of complaints about dishonest practices, the federal government enacted four major laws regulating the consumer credit function.

Before federal legislation was passed, women and members of minority groups were frequently discriminated against in the granting of credit. The federal Equal Credit Opportunity Act's goal is to provide equal access to credit regardless of sex, marital status, race, color, religion, national origin, age, or the receipt of welfare funds.

A business must take care to ensure that the provisions of the Equal Credit Opportunity Act are not violated during any stage of the credit application process. Not only must forms be carefully designed, but interviews must be conducted to avoid collecting information that could be used in a discriminatory manner.

Other federal laws regulate other aspects of consumer credit. In addition to expanding access to credit, the federal government is also interested in policing many potential abuses in the system. The Truth in Lending Act, Fair Credit Billing Act, and Fair Debt Collection Practices Act were all enacted because some businesses, credit bureaus, and collection agencies were either sloppy or dishonest.

How to Get Paid

INTRODUCTION AND MAIN POINTS

The other chapters in this book focus on specific aspects of a credit and collection system. This chapter focuses on one thing: how to get paid. After all, this is the goal of your entire credit and collection system.

Businesses that nearly always get paid have one thing in common: they don't take getting paid for granted. Getting paid takes work, but there are a number of strategies and techniques that can help.

After studying the material in this chapter, you will understand the following

- The need to focus on debt collections
- The need to pay attention to individual accounts
- The need for itemized billings
- When and how to offer cash discounts
- How personal contacts can increase your collections
- How telephone contacts can aid collections
- How to compose standardized collection letters
- When you need to get tough
- How to use credit insurance

THE NEED TO FOCUS ON YOUR COLLECTIONS

Many managers and business owners feel that the most important number on their financial statements is "Sales." More sophisticated persons may believe that "Net Income" is the real key to success. Because generally the more you sell the more you make, sales volume looms large for most managers and business owners.

However, for most smaller businesses, the real key to success is often the handling of "Bad Debt Expense" (also called "Uncollectible Account Expense"), which reveals how many of your sales dollars go uncollected. When you make a sale and cannot collect, the amount is booked as "bad debt expense." Accordingly this figure is a prime indicator of how your credit and collections system is operating and whether you're getting paid.

Looking at one month's or one year's bad debt expense won't tell you much, but looking at a series of months or a series of years can be revealing. For example, if your bad debt expense looks like this, you probably don't have too much to worry about.

Period 1	Period 2	Period 3	Period 4	Period 5	Period 6
$1,000	$900	$1100	$1200	$800	$1050

On the other hand, if your bad debt expense looks like this second example, you probably have a problem.

Period 1	Period 2	Period 3	Period 4	Period 5	Period 6
$1,000	$1200	$1100	$1500	$1800	$2150

In this example we see the bad debt expenses rising in a pretty steady upward trend. This means trouble: you are increasingly unable to collect your bills. The numbers themselves don't tell you *why* you have this problem, but they do indicate that you are not being paid.

When your bad debts or uncollectible accounts are rising and your sales volume is holding steady, either your credit customers are increasingly unreliable, or your collection system is no longer functioning efficiently. Of course, if your sales volume has roughly doubled during the course of this period, you'd naturally expect the uncollectible accounts to double as well, unless you've restricted the availability of credit to only the best risks.

The key to success is not just selling, but selling and collecting the money. Despite the obviousness of this statement, an alarming number of businesses pay scant attention to their collections and as a result collect less than they could. If you don't seem interested in getting paid, some customers will pick up the signal and will surely take advantage of you.

Memories are short, and that is especially true when it comes to debts. As unpaid debts get older, they are far less likely to be paid. Some customers will honestly forget to pay an old bill. Others will sometimes rationalize and invent reasons to postpone paying—either for a time or indefinitely. Still other customers will pay only when hounded. Some customers never intend to pay unless they are called on the carpet—sometimes in court.

In fact, some authorities suggest that only a little more than half the bills that are six months overdue will ever be paid. As bills age this figure drops alarmingly. Only about a quarter of bills that are twelve months old will ever be paid. In other words, if you have 20 customers that in total have owed you $10,000 for more than a year, you will probably never see $7,500 of that money.

The lesson here is that vigilance counts. Not only do you have to act, but you have to act promptly if you want to get paid. You need to have an organized collections policy and a procedure that will monitor your accounts so that you will quickly learn which customers are falling behind, and by how much. Once you are armed with this information you can not only start collecting the bills sooner, but you will also know that you have to be cautious before you sell more goods or services to the delinquent customers.

You need to train at least one staff member to handle your collections. Larger businesses should assign a person to this job permanently, while smaller businesses should assign a person to spend an afternoon or two per week to monitor collections. You may feel that this is too big a commitment of your staff's resources if collections don't seem to be a big problem. However, most managers overlook the fact that the most efficient way to raise cash is to collect your unpaid sales. The next time you need to get short-term financing, examine how much more cash would be on hand if you had persuaded all of your customers to pay.

THE NEED TO PAY ATTENTION TO INDIVIDUAL ACCOUNTS

You no doubt spend lots of effort selling or promoting your business. You need to expend the same effort in turning your successful sales into cash. One key strategy is to pay attention to each individual account.

Unfortunately, it is easy to ignore individual accounts when you delegate credit and collections responsibility to someone on the staff. Without your day-to-day personal attention, you won't realize when an individual customer is not paying. Even though your bad debts expense is constant, there may still be accounts that are turning into real problems. Early attention is the best approach to maximizing collections.

For these reasons you need to develop a clerical routine that will alert you to problem accounts. The person handling billing and collections could prepare a list on a monthly or weekly basis of bills that are more than 30 days overdue. Better yet, your own computerized accounting system should be able to generate such reports as a normal routine. These reports can also be used to build your own in-house data base that will document the credit history of your customers. The business owner or manager should take an interest in the progress of these collections. Certainly the sales staff should be alerted to any problems. If you have sales reps who call on customers, they may even be able to help with the collection efforts while they are at the customer's place of business. When customers fall badly behind in making payments, you have to think twice about selling them more goods before they have paid their balance in full.

ITEMIZED BILLINGS

One way to speed up your collections is to adopt itemized billing. An itemized bill specifically lists each portion of the bill. For example, your long-distance telephone company provides an itemized bill, providing not only a detailed listing of the charges, but also each telephone number called, the time of day, the duration of the call, and any discounts that apply to the charge. However, as the telephone billing analogy suggests, itemization does not guarantee that a bill will be more comprehensible. Indeed, the more details, the more potential for misunderstandings.

At the other extreme is so-called "country club billing" in which a few charges are noted but with little detail. Service providers still send this type of bill to a customer. Attorneys were once notorious for resisting itemized billing. It was not uncommon for a large law firm to send a handwritten bill that might say only "For legal services rendered: $25,000." However even large law firms have now abandoned this type of horse and buggy billing system.

Some customers will not pay a bill that they believe is incorrect. These customers will request a corrected bill. Other customers will refuse to pay a bill that is incomprehensible. Although the country club billing is clear, a customer might balk at paying because it may be unclear what charges are included.

Because of client complaints, most larger firms have adopted itemized billing not only to inform the client about what services have been performed, but also to justify the size of the bill. Itemized billing also has the happy side effect of speeding up collections, because customers and clients are generally more willing to pay if they understand the bill.

Itemized billing has its drawbacks from the sender's standpoint. When customers or clients have itemized details, they can more easily spot mistakes and overcharges. Although there is no hard evidence, it seems clear that billing disputes are probably increased by itemization.

Additionally, itemized bills that are too detailed cause customer confusion. There are both professional form designers and amateur form designers. An amateur effort will probably produce amateurish results. A poorly designed bill may actually slow down collections if customers have to call for explanations or if they simply put the bill aside because they can't understand it. A surprising number of bills probably fall into this category.

More importantly, itemization is expensive for the business. Preparing the itemization takes time even if you are using a computerized billing system. This is a straight administrative cost that eats into profits and robs your staff's attention from more profitable tasks.

Many firms include self-addressed envelopes with their bills, which encourages prompt payment. Using your own envelope also helps ensure that the bill and check will be returned to the right address. Although they are somewhat more expensive, you can also obtain business reply envelopes, which have the familiar slogan "Postage will be paid by addressee." These envelopes can be obtained from the post office. Your business will pay a flat fee plus a charge for each envelope you actually receive.

Although itemized bills have their drawbacks, customers have come to expect them. If you haven't been using itemized billing, the change will probably speed up your collections and help you to get paid.

CASH DISCOUNTS

A cash discount is a reduction in a customer's bill in exchange for prompt payment. The idea is to encourage prompt payment even if you realize less profit on the individual transaction. Experience has shown that this technique will increase your overall profits, even though your effective profit on the particular sale has dropped.

For example, assume that a merchant sells a $100 item on credit, but allows a 2 percent cash discount for prompt payment.

The merchant paid $80 for the item and marked it up 25 percent to its sales price ($80 × 25% = $20; $80 + $20 = $100). The customer who pays promptly gets a 2 percent discount and sends a check for $98. The merchant's profit has dropped from $20 ($100 – $80 cost) to $18 ($98 – $80 cost). Although the $2 discount amounts to only 2 percent of the customer's cost, it represented 10 percent of the merchant's profit.

Despite this loss in profit, offering cash discounts will increase your profitability. There are two reasons for this seeming contradiction. First, by speeding up collections you will have less need for short-term borrowing, so you can reduce your interest costs. Even if you don't need to borrow, you can put the cash in the bank to earn interest, or even better, you can invest in more inventory which you can sell to make 18 to 20 percent returns.

Also, remember that many bills that linger without being paid will never be paid. It is more profitable to offer a cash discount that eats into your profit potential, but insures that you get your cash in hand.

Cash discounts could be offered in a number of ways, but two methods are most common.

1. Allow the customer to deduct a percentage of the retail price (2–5%) if cash payment is made by a particular date.
2. Waive shipping and handling costs if payment is made in cash.

PERSONAL CONTACTS

Owners and managers of small businesses often complain that they are at a competitive disadvantage with big corporations. However, one area in which small businesses have a distinct advantage is in collections work. A small business is much better equipped to establish personal contacts with its customers that will help ensure that bills get paid and paid promptly.

Although owners and managers may establish the personal contacts, the more likely candidate is the staff person who will be taking care of collections. In a medium-sized business there may be one person who handles collections full time, but in many smaller offices one person will devote an afternoon or perhaps several afternoons per week to collection matters. This may also be the person who takes care of credit matters for the business.

This staff person has a distinct advantage over collections people in large corporations. Typically your customers will be close by and small in number. Accordingly, the number of problem accounts will be relatively small and the collections person will learn about the customers' bill-paying habits.

You should encourage the collections person to learn as much about a customer as possible, including all about the customer's business. Does the customer normally pay bills on time, late, or only with prodding? Does the customer have regular periods when cash is short and when cash is abundant? Obviously collection efforts should be timed to coincide with the cash flow.

Also, the collections person should ascertain who at the client business has the authority to approve bills and to sign checks. Sometimes one person has responsibility for both; sometimes this responsibility will be split between two persons. When a customer wants to avoid paying a bill, one of those two persons who must approve the bills and sign the checks will be conveniently absent.

If you have a really recalcitrant customer who refuses to pay a bill, a personal visit at work has been known to yield good results. But a personal visit can also be a complete waste of time.

TELEPHONE CONTACTS

The Yellow Pages used to use the marketing slogan "Let your fingers do the walking." This slogan sums up the advantage of making personal telephone contacts with slow payers—it is efficient. Time for personal visits is costly, and visits probably don't work much better than other collection methods. Even standardized letters can take a significant amount of time to send. A telephone reminder has two distinct advantages:

1. It is quick and cheap.
2. It may provide other useful information.

Unless the nonpaying customer is especially talkative, the call will be relatively short, and you get to make your point without much wasted effort. If the call is long distance and you do not have a WATS line (800 number), you need to consider the cost of the call or calls. You should also take care to call during business hours if the customer is in a different time zone. Calls during lunch and at the very beginning and end of the day can also catch people out of the office, which will double your long-distance costs if you have to call back later.

You should always consult directory assistance to determine if the customer has a toll-free 800 number. A surprisingly large number of small businesses have such numbers. Even if they are designed for telephone sales, oftentimes you can be transferred to other offices.

When you call, you should have all the information before you so you can discuss the debt and any disputes about the bill. Always let the person on the other end of the line talk. You want to learn the real reason for nonpayment. In some cases the customer may be willing to pay, is merely short of cash, and may be perfectly willing to pay in the future. On the other hand, when customers lie or appear to be dishonest, you can probably conclude that they are dishonest and may have no real intention of paying.

You can discover things during a phone call that would never be revealed by mail. You may learn that an individual is about to be divorced. You may find out that an individual or business is about to file for bankruptcy. Both of these facts mean that you need to take immediate collection action if you want to see any of your money. Customers would normally not reveal either of these facts in a letter.

STANDARDIZED COLLECTION LETTERS

Large businesses are well equipped to send out computerized bills and reminder letters. Although smaller businesses will find this process more burdensome, it dramatically increases your chances of being paid. If you don't act as if you want your bill paid, chances are it won't be paid. Recall that speed is essential in collections work, because the longer the bill goes unpaid the less likely it is that you will ever be paid.

At a minimum you should send a duplicate bill each month. The collections person could use a red felt-tip pen to write a reminder such as:

"Just a reminder . . ." or "Second reminder"

Handwriting gives this appeal a personal touch that will make certain customers feel guilty that they haven't paid on time as they have implicitly promised. You can also get preprinted stickers for this purpose from stationery stores and mail order houses. The messages range from cute to firm to almost nasty. Nasty messages should be used only when you don't anticipate ever doing repeat business with the customer. For example:

"We're ready to refer this account to a collection agency."

or

"Act now to protect your credit rating."

or

"Legal action will begin if payment is not received by May 1st."

Although second bills and individualized notes or stickers can induce payment, a well-designed reminder may be more effective. These letters can be standardized so the only changes required will be the customer's name and address and the amount due. The initial time spent composing the letter can be spread over many years as you repeatedly use the same letter.

If you decide to use letters instead of phone calls, you should compose at least two: one that is a pleasant reminder and one that is firm. Your first letter should be a friendly reminder. Some customers do forget to pay bills on time, and some may have to wait for others to pay them before they can pay.

Your second letter should be polite but more impersonal. You might mention that you were "surprised" or "disappointed" that they hadn't sent in their payment as they promised. Again, this will work on their guilt feelings. For those without guilt feelings, you may need a third and almost threatening letter, pointing out that your previous letters have been ignored. In this letter you may want to bring up the possibility of using a collection agency or mention that they may find themselves with an unfavorable credit rating. Of course you should delete this part if you know that the customer would sincerely like to pay but is in financial distress.

Letters should always mention that the customer is to disregard the letter if payment has been made or mailed. Naturally a number of letters cross in the mail. If a customer receives what is seen as an insulting collection letter after a late payment has been sent, you may lose a customer. It may be better to make a phone call to chat about the bill instead. Again, the key is to treat each customer as an individual. What worked with one customer may not work with another.

WHEN TO GET TOUGH

You should get tough

1. after three contacts in 60 days.
2. if the customer has tried to lie to you.
3. if there has been a history of problems with the account and one contact has been ignored.

Generally if you send a bill, then follow up with two phone calls, two letters, or a combination of calls and letters and get no response, it's time to get tough. If you did get a response and the customer wants to pay but cannot, you may want to take a chance and wait for a check. If you're being ignored, it's time to make a final demand and then to hand the matter over to a collection agency or collection attorney.

If your customer has lied to you, you might as well get tough now. There's no reason to expect that person to be honest and trustworthy later. If the delinquent customer won't pay you now, there's no reason to think you'll be paid later.

Of course you need to distinguish a lie from a "face-saving excuse." Although "the check is in the mail" story is used by customers who have no intention of paying, it is also a means of saving face for those who have forgotten the bill or those who are temporarily short of cash. Many individuals and small business owners don't like to admit that they are forgetful, or even worse are temporarily strapped for cash. Don't forget that some people always show up for the party late. Some customers will be late but will always pay—at least by the time they send in their next order.

CREDIT INSURANCE

Many sellers are unaware that they can minimize their risk by purchasing credit insurance, which is available to companies who are selling goods or services to other businesses rather than to the general public.

In a credit insurance arrangement a seller buys insurance from an insurance company that agrees to reimburse the seller if a customer fails to pay. The seller must pay a premium for this protection—generally about one percent of the insured accounts. If you are insuring $10,000 of accounts, the premium would probably be about $100.

Insurance companies are not in the business of losing money, so they will be choosy about which accounts they will insure. If one of your customers is heading for bankruptcy and hasn't paid you, you can be sure that this account will not be acceptable to the insurer. Likewise, accounts from small businesses with no track record will normally not be insurable.

A credit insurance policy will typically include a deductible amount. If a customer fails to pay a $10,000 bill, the insurer will not reimburse you for the entire amount; you might be reimbursed only $9,000 after you absorb a $1,000 deductible. Insurance companies sometimes limit their risk by insuring only a percentage of any customer's accounts. For example, the policy may provide that you have a fixed deductible, and in addition, the company will insure only 70 percent repayment of default. As with most insurance, the more risk you accept the lower your premiums will be.

Generally you will want to insure only your riskiest accounts, while the insurer would like to insure all of the less risky accounts. Typically the insurer will negotiate an arrangement that includes some of both.

You probably need to consider using credit insurance in the following cases:

1. One or two companies make up the bulk of your sales. If one of these companies fails to pay, the financial health of your business could be at stake.

2. You have sold specially manufactured goods that cannot be resold to anyone else should the buyer default.

Credit insurance is written only by a few companies, but a knowledgeable local insurance broker should be able to locate a carrier for you. You may also be able to get a reference from a trade association to which you belong.

CHAPTER PERSPECTIVE

Businesses that nearly always get paid have one thing in common: they don't take getting paid for granted. Getting paid takes work, but there are a number of strategies and techniques that can help.

Business managers and owners need to focus on collections. If your customers perceive that you are not interested in getting paid, some of them will invariably take advantage of you. You need to remember that the older the bill, the less likely it is to be paid. While it is important to pay attention to indicators such as your overall bad debt expense, it is also vital to pay attention to individual accounts. This individualized attention is required if you want to increase realization on your billings.

Certain techniques can also help you to get paid. The use of itemized bills can increase your chances of being paid. Although it takes time to itemize your charges, the result is normally increased collections. Cash discounts can increase your collections and profits. A cash discount allows the customer to get a small discount—typically 2 percent of the sales price—for prompt payment. Although this may reduce your profit margin, it speeds up collections and cash flow. Experience has shown that cash discounts improve profitability.

Personal contacts can help a business collect its bills. It is important to develop firsthand knowledge of your customers and their businesses so you can plan your collection activities for maximum results.

Telephone contacts and reminders of overdue bills are cheap, quick, and often effective. Similarly, the use of standardized collection letters at regular intervals will provide a reminder to customers that they have overdue accounts. If you act as though you care about the bill, you will usually be paid.

Finally, the purchase of credit insurance makes sense for many companies. If the customer does not pay bills, the insurer will. The use of credit insurance is especially appropriate for a major account.

Sample Collection Letters

[First Notice]

February 1, 1995

Dear XYZ Company:

Our records indicate that your account has a $750 unpaid balance. Please check your records to verify this amount and promptly send us a check for the balance. If you have recently mailed payment, please disregard this notice.

Regards,

Sam Stone
Credit Manager, ABC Co.

[Second Notice]

April 1, 1995

Dear XYZ Company:

Our records indicate that your account has a $750 unpaid balance. Despite our previous reminder, we have received no payment to date.

Please check your records to verify this amount and promptly send us a check for the balance. We would like to avoid forwarding this account to our collection agency for action. If you have recently mailed payment, please disregard this notice.

Regards,

Sam Stone
Credit Manager, ABC Co.

Understanding Accounts Receivable

INTRODUCTION AND MAIN POINTS

This chapter explains the operation and importance of accounts receivable—money that your customers or clients owe you for goods or services that you have already provided. The accounts receivable figures are among the most important data in your accounting system; they directly affect not only your cash flow but also your profit and loss position. Accounts receivable are the most important corporate asset.

Once you understand the operation of your accounts receivable, you will also be able to use the accounts receivable information as an important management tool in operating your credit and collection system. You will gain important insights into future cash flow, sales trends, and even information about individual clients and customers. A periodic analysis of your accounts receivable will tell you how your credit system is actually operating and whether changes need to be made in credit policies.

After studying the material in this chapter, you will understand the following

▬ The effect of credit sales on accounts receivable and income
▬ The relationship of your accounts receivable and the allowance account
▬ How to create an aging of your accounts receivable, and how to use the aging as a management tool
▬ The effect on your accounting records of writing off a bad debt
▬ How the tax rules governing receivables operate

CREDIT SALES AND ACCOUNTS RECEIVABLE

Although your bookkeeper or accountant will probably be keeping track of your accounts receivable, it is essential for a business owner to understand precisely how accounts receivable operate, because the status of your accounts receivable will tell you a lot about the operation of your credit and collections system and also about the general financial health of your business.

Accounts receivable can be used to predict your future cash flow, which is essential in running any business, big or small. By analyzing the composition of your accounts receivable you will know when changes need to be made in your credit and collections policies.

Cash versus Accrual Accounting

To understand the effect of credit sales and accounts receivable on your financial results, it is important to know if your business's accounting data is kept on a cash basis or an accrual basis. Most larger businesses are on the accrual basis, although some large service businesses operate on the cash basis. Generally, if you have an inventory of goods for resale you will probably be on the accrual basis, since the IRS requires tax reporting on the accrual basis for businesses with inventories. If you do not know if your accounting is done on a cash or accrual basis, consult your bookkeeper or certified public accountant (CPA). If your company conducts business on a cash basis, there are no accounts receivable.

With a cash basis accounting system, income is recognized at the time cash is received. Likewise, an expense is recorded when cash is actually spent. Accordingly, there is a close relationship between the cash position and the profit and loss for a period. Your income statement (also known as the profit and loss statement) typically will show a large profit when your cash receipts greatly exceed your cash disbursements for the period. Although a large profit in any period is generally good news, the data may be misleading, as we shall see below.

The cash basis of accounting is the system that nearly every individual uses for income tax purposes: recognition of income when cash is received and recognition of a tax deduction when cash or a check is sent. For example, if your business keeps its books on the cash basis, revenue is recognized when a customer or client pays for goods or services. Similarly when you send a check to one of your suppliers, pay a professional fee for services, or pay your taxes, you recognize an expense which reduces your income.

The basic accounting profit equation for a service business looks like the following:

Revenue – Expenses = Net income

The equation for a business that retails its inventories is somewhat more complicated:

Net Sales – *Cost of Goods Sold* * = Gross Margin
Gross Margin – *Operating Expenses* = Net Income
(* Beginning Inventory + New Inventory – Ending Inventory)

The cash basis of accounting has its pluses and minuses. One advantage is that it presents a realistic, if conservative, picture of *solvency*. Solvency is your ability to pay debts as they fall due. However, the minuses generally outweigh the pluses. In fact, the cash basis is considered unacceptable by CPAs for clients with inventories. This is primarily because of the distortions caused by credit sales. The cash basis measures profit and loss based on cash receipts and disbursements rather than the activities that generate profit. Not infrequently, this can lead managers to believe that they are doing better or worse than is really the case.

Under the cash system, a credit sale is not counted as a sale until the cash is actually received. In some cases this would have the effect of shifting income from one year to another; for example, when a sale is made in November but not paid until January of the following year. Theoretically, this deferral of recognition is unsound. Good accounting matches income to the activities that produce it. In this way managers can determine if their efforts are successful during a particular period. When a cash basis accounting system defers the recognition of income to the period in which the cash comes in, rather than when the sale or service took place, the operating results of the two periods are distorted.

Because of the distortions associated with the cash method, most larger businesses use the accrual method, which recognizes income when it is earned—that is, when the event that will yield cash takes place. To present a realistic profit and loss picture, all expenses must be matched against the revenues they help to produce. You should note that all of this is done without considering whether any cash has been received or paid out. Instead of measuring profit and loss in terms of cash receipts and disbursements, the accrual system looks at activity: the activity of earning a profit.

Generally, revenues are recorded when the goods are shipped to a customer. All the expenses that were incurred in making that sale will also be recognized in the same period. This is known as the *matching rule*.

Although both cash basis and accrual basis businesses have accounts receivable after a credit sale, only the accrual basis business will have booked any revenue for the transaction.

Effect of a Credit Sale on Income

A credit sale increases the firm's revenues and accounts receivable. Accounts receivable is an *asset account* and sits on the balance sheet (sometimes referred to as the "statement of financial position"). When the customer pays the receivable with cash or a check, the company's cash is increased and accounts receivable decreased. For example, if a $100 credit sale is made, the double-entry accounting system will increase revenues on the income statement and accounts receivable on the balance sheet by $100. When the customer pays the bill, cash is increased by $100 and accounts receivable is decreased by $100, and revenue remains the same. Revenue then is recognized when the sale is made, not when the cash is received.

Bad Debts and the Allowance Account

All businesses that sell goods or services on credit will have a number of bad debts—bills that never get paid. Businesses with tight credit policies will have fewer bad debts, while businesses with looser credit requirements will normally have a larger portion of their accounts receivable turn into bad debts.

Of course, no business would knowingly provide goods or services to a client or customer who they suspect would not pay. However, bad debts are a normal expense of doing business. Credit experts are convinced that if a business has very few or no bad debts, its credit policy is too restrictive and its business is hampered. It is more profitable to grant credit to a wider range of customers and suffer a few losses.

At the end of the year (or period) a business will have a balance of accounts receivable from its credit sales. Most of these ultimately will be paid, but a portion of those accounts receivable will not be paid and will turn into "bad debts," which are also known as "uncollectible accounts." Accordingly, at the end of the period the net realizable value of the firm's accounts receivable will be overstated by the amount of these bad debts.

For example, if the business has made $100,000 of sales, the accounting system will also have booked $100,000 of accounts receivable that managers will be expecting to turn into cash. The $100,000 figure is unrealistically high because some of those bills will never be paid. Of course, the business does not know exactly how many accounts will go unpaid, but it knows that at least some of them most likely will not be paid.

Not only is the balance of the company's accounts receivable overstated, but also profit (net income) will be overstated as well. You will recall that when a company with an accrual basis accounting system made a credit sale, it recognized income. Later, if one of the firm's accounts receivable goes unpaid, this will cause income to be overstated. The P&L will need to reflect bad debt as an expense item so that net income will not be overstated.

For example, let's assume that late in 1993 the company had a credit sale of $100. At the time, the company's accounting system increased accounts receivable by $100 and also increased revenues by $100. If that particular bill was not paid during the remainder of 1993 or in 1994, the company's profit for 1993 is overstated by $100. The company booked revenue of $100 when it made the sale, but if it never received the cash, the reported income is too high by that amount.

For financial reporting purposes the firm faces a dilemma at year end. If it reports all of its accounts receivable and revenues from credit sales, it will surely be overstating both of these accounts, because some of those sales will never be paid for. However, the company will not know precisely how many of these sales will be written off until later the following year. Although there is no perfect answer to this dilemma, the company's accountants do their best to make an estimate of bad debt expense. At year end, the company decreases its profits and its accounts receivable by an estimated amount of bad debt expense.

Accounts receivable are reduced at year end by creating an *allowance account*. This is a negative account that reduces the net amount of accounts receivable. For example, if the amount of accounts receivable at year end is $100,000, and the company's accountant determines that the allowance account is to be $5,000, then the net amount of accounts receivable on the firm's balance sheet would be listed as follows:

Accounts receivable	$100,000
less: Allowance for uncollectible accounts	– $5,000
Net receivable	$ 95,000

Bad Debt Estimation Techniques

At the end of the year or period, management must determine
the proper amount to place in the allowance account—the
amount of the firm's accounts receivable that will probably
never be paid. To determine this amount, managers typically
estimate the probable amount of bad debts by one of two methods:

1. The percentage of sales method
2. The aging method

Managers may also use a combination of the two methods in
arriving at their estimate of uncollectible accounts for the
period.

The *percentage of sales method* estimates the number of
future bad debts by multiplying the credit sales for the period by
a fixed percentage. For example, the firm may estimate that 5
percent of its credit sales will never be paid. Selection of the
actual percentage is determined with reference to past periods
and changes in both the national and local economy, the business customers, and any changes in credit policy made during
the last year.

For example, if a business has net annual credit sales of
$200,000 at year end, management might multiply this amount
by 7.5 percent to arrive at an estimated uncollectible account
amount of $15,000. This amount is recognized as an expense at
the end of the year.

$200,000 net annual credit sales
$\times 7.5\%$
$15,000 estimated bad debts for the year

Aging of Accounts Receivable

Another method used to estimate the amount of the firm's bad
debts is the aging method. Whereas the percentage of sales
method looks at annual credit sales, the *aging method* analyzes
the firm's actual accounts receivable at year end to see how long
the accounts have been unpaid. The theory here follows common sense: the longer a customer neglects to pay a bill the less
chance there is that it ever will be paid. Using this information
and an algebraic formula, management is able to derive an estimate of the current bad debt amount.

There are three steps in preparing an aging:

1. Sort the accounts by age.
2. Total the sorted accounts.

3. Multiply the summed totals by a percentage, and add the result.

The aging in Figure 8-1 illustrates how the accounts are first grouped by age and totaled. These totals are then multiplied by percentages to determine the total estimated bad debt expense. Notice that the percent of the accounts that are considered doubtful increases dramatically with the account's age. Experience has demonstrated that when accounts grow old, the debtors are far less likely to pay. Different firms use different percentages in this computation, based on their past experience.

Client	Credit Balance	0–30 days	31–60 days	61–120 days	121–182 days	Over 6 months
A Corp.	$20,000	10,000	10,000			
B Corp.	10,000					10,000
X Corp.	10,000			10,000		
Y Corp.	20,000	20,000				
Z Corp.	40,000	20,000	10,000		10,000	
	$100,000	50,000	20,000	10,000	10,000	10,000

	Amount	% Doubtful	Allowance Amount
0–30 days	$50,000	1%	$ 500
31–60	20,000	3%	600
61–120	10,000	10%	1,000
121–182	10,000	25%	2,500
182 +	10,000	50%	5,000
		Total Allowance:	$9,600

FIGURE 8-1 *Aging Analysis*

Using the Aging Analysis as a Management Tool

Besides being a convenient way to estimate the amount for the allowance account, an aging analysis is also an important credit tool for managers. An aging is especially valuable when it can be compared to similar documents prepared on a monthly basis over the last year. In fact, the aging analysis should be required monthly reading for every manager with responsibility for either sales or credit functions.

The aging of accounts receivable reveals payment patterns by your customers as a group and by individual clients. Managers will be able to tell at a glance whether their overall credit policy is too loose or too tight. If the percentage of overdue accounts is inching up, steps should be taken to restrict credit so the firm does not face an unexpected cash flow shortage down the road.

The aging will quickly reveal which clients are not paying promptly. Although the bookkeeper may be aware that a particular client has become slow in paying bills, the sales force may not realize this. The problem should be investigated before the client amasses a large bill that will never be paid. Notice that communication is important. Even a good credit and collection system will not function if the information is not given to those who need it.

The sales staff can perform an important function in the collection process. The salesperson has a personal relationship with the client and can often assist in speeding up payments. Many times the salesperson—not the credit and collections department—will be instrumental in collecting outstanding amounts. However, the sales staff cannot perform this valuable service unless they receive accurate and timely reports about overdue payments.

Effect of Writing off a Bad Debt

After a period of time, a manager may conclude that a specific account receivable will never be collected. Generally, when collection efforts have been ignored for over six months, it is highly unlikely that the client or customer will ever respond. When a manager finally determines that a specific bill is uncollectible, the amount must be written off. This is accomplished with a bookkeeping entry.

Surprisingly, the process of writing off an account receivable as a bad debt has little effect on the business's financial position and no effect on the overall balance of accounts receivable. This is because the process of writing off a bad debt or uncollectible account decreases both the total of accounts receivable and also the allowance account; the net balance of accounts receivable remains unchanged after the write-off.

Figure 8-3 illustrates the effect of writing off a $1,000 accounts receivable as uncollectible. Notice that the overall net balance of the accounts receivable account remains unchanged.

Tax Accounting versus Financial Accounting

Although proper financial accounting requires the use of an allowance account, the requirements for federal tax purposes differ greatly. In fact, the use of an allowance account for accounts receivable is now prohibited in business statements for tax purposes.

	Accounting Records Before Write-off	Accounting Records After Write-off
A/R	$100,000	$99,000
Allowance for doubtful accounts	8,000	7,000
Net balance A/R	$92,000	$92,000

FIGURE 8-3 *Writing off a Bad Debt*

The Internal Revenue Service requires businesses to use the *direct write-off method* in calculating their current bad debt expense (also known as uncollectible account expense). This method requires you to write off an account when you actually decide it cannot be collected: estimates are not allowed. Interestingly, the direct write-off method is considered unacceptable by CPAs. Figure 8-4 illustrates the differing treatment.

	Financial Accounting	Tax Accounting
Allowance method	preferred	not allowed
Direct write-off method	unacceptable	required

FIGURE 8-4 *Bad Debt Estimation Techniques*

Why the different treatments? Because the goals of financial accounting and tax accounting are quite different. When a CPA prepares your books for financial reporting, the stress is on the most accurate reporting of results. If a business is given too much discretion it may not write off its uncollectible accounts, and the result will be an overstatement of profit. Accountants strive to be conservative, so they require the use of an allowance account, which tends to depress reported profits.

The IRS, on the other hand, is in business to raise money for the U.S. Treasury by collecting federal income taxes. If the direct write-off method of estimating bad debts increases a firm's reported profits, then it also increases the firm's taxable income and the amount of tax that must be paid.

There is another important reason why the IRS insists on the direct write-off method on tax returns. The IRS is also worried that unscrupulous taxpayers may use the allowance account to create unrealistic high expenses. Such expenses would decrease taxable income and the amount of the tax that the taxpayer would owe. Of course since these expenses are noncash expenses, the net effect might be lower taxes and more cash left in the firm.

To comply with these two varying rules, a business must generally maintain two sets of accounts receivable records. One set, on the direct write-off method, is for tax return reporting, and the other set, using the allowance account, is for financial reporting purposes.

Accounts Receivable Control

Managers need to understand the close relationship of accounts receivable and cash flow. In fact, for most businesses that make credit sales, accounts receivable are the largest source of cash flow on the balance sheet. In the normal operating cycle, cash is turned into inventory that is sold and turned into accounts receivable. These accounts receivable are in turn transformed into cash when the bills are paid by customers.

Cash → Inventory → Sales and Accounts Receivable → Cash

FIGURE 8-2 *The Operating Cycle*

Managers need to remember that cash flow depends not just on the size of the accounts receivable account, but on the quick realization of those receivables, that is, the prompt collection of customer's bills. Prompt collection accompanied by a minimization of bad debts can greatly increase a company's cash flow.

Additionally, better control over accounts receivable will minimize reliance on short-term financing or a bank line of credit. Once accounts receivable collections are under control, there should rarely be a need for short-term bank borrowing.

Because accounts receivable are so important, managers normally keep a close eye on the *age* of accounts receivable. As discussed earlier, the older the bill, the less likely it is to produce cash for the business. Managers have to go beyond looking at totals and averages and examine individual customer accounts on a regular basis.

Managers need to be alert to look for trouble signs. If your customers are getting slow in paying you need to know why. There are a number of causes. Some regular customers may be in financial difficulty themselves. A large business may have adopted a policy of paying bills slowly, knowing that you want their business even if they pay slowly.

On the other hand, if your accounts receivable realization is slowing down, you may discover that you have accepted a number of marginal customers who are unable to pay for what they have ordered. You may be offering payment terms that are too generous and that defeat your aim of producing cash flow. You need to remember that collectibility of your accounts receivable is an important component of your cash flow. Also, only the strong accounts receivable will qualify for factoring (see Chapter 12, "Factoring Accounts Receivable"). Even if you have lots of accounts receivable, it's the ones that get turned into cash that count.

Whenever you determine that a particular bill should be treated as a bad debt, you ought to investigate the cause of the bad debt. In effect this was also a failure of your credit function: you sold to an unworthy customer. For control purposes you should keep track of your company's bad debt experience: what percent of your credit sales went uncollected each year? Of course, external factors over which you have no control such as the health of the national and local economy will always affect this number.

Besides keeping a historical record of your own company's bad debt experience, you should obtain some averages for your industry from trade associations or standard library reference works. If your bad debt experience is significantly worse than the industry average, you should reevaluate your credit policies to try to minimize the losses. This will usually have a positive effect on your next period's cash flow. On the other hand, if your experience is much better than average, you may need to loosen up your credit policies to maximize profits through greater volume.

CHAPTER PERSPECTIVE

The information in this chapter on the operation of your accounts receivable is essential in understanding the operating cycle of your business—the process of turning your cash back into cash. If you are a retailer or wholesaler, you will be buying inventory and selling it to customers on credit. The cycle is complete when the accounts receivable created by the credit sales are turned into cash. If you provide services, your operating cycle will be shorter, but you still must realize your receivables.

Although a business owner may employ financial professionals, advisers' expertise cannot substitute for an understanding of the credit cycle. Accounts receivable are basic to any credit and collection system, and mastery of their operations is essential if you want to be in control of the process.

Your accounts receivable data provide you with your most important financial management tools. By consulting this data, you will be able to predict cash flow and the need to borrow operating capital in the months ahead. You will be able to detect if your credit policies are too restrictive or too loose. You will also be able to monitor the payment habits of particular customers to determine not only who pays, but how promptly. With this type of specific information at hand, managers can make decisions that will enhance the firm's profitability.

Managers need to closely monitor not only the average age of the accounts receivable, but also the activity of each customer's account. When the average age of the accounts starts to lengthen, this is a danger signal and the cause should be identified. Once the causes are detected the firm's credit and collections policies should be modified to cope with the situation. Failure to take steps will have an adverse effect on the company's cash flow.

Bad Debts

INTRODUCTION AND MAIN POINTS

In Chapter 8 you learned about accounts receivable and the effect of writing off bad debts. Your bad debts expense account is a crucial indicator of how your credit system is operating. It also provides a valuable benchmark for your collections activities.

This chapter will focus more precisely on bad debts: how they arise, how to interpret them, and how to use this information as a management tool.

After studying the material in this chapter you will know the following

— The importance of bad debt to your credit and collection system
— Why you do not want to entirely eliminate bad debts
— How to estimate bad debt expense with both the percentage of sales method and the aging method
— When to write off a bad debt
— The mechanics of writing off a bad debt
— The effect of the write-off on the income statement and on the balance sheet
— How bad debts are handled for tax purposes

WHAT IS A BAD DEBT?

Chapter 8, "Understanding Accounts Receivable," discussed the concept of bad debts, or uncollectible accounts. A bad debt or uncollectible account is a credit sale for which the revenue will never be collected. For example, assume that the Farmer Company has sold goods to Baxter Company on credit. Despite numerous collection attempts, the buyer has been resistant to paying the debt and the seller has determined that collection is unlikely because of the buyer's precarious financial position.

The seller determines to hand the matter over to a collection agency, but feels it is unlikely that the revenue will ever be collected. This is a bad debt.

Under more modern accounting terminology, bad debts are called "uncollectible accounts," which is probably more accurate. However, in this book we will use the more familiar term "bad debt." Just remember that they refer to the same thing: a credit sale that will not be collected.

Accounting Rules

You should recall that because most businesses are on the accrual basis of accounting, revenue is recognized when credit sales are made, not when the cash is actually received. In other words, companies record income when the sale is made and the invoice is sent to the customer, not when the invoice is paid. Accordingly, a business may show lots of sales revenues, but have little cash to show for it. This fact is one of the major causes of business failures, even in light of increased sales revenues and increased activity by the sales department.

For example, assume that Farmer Company plans a drive to increase its income. Farmer's sales reps respond with increased orders, including a $100,000 order by a new customer, Edgewood Supply. Farmer Company records the income as the credit sales are made and it appears that Farmer will have increased its annual sales and revenues by about 20 percent. Unfortunately, a few of Farmer's old customers, and more importantly, Edgewood Supply, all fail to pay their bills. In fact Edgewood files for bankruptcy before it pays Farmer. Although Farmer's sales increased, its collections dropped and Farmer may find itself in financial straits.

In fact, the only safe receivable is one that has been collected. Although increased sales are a positive sign, managers need to pay close attention to the collection of their accounts receivable to determine true operating results.

WHY NOT ZERO BAD DEBTS?

At first blush, it would seem that a manager's goal would be to minimize bad debts. Shouldn't the goal be zero bad debts? On the contrary, having zero bad debts would be an obvious sign that the company's credit policy is in serious need of overhaul.

Although rational business people would never sell goods or services to a client or customer they suspect would not pay, all well-run businesses will sell to some customers who will fail to pay. Although it may be possible to create a credit policy that will completely eliminate bad debts, this is not the wisest decision.

Effect of Tight Credit Policy

It would be possible to completely eliminate bad debts by refusing to extend credit to anyone who might fail to pay. For example, a business could decide to make credit sales only to customers with a net worth of over one million dollars and spotless credit ratings. Obviously, this would greatly reduce the number of potential credit customers. Such a business would have a very low sales volume and hence lower profits.

Credit Policy versus Sales Volume

This simplistic illustration does reveal the purpose of an appropriate liberal credit policy. A seller with too strict a credit policy will be giving up sales volume. The tighter the credit policy the lower the sales volume and potential profits. On the other hand, if a credit policy is too loose, the bad debts will mount as some of the unreliable customers fail to pay their bills. When bad debts get excessive it's time to tighten your credit policy a bit, but not too much.

The goal for a business is to find a happy medium, and to have a credit policy that allows just enough bad debts to maximize profits. For example, you might want to establish a policy that will produce about five percent bad debts and 95 percent payments. If you find that your bad debts are only two to three percent of credit sales, you can probably accept a few more unpredictable credit customers. On the other hand, if you find that your bad debt expense has risen to between 15 and 20 percent, you should immediately tighten your requirements to improve the quality of your credit customer base.

Although arriving at a credit policy that will reach expected goals can be hard when you first start a business, it will become easier over time for two reasons. First, you will have more experience in making credit decisions; second, your customer base will be more stable. Over time, your credit policy and credit policy changes will yield more predictable results.

ESTIMATING BAD DEBTS: THE PERCENTAGE OF SALES METHOD

As you will recall from Chapter 8, "Understanding Accounts Receivable," a company's books include two accounts that relate to bad debts: 1) the uncollectible account expense or bad debt expense account, and 2) the allowance account. At the end of the year (or accounting period), a business on accrual basis will recognize that a certain number of its credit sales will be uncollectible.

For example, if a business has $100,000 of credit sales and determines that 9 percent of those sales will be ultimately uncollectible as bad debts, then the business will recognize $9,000 of bad debt expense to show that those revenues will probably never be realized.

This accounting rule grew up during the Great Depression of the 1930s, when accountants strove to be conservative in their reports. By making a business reduce its income for estimated bad debts, the bottom line or net income of the business is reduced and presents a more conservative figure to both potential lenders and potential investors. Although this is an old rule, it still applies and for the same good reasons. Accountants don't want to be misleading about the true financial health of the business.

There are two methods of estimating bad debts expense:
1) the percentage of sales method and
2) the aging method.

In practice, many companies use both the percentage of sales method and the aging method in estimating their bad debt expense for the year. We will look at both of these methods in some detail.

In preparing an estimation of bad debts using the percentage of sales method, a credit seller will estimate bad debts by taking a percentage of net credit sales for the year. Net credit sales are sales made on credit minus sales discounts. The percentage to be applied to the net credit sales will be based on the company's historical experience, the type of business, and also the local economy. As the company's credit sales rise, the bad debt estimate will rise, because it is a fixed percentage of the credit sales figure. For example, if a firm is using 5 percent of its net credit sales, at $100,000 of sales volume estimated bad debt expense will be $5,000 ($100,000 × 5%). If sales volume doubles to $200,000, bad debt expense will also double to $10,000 ($200,000 × 5%).

Certain types of businesses have a greater likelihood of bad debts. For example, a retail furniture store would typically have a higher percentage of bad debts than a wholesale hardware outfit. Similarly, during a business recession, the percentage should increase because people in businesses are more likely to fail or to be unable to pay debts as they fall due.

ESTIMATING BAD DEBTS: THE AGING METHOD
In contrast to the percentage of sales method, the aging method looks at the age of current accounts receivable rather than the volume of annual credit sales.

There are three steps in preparing an aging:
1. sort the accounts by age;
2. total the sorted accounts; and
3. multiply the sorted totals by a percentage, and add the result.

The accounts are first grouped by age and totaled. These totals are then multiplied by percentages to determine the total estimated bad debt expense. (See Figure 8-1 on page 99 for an example of Aging Analysis.)

RECOGNIZING WHEN TO WRITE OFF A BAD DEBT
One of the hardest things to do in a business is to recognize when to write off a bad debt. Many business owners and managers are reluctant to write off bad debts; they continue to carry accounts receivable on their books far longer than they should. This may be more a reflection on human nature than on business judgment. Managers may feel responsible for approving credit customers and have sincere confidence that a customer will pay. This, however, may be a triumph of optimism over experience.

Why Some Older Accounts May Still Be Collectible
On the other hand, an old account may sometimes be collectible, because not all payers pay promptly. For example, government units—the federal government, states, counties, municipalities—always pay their debts, but they are also very slow in paying.

Large companies are often similar to the government; they nearly always pay their bills. However, even some larger companies have adopted the process of "lagging" their accounts payable as part of their cash management procedures. When a company lags its accounts payable, it merely postpones paying its bill for a month, two months, or even three months. In effect, the company is getting the use of owed money and its interest for an additional period, while depriving the creditor. Some large companies can do this with impunity since people still want to do business with them for their ultimate reliability and substantial purchases.

Rules of Thumb

Companies range from reliable to risky. It takes an experienced credit manager to determine the date when an account receivable will be deemed uncollectible. Even experienced credit managers make mistakes each year when overdue receivables are indeed paid long after the credit managers have given up all hope of collection. Generally, however, a nongovernment receivable that is more than six months old is a highly unlikely prospect. Because there can be practically no expectation of collecting an account receivable that is more than 12 months old, you should probably write off any such accounts. Other candidates for write-off are accounts for which you have evidence of uncollectibility. For example, if a company has declared bankruptcy you should probably write off its account receivable even if you think you may realize part of it.

MECHANICS OF WRITING OFF A BAD DEBT

The mechanics of writing off a bad debt are rather simple. By an internal bookkeeping memo the accounts receivable for the particular customer is simply stricken from the books, while the allowance account is lowered. For example, suppose Bush Company owes you $300 and fails to pay. After one year, you may determine that Bush is never going to pay. The bookkeeping entry to write off the debt will set the Bush account receivable to zero while reducing the allowance account by $300. There is no effect on the income statement because the write off is included in the estimated bad debt expense as described on page 111.

Don't Send a Notice Informing the Debtor of the Write-Off

Note that you should never inform Bush Company, the debtor, that the account has been written off. It is unlikely that the debtor would ever pay an account receivable that it knows has been written off. There may still be hope that payment will eventually be made. Your internal bookkeeping entry for accounting purposes does not change the legality or the collectibility of the debt.

Even if your bookkeeping system has written off the debt, your firm or a collection agency can still collect the debt if that proves practical, so long as the state's statute of limitations for the debt has not expired. In some states, the statute of limitations for open accounts is only a few years. Businesses therefore need to act promptly in collections.

EFFECT OF A WRITE-OFF ON YOUR INCOME STATEMENT

The actual writing off of a bad debt makes no change whatsoever in the bottom line of your income statement. What does change your annual income is the estimated bad debts expense that is recorded at the end of the year. For example, suppose again that you have written off $300 of bad debt expense for the Bush Company. That bookkeeping entry in no way changes your bottom line. Your bottom line will be determined by the bad debt expense that is estimated with regard to the percentage of sales method or the aging method that was discussed on page 108.

EFFECT OF A WRITE-OFF ON YOUR BALANCE SHEET

The effect of writing off a bad debt on a balance sheet is the same as on an income statement. The actual process of writing off an individual bad debt has no effect on any balance sheet account. What does affect the balance sheet is the estimated bad debts at the end of the year. This estimate also becomes part of the allowance account, which reduces the net balance in accounts receivable.

Analyzing the Allowance Account

The amount of accounts receivable is important for a number of reasons, both internal and external to the firm. As you will recall, accounts receivable are an important component of the firm's cash flow over the next few months. Accordingly, the allowance account helps to evaluate realistically those accounts receivable and thus anticipate what cash flow the business will have during the next few months.

If the company is forced to recognize a large bad debt expense because of economic conditions or trouble with particular customers, these particular accounts receivable will be written off and the allowance account reduced. Managers looking at such accounts receivable should recognize that their cash flow may be restricted during the months ahead. While this news may be bad for the company, it would be worse if the situation took the managers by surprise. If the managers know that a cash flow shortage lies ahead, they will be able to plan for it by borrowing money or by curtailing expenses until the crisis is over.

On the other hand, if bad debts and the allowance are underestimated, the amount of accounts receivable and potential cash flow will be overestimated. This is a far worse situation for managers who expect to have a cash cushion in the months ahead and who may be faced instead with a severe and unexpected cash shortage that may necessitate firing employees, failing to pay payroll taxes, or, in extreme cases, even filing for bankruptcy.

BAD DEBTS AND THE IRS

For financial accounting purposes bad debts are recognized as an expense at the end of the year. Income tax accounting for businesses also recognizes bad debt expenses. However, the treatment for tax accounting purposes is far different from the treatment for financial accounting purposes.

For financial accounting purposes, bad debt expense is estimated at the end of the year. As discussed (see page 107), this bad debt expense reduces net income and also reduces the carrying value of the firm's accounts receivable on the balance sheet. The purpose of this treatment is to be conservative. This treatment reduces the amount of reportable net income and also reduces an asset, accounts receivable, that is carried on the firm's balance sheet. Again, accountants strive to be conservative in their reporting.

On the other hand, tax accounting of bad debts for income tax purposes is done differently. For income tax purposes, bad debts can be recognized only when they are actually written off. This is called the "direct write-off method," which is considered unacceptable for financial accounting purposes.

For tax purposes, this will tend to reduce the amount of bad debts because most business owners are very reluctant to write off a debt. In fact, at one time, the government tax treatment was the same as for financial accounting purposes. The government changed its system to recognize a deduction only for bad debt expense when an account was written off merely to increase tax collections. Because taxpayers are normally reluctant to write off their bad debts, this results in a lower tax deduction, a higher taxable income, and a higher income tax.

MANAGEMENT INFORMATION

Bad debts and other accounts receivable information can be used to assess the effectiveness of your credit and collection operation. Over the years credit managers have devised a number of measurements derived from your firm's financial information that will quickly point out strengths and weakness in your operations.

Bad Debt Loss Index

One measure of the efficiency of your credit system is the number of bad debts it generates. However, the bad debt number itself is not especially useful unless it is compared to something. In this case the bad debts are compared to credit sales:

$$\frac{\text{Bad debts}}{\text{Net credit sales}} = \text{Bad debt loss index}$$

This number can be used by management to determine what percentage of sales are not collected. If the number starts to jump up, then the firm's credit policy should be investigated and changed if warranted.

A rise in this index does not necessarily mean that the credit department has not been doing its job. There are a number of internal and external factors that affect this index. If management has been writing off more doubtful accounts, this percentage will rise. Likewise, a downturn in the economy as a whole will normally cause the index to rise.

Although this number must be used with care, it is helpful in quickly pointing out trends, which must then be analyzed to see if appropriate changes are required in the credit and collection system. Here it would be useful to see Using the Aging Analysis as a Management Tool, page 99.

Percentage Past Due

The data compiled in the aging can be used to compute the Percentage Past Due. This is merely the percentage of your accounts receivable that are "past due" (unpaid after the due date of the bill). This measure is helpful primarily in tracking your own collection progress.

$$\frac{\text{Past due receivables}}{\text{Total receivables}} = \text{Percent past due}$$

Receivables Turnover/Average Collection Period

One important measure of the efficiency of your credit operation is your "receivables turnover." Your turnover rate tells you how many times you "turn over" your accounts receivable in a year. If your turnover rate is high compared with other firms in your industry, you are collecting your receivables quickly and efficiently. If your turnover rate is slow, your credit system is relatively inefficient.

Receivables turnover is calculated by dividing net credit sales by your receivables, net of the allowance account:

$$\frac{\text{Net credit sales}}{\text{End of period receivables (net of allowance)}}$$

Average collection period is another measure that uses the same numbers in a different way. Sometimes called "days sales outstanding" this measure demonstrates how many days on average your receivables require for collection. To calculate the ratio divide your end of period receivables by your sales and multiply by 365 days.

$$\frac{\text{End of period receivables}}{\text{Net credit sales}} \times 365$$

To determine your relative efficiency you should use the following formula.

$$\text{Net credit period} \times 1.33$$

Your "net credit period" is the average period which you allow customers to pay their bills, typically 30 or 60 days. If your average collection period exceeds this period by more than one third, then your credit system is relatively inefficient at collecting your bills.

For example, assume the Black Company has net credit sales of $950,000 and year-end receivables of $100,000. Their turnover and average collection period are as follows:

Turnover:

$$\frac{\text{Net credit sales}}{\text{End of period receivables}} = \frac{\$950,000}{100,000} = 9.5 \text{ times}$$

Average Collection Period:

$$\frac{\text{End of period receivables}}{\text{Net credit sales}} \times 365 = \frac{\$100,000}{\$950,000} \times 365 = 38 \text{ days}$$

Safety Zone:

$$\text{Net credit period} \times 1.33 = 30 \text{ days} \times 1.33 = 39.9$$

If Black Company's normal terms of sale were 30 days, the rule-of-thumb measure would require about a 40-day average collection period. Here Black Company's collection period is 38 days, so it is just within the safety limit. If receivables rose to just $110,000, the average collection period would have risen to 42 days, which is over the safety zone ($110,000/$950,000 × 365 = 42.3).

CHAPTER PERSPECTIVE

A bad debt is simply an uncollectible account. You have made a sale and are unable to collect the cash. If your firm is on the cash basis of accounting, you will not have already recorded the income from that sale. Since you will not be paid, that income is forever lost. If you are on the accrual basis, you would have recorded income when the sale was made initially. Accordingly, you will have to reduce that income by the amount of the bad debt because you will not be paid for that sale.

A company with no bad debts is actually worse off than a company with a manageable amount. Having no bad debts is an indication that your credit policies are too strict. You are rejecting potential credit customers that could contribute to your bottom line results. By loosening your credit terms, you will add sales volume that will more than compensate for the increased bad debt losses.

There are two methods for estimating bad debts: the aging method and the percentage of sales method. In practice it is a good idea to calculate both figures. The aging method has special significance as a management tool in maintaining control over the credit and collections function.

Managers need to recognize when to write off a bad debt. Generally when a debt is more than twelve months old or you have strong evidence that the debtor will not pay, you should write off the debt. Writing off a bad debt normally does not change your accounting income or loss. This is because bad debt expense is actually estimated at year end. However, the actual write-off does establish which of your accounts receivable is not collectible. Once you have written off a customer's debt as worthless, you should have controls in place to assure that you don't ship another order or perform more services for that customer.

Although writing off a bad debt doesn't change your operating results, it can lower your income taxes. Writing off a bad debt lowers an accrual-basis taxpayer's taxable income and tax liability. For this reason alone you should periodically review your overdue accounts to see which are ready to write off. Using bad debts and other financial data can provide valuable management information about the efficiency of your credit and collections operation.

Establishing a Collections Policy

INTRODUCTION AND MAIN POINTS

This chapter provides an overview stressing the importance of collections to the financial life of a firm. The chapter details how the collections function should be organized and managed.

After studying the material in this chapter, you will understand

- The need to manage the collections function
- The importance of prompt collections to the firm
- How to establish in-house collections procedures
- How to encourage prompt payments
- Why a partial payment is preferable to no payment
- When to use a collection agency
- When to enforce a debt in court

INTRODUCTION TO COLLECTIONS

At one time, businesses may have been able to regard their collection activity as a secondary part of their financial activities. Today, however, the collections function needs to be seen as a vital part of a business financing. In fact, for many businesses, the successful design and operation of a collections system may mean the difference between success and failure.

Effect of Apathy

Many smaller businesses are successful at providing goods or services, but unsuccessful at making timely collections. This failure to collect bills can lead to cash flow shortages that can be fatal to a smaller business. During recession and business downturn, the results of a poorly conceived credit function will be felt quickly and painfully by a small business.

For example, suppose Susan Saunders operates a small business specializing in food catering for businesses. Saunders had previously worked for a commercial caterer and was highly skilled not only in preparing and planning events, but also in other aspects of the business. She did not have any formal training in business administration, however, and initially had not thought much about collections.

Saunders was especially successful during her early years, when she mainly worked alone and hired people on a part-time basis. Because of her exceptional work, Saunders' reputation grew and with it her business. Over time, she added first one full-time person and then several more. All this time, she not only acted as manager of the business, but she was also personally involved in planning and selling her services to various business clients, planning the events, and supervising the actual catering.

During the last recession, however, many businesses started to forgo the use of caterers as they cut their business expenses. Because Saunders had moved into more attractive quarters, she had to pay higher rent. Additionally, she now had four full-time employees who were on a salary and had to be paid no matter what.

Saunders' biggest problem, however, was not the business she lost but defaults for catering she performed. One of her clients, a large local company, contracted for approximately $40,000 of catering during the year but was very slow in making payments. Because it was a big client, Saunders was reluctant to press for payment because she feared this would annoy the client, who would take its catering business elsewhere. The $40,000 bill continued to be held on the books and Saunders never did more than send one or two reminders to the company. Because she was on a friendly basis and continued to do business with the company, she assumed that the debt would be paid in full.

In October, Saunders was shocked when she received a notice from the bankruptcy court, noting that the customer had filed for Chapter 7 bankruptcy and that she was listed as one of the outstanding creditors. After consulting an attorney, she discovered that she was unlikely to get more than ten cents on the dollar for the $40,000 debt. This caused not only a cash flow shortage but also a severe change in her business plan, as she was forced to lay off two employees and to look for less attractive business quarters.

The Need to Manage the Collections Function

Managers and business owners need to understand that they must actively manage the credit and collection functions within the business. The collections function must be planned to maximize benefits to the business. There are at least seven steps to effective management of the collections function:

1. Understand how dependent the business is on credit sales.
2. Analyze the current state of collection procedures.
3. Based on the analysis of the credit sales and overdue accounts, determine how to handle collections in house.
4. Once the scope of the work is determined, organize staffing.
5. Design a system to track overdue accounts.
6. Design a system to send reminders to customers with overdue accounts.
7. Provide a mechanism to determine when to refer overdue accounts to collection agencies or law firms.

The Need to Delegate

Although there is a tendency for small business owners and managers to try to do everything themselves, this often results in things not being done very well or not being done at all. Collecting overdue accounts is a time-consuming process, especially if it is done on an ad hoc basis. Delegating some of the responsibilities for collections to another staff person and standardizing collection forms and procedures save much time and effort and achieve more efficient collections and faster cash flow for the firm.

Importance of Prompt Collections

We can hardly overemphasize the importance of prompt collections, especially to a small firm with a significant amount of credit sales. Based on the experience of others, the age of accounts receivable generally determines whether they will be collectible at all. When a bill is more than 60 days overdue, it is far less likely to be collected. When a bill is more than 12 months overdue, the prospects for collection are very slim indeed.

Pestering Gets the Check

The race for collection goes to the swift. Businesses and individuals are not always able to pay all their bills, but they normally will pay a bill if they are pestered into paying. This is essentially the technique of collection, to nag customers to live up to their obligation to pay their own bill.

Building Your Reputation

Firms that neglect to collect debts will soon get a reputation for this laxity. Some individuals and businesses will take advantage of a company that is not aggressive in collecting its bills. Sometimes these businesses and individuals prey on firms that are lax in their collections and will purposely order goods and services with no intention of paying or with the intention of paying only after a long drawn-out fight.

It is better to avoid from the start getting a reputation for laxity. In most cases, customers who are going to pay you would just as soon pay you now as later. Conversely, if they are not going to pay you now, it is unlikely that they will pay you later. Good collections procedures not only minimize bad debts but result in good accounts receivable turnover.

Establishing In-House Collections Procedures

Even small businesses need to establish an in-house collections policy and procedures. The first step in establishing a collections policy is to understand the significance of credit sales to the business. Obviously, if the great bulk of your transactions are for cash, with only a few credit sales, you need not be deeply involved with collections. On the other hand, if the bulk of your business is credit sales, your collections activities will be a vital part of the business.

For example, assume that a candy store has 90 percent of sales over the counter in the form of cash sales. However, approximately 10 percent of the store's sales are to businesses on a credit basis. This type of store does not have to be very involved with collections because of the small proportion of the credit sales in comparison with cash sales. On the other hand, if the store made 90 percent of its sales to credit customers, say various types of businesses and other retailers, a slight drop off in collections would have a severe impact on this firm's cash flow and financial health.

If the collections work is going to be fairly substantial, even a small business needs to formalize the procedures. This will require identification and a current list of accounts that are overdue. It is essential that overdue accounts be given focused and prompt attention from the person handling the collection work.

Who Should Supervise Collections?

One or more staff persons should be assigned the task of running the collections activities. In many small businesses, one person may be handling all the collection activities. The person who handles the accounts receivable would be a good choice in a small business. That person is aware when bills are sent out and knows which customers are paying and which ones are not. The person handling the accounts receivable also will typically have direct contact with the customers and may be on good terms with customers' bookkeepers.

Personal Contacts

Sometimes human contact can greatly speed up bill paying. You should encourage your accounts receivable and collections staff to build sound relationships with bookkeepers at customers' offices. These relationships can often mean the difference between being paid promptly and not being paid at all.

As part of in-house collection procedures there should be a standardized plan to collect overdue accounts. When an account is found to be overdue,

1. a file should be created
2. the amount of the overdue account should be transferred to a master list that can be used by the managers and owners of the business.

This master list should be given to a responsible person in sales to make sure that no more sales and shipments are made to customers who have not paid their old bills. A lack of communication in this area can prove very costly to a small business.

Checklists and Flowcharts

The business owners and managers should establish a flowchart or checklist for the person running the collections activity. For example, the checklist or flowchart should tell exactly what to do at what stage. This has two advantages:

1. This allows staff to do the tasks routinely, especially if staff hasn't done them for some time.
2. This list can be used by a new or temporary employee if the regular collection person is not available.

The firm should carefully develop letters that can be sent to client customers as reminders to pay. See Chapter 7 for more details. The person handling collections and the manager will probably need to determine which type of letter is appropriate for your firm and for the individual client. While some clients may need a firm letter, others may find a hard approach distasteful.

More Standardized Procedures

Finally, your business needs to develop a procedure that will determine when to refer overdue accounts to third parties such as letter-writing firms, collection bureaus, and law firms. A standardized procedure has two primary advantages. One, this will speed up the decision making; and two, this will treat all customers more fairly.

Speed is important in collection work: the longer you wait, the less likely the bill will be collected. Having a standard procedure for determining when overdue accounts should be referred will speed this process immeasurably and should lead to higher collection success.

ENCOURAGING PROMPT PAYMENT

There are a number of ways to encourage prompt payments. As we discussed, the key to a collections policy is to encourage prompt payment by all reasonable means. The use of letters to encourage customers to pay can be very effective. At first the reminder letters should be gentle in tone and sometimes humorous to help encourage a slow payer to pay bills. Over time, the letters can get more firm. Remember, some bills are paid only when several demands are made.

When to Call

If letters don't work, follow-up phone calls from the collections person to bookkeepers can be very effective—especially when there is a personal relationship with the bookkeeper or someone else who has authority to write or approve checks at the customer's place of business.

Cash Discounts

Another approach is to use cash discounts to encourage prompt payments. Many large companies use cash discounts quite successfully in business-to-business transactions. When a cash discount is offered, a seller will allow a credit buyer to pay a smaller amount if the bill is paid promptly.

Many sellers allow a two percent or three percent cash discount if a bill is paid within ten days. Many companies use a shorthand notation to alert customers to these credit terms. The term "2/10, net/30" indicates the discount is two percent off the price if the bill is paid within ten days. In any event, the entire amount is due within 30 days.

For example, if a seller sells an order to a buyer for $1,000 and offers 2/10, net/30, the customer can elect to pay the bill within ten days, and send $980 (98% × $1,000 = $980). Many purchasers are eager to take cash discounts even though they may seem modest.

Of course, if your clients are unfamiliar with the terminology of cash discounts, you need to explain their operation. Generally, only businesses that deal in goods and order goods from other businesses on a regular basis would be familiar with this shorthand cash discount terminology.

Encourage Prompt Payments

Although interest earned on credit sales is beneficial, it is also desirable to speed your collections to make sure that you receive the principal amount, so credit should be designed to encourage prompt payments.

For example, when you send out bills, note when the amount is due and what credit charge will be assessed on the overdue bill. If you send out a bill for $1,000, you could offer a cash discount, but you could also indicate a one percent per month credit charge will apply to all amounts paid after 30 days beyond the billing date. Some companies carefully avoid interest charges on purchases, even though the amount may be tax deductible to them. By alerting these buyers that your particular bill will carry a credit charge, you may encourage them to pay the bill more promptly.

Your interest percent should not be too low. If the interest charge on your overdue account is much lower than the cost of borrowing funds, the customer may determine that you are a good alternative to a bank loan. For example, suppose you have an annual rate of 12 percent and your customer currently pays 16 percent at the bank. The debtor may decide not to pay your bill, but use that cash for other operating expenses, paying you the 12 percent interest.

On the other hand, you don't want to have your interest rate so high as to run afoul of the state usury law, which may establish a lawful maximum rate of interest. Because usury laws vary state by state, this part of your collections activity should be designed after consulting a knowledgeable local attorney or the Small Business Administration.

Trade Discounts

Trade discounts allow a seller to offer predetermined discounts to favored customers—typically those who buy in larger quantities. Trade discounts are offered for two reasons:

1. To encourage larger purchases of an item
2. To encourage the sale of slower moving items

For example, you might print a catalog describing your products and listing a normal "retail" price for each item. However, you could then include an insert that lists the trade discounts available on particular items. The trade discount could be listed as a reduced dollar amount for the item or the discount could be expressed as a percentage of the suggested retail price.

Suppose that items X, Y, and Z are each listed in the seller's catalog for $100. An accompanying enclosure could list the available trade discount on each item:

Item	Discount
Model X	0
Model Y	10 percent
Model Z	30 percent

Thus the effective price of Model Y is only $90 ($100 retail price less $10 discount = $90), while the price of Model Z is only $70 ($100 retail price less $30 discount). However, no discount is offered for Model X.

This example illustrates the flexibility of using trade discounts, which can be limited to the slower-moving inventory items. If an item is literally flying off the shelf there is no reason to discount it. On the other hand, if an item is not selling well, it may sell better at a lower price. This type of flexibility is not available when using straight cash discounts.

Trade discounts also let you tailor your discounts to individual customers. You might want to make two trade discount schedules—one for regular customers who buy in smaller quantities and one for customers who normally place larger orders.

A Partial Payment Is Preferable to No Payment

Generally, a small payment is better than no payment at all. If a customer is having trouble paying a bill, try to arrange a schedule that will allow payment in smaller installments. The best policy uses a promissory note that can be enforced in court. That way, if a scheduled payment is missed, the obligation can be more easily enforced.

For example, if a small business owes you $30,000, it may be psychologically difficult for that business or individual to send you a check if there is a financial problem. In fact, other smaller bills totaling more than $30,000 may be paid before your bill.

It may be far easier to collect a large bill in a series of small installments than getting one large payment. It would be simpler to collect the entire bill at once than in five or ten installments, but you have to compare the efficiency of one large windfall to the more likely collection of ten smaller payments. Again, the personality and financial ability of a particular debtor will have to guide you in making this decision.

WHEN TO USE A COLLECTION AGENCY

One of the hardest decisions for a small business is trying to determine when to refer a matter to a third party such as a collection agency or a law firm for collection. Generally, a matter should be handed over to a collection agency for any of these reasons:

1. You determine that the customer is unresponsive to your request.
2. The firm is unlikely to be a customer in the future.
3. The matter is so large that its noncollection threatens the financial health of your business.

Why a Referral Should be Avoided

Because the use of a third party such as a collection agency will jeopardize your relationship with the client, you should carefully consider when to refer a bill. On the other hand, the longer a bill is outstanding, the more unlikely it is to be collected.

Generally, a bill three months old is a prime candidate for referral to an out-of-firm third party for collection. Certainly when a bill is 12 months old, you should abandon failed in-house collection efforts. It is important to have a standardized procedure to determine when bills should be referred for outside collection. Again, this should be done so that these referrals are made swiftly and fairly. This will help your cash flow and can help establish your reputation with your customers too.

Before an overdue account is referred to a third party, the decision should be discussed personally with the manager or the business owners. The person in charge of collection should not normally make a unilateral decision, but in consultation with the owner/manager or a person in the sales department. Sometimes, the owner/manager or a salesperson can help make additional contacts that can speed the collection efforts in-house. Failing that, however, the matter should be referred as soon as possible.

CHAPTER PERSPECTIVE

This chapter provides an introduction to collections. Because cash is the lifeblood of a firm, managers and business owners need to actively plan and manage the collections function. If collections are de-emphasized, realizations will be low and the firm's finances can suffer.

One can hardly overstress the importance of prompt collections to the firm. Bills that are more than six months overdue are seldom paid. If the firm does not seem interested in collecting its bills, customers may take advantage of the situation.

Because collections are a perennial function, it makes sense to establish standardized in-house collections procedures. The firm can adopt a number of techniques to encourage prompt payments, including cash discounts and trade discounts.

Although many collection routines should be standardized, the manager in charge of collections needs to work with debtors so they can be maintained as profitable customers. Many times a partial payment is preferable to no payment. Whenever possible, customers should be encouraged to agree to installment payments when it seems unlikely that they will be paying their bill in full.

Although you should try to maintain good relations with late-paying customers, you should not be afraid to use a collection agency when the customer has no intention or ability to pay, or when the overdue amount threatens the financial safety of your business. If normal collection efforts fail, you should not be afraid to enforce debt payment in court.

Handling Billing Disputes

INTRODUCTION AND MAIN POINTS

There are few things more aggravating than a billing dispute—both for the seller and for the buyer. Billing disputes certainly waste time and create bad feelings, lost sales, and lower profits. Yet occasional billing disputes are inevitable, and business owners and managers need to control such disputes to improve bottom-line performance.

This chapter examines the causes of billing disputes and offers some techniques and strategies that can provide solutions.

After studying the material in this chapter you will understand

- What causes a billing dispute
- Four types of billing disputes
- Solutions to the four types of disputes
- How to evaluate the customer's claim fairly
- The importance of handling the claim promptly and courteously
- How to proceed when handling claims by established customers
- When and how to apply cost/benefit analysis to disputed bills
- The value of suggesting arbitration of disputed claims
- The advantages of avoiding litigation over disputed bills
- The provisions of the Fair Credit Billing Act (FCBA)

WHAT CAUSES A BILLING DISPUTE?

There are a number of reasons for a billing dispute with a customer, and they all need to be addressed. Even if no money can be gained from the disputed account, you can always learn something when handling a dispute with a customer. There is no substitute for experience; the lesson may be profitable in the future even if it is not currently.

Analyzing a Dispute

In analyzing a dispute, it is useful to determine first whether the dispute is with a consumer or with a business; causes often differ. Likewise, it is important to know whether the dispute is a result of an initial misunderstanding or a dispute about the value of your product or service. In other words, is the problem that the customer expected something different from what was provided, or is the customer dissatisfied with the quality of the performance?

Consumer Complaints

Within the last twenty years, consumers have become a lot more vocal about disputes, and they have a lot more power under state consumer protection statutes. Problems include bookkeeping errors, misunderstanding of sales terms, and unsatisfactory merchandise or service.

Business Complaints

If the complaining customer is a business, the dispute is more likely to involve the quality of goods received or the quality of the performance rendered. As a general rule, businesses are less price-sensitive than consumers. However, they may be more concerned about the quality received for their money. Business people expect their customers and suppliers to be somewhat more flexible about their contracts. If the goods or services you supplied were found wanting, a business may want you to reduce the price or to provide more favorable terms on the next order.

A contract of sale establishes a relationship between two parties. Although most contracts state what both sides are to receive, that is not always the case. For example, with dental work, it is unusual to bargain with a dentist beforehand. It is implied that the patient will pay the reasonable and customary charges for treatment. This is known as a contract "implied by law." The patient owes the dentist the customary fee even if there was no discussion about fee.

FOUR TYPES OF DISPUTES

Let's look at four typical complaints, and then we'll suggest how these disputes could have been prevented.

The first type of complaint involves the price charged. In many cases the customer is unprepared for the size of the bill.

Not surprisingly, this type of complaint is most commonly associated with contracts for services.

In a service contract, the total fee is not always stated. In some cases, an hourly rate is quoted; in some cases, an estimate of the time involved may be quoted. But in some cases, a total fee estimate is not given. This can lead to a dispute when the fee is more than anticipated, or if the fee is more than the customer or client feels should be charged.

For example, suppose a carpenter has agreed to a remodeling project for a homeowner. The carpenter gave the homeowner a rough "ball-park estimate" that the job would cost about $15,000. After receiving a $3,000 down payment the carpenter and an assistant went to work. During the work the homeowner specified several changes that added to the cost. When the job was completed the carpenter submitted a bill for $22,000, bringing the total for the job to $25,000. The total bill was $10,000 over the initial ball-park estimate. The homeowner disputed the amount and refused to pay. Before we look at techniques that help prevent these disputes, let's examine the second type of dispute.

The second type of billing dispute is not about price, but about the quality of the service rendered or the goods provided. These disputes can occur in contracts for services or for the sale of goods. For example, in the sale of goods, the price is normally disclosed in advance. In fact, in a commercial transaction, the price is also often a negotiating point. Accordingly, in most sales of goods, the buyer and seller know the price precisely. However, disputes can still arise even over price when the quality of the goods is less than expected.

For example, assume that a retailer has ordered twenty dozen wool sweaters from a woolen mill. The retailer placed the order after examining a sample at a trade show. The retailer paid a wholesale price of $30 per sweater after estimating that the sweaters could be priced at $50 each retail. The retailer anticipated making a 10 to 15 percent profit after end of season markdowns and returns. However, when the sweaters arrived, the retailer realized that the $50 price was unrealistically high considering the quality of the goods, which did not conform to the original sample.

Although the sweaters would have passed without objection in the trade, they were clearly of only average quality and couldn't be marketed for $50. The retailer demanded that the woolen mill make a 30 percent price adjustment or take back the sweaters. The woolen mill insisted that the retailer fulfill the contract as agreed.

The third type of billing dispute involves the bill itself. In some cases, the bill is hard for the customer to understand. Anyone who has received a phone bill over the years understands this problem. The bill might provide lots of detail but not enough useful information. A bill that merely lists an amount due is inadequate. The customer should see at a glance the previous balance, details of current charges, and how recent payments have been applied. Confusing bills are near the top of the list of consumer complaints.

The fourth type of problem involves a billing error by your own bookkeeping system. Nothing is more infuriating to a customer than to be billed again for an amount already paid. Businesses that have to deal with "third-party payers" (typically insurance companies) realize that disputes are an almost inevitable cost of doing business. Many of the disputes will be caused by the carelessness or inefficiency of these third parties. However, unsophisticated customers are likely to blame your business for the problem.

EVALUATING THE CUSTOMER'S CLAIM

The first step in handling any billing dispute is to understand the facts. Far too often, decisions are made without fully understanding the facts. It is essential that someone takes the time to evaluate the customer's claim without prejudice. Sometimes the customers are right and they should be treated as such. Although it is your money at stake, look at the matter as a disinterested third party. This will help you in evaluating whether the customer's claim is partially or completely justified, or whether the whole claim is erroneous.

There are certain customers who merely have an aversion to paying bills, although, of course, they like getting services and goods. Worse, certain customers plan on not paying bills. This is especially true of certain customers who operate on credit. They may pay the first of three or four installments, but have no intention of paying the last installment. It is vital to know when you are dealing with people in this last category.

IMPORTANCE OF HANDLING THE CLAIM PROMPTLY AND COURTEOUSLY

One cannot overstress the importance of handling a customer's claim promptly and courteously. Unless you provide a unique and needed product or service, the customer has alternatives. Your business depends on personal attention to the customer.

This is especially true when you provide either technical equipment or technical services. Very often, the customer will not understand completely what you do. For example, if you are an installer of local area networks for personal computers, it is unlikely that the client understands your business as well as you do. The customer, with no frame of reference, may be in no position to judge the quality of your work. However, the customer can judge how promptly and courteously you attend to a problem. One of the main problems for customers can be a billing dispute, and it deserves your immediate attention. Some businesses spend far too little time on handling billing disputes and the result is dissatisfied customers who take their business elsewhere.

On the other hand, if a billing dispute is handled promptly and courteously, you may create a loyal customer that had formerly chosen you by accident. For example, suppose a plumber had billed a client $400 for installing a bathroom sink. The customer thought this was an overcharge and complained about the bill. The office manager of the plumbing contractor reviewed the bill, called the consumer, and agreed that the hourly charges looked out of line and included several trips back to the office for parts that were forgotten by the plumber. Accordingly, the contractor reduced the bill by $100. The overjoyed consumer was impressed not only by the prompt and courteous service, but also by the willingness of the contractor to listen to the problem and provide a fair and meaningful solution. Not surprisingly, not only did the customer call the same contractor for the next plumbing problem, but also passed along the story, which resulted in additional business for the plumber.

HANDLING CLAIMS BY ESTABLISHED CUSTOMERS

Whenever an established and loyal customer disputes a bill, a business should be very careful to evaluate the customer's claim fairly and make every effort to satisfy the customer in some way. It is far cheaper to cultivate established customers than to attract new ones through advertising and promotional efforts.

In some cases, you should agree to settle disputes with customers even if you feel they are in the wrong. Some larger firms really do implement the motto "the customer is always right— (even if they're really wrong)."

APPLYING COST/BENEFIT ANALYSIS TO DISPUTED BILLS

It is important to apply cost/benefit analysis to billing disputes. In many cases, the time costs of evaluating the customer's claim and the potential for losing the customer's goodwill far outweigh the benefit of collecting a disputed bill. For example, assume a customer has disputed a bill for services. The customer has argued that the bill was about $200 over the estimate and additionally at least $100 over what would have been charged elsewhere.

On the one hand, the business could simply refuse to discuss the matter and demand payment for the bill. The result would probably be a dissatisfied customer and an end to a relationship. If you tend to do one-time-only services or one-time-only sales, this might not be a great disadvantage. If you rely on repeat business and word-of-mouth advertising, the take-it-or-leave-it attitude will not be profitable in the long run.

The $20 Solution

If the disputed amount is less than $20, you should always side with the customer. The costs of even thinking about an amount less than $20 always outweigh any benefit that you will receive from a customer. Make the adjustment quickly and cheerfully, and most customers with that experience will return and bring profits with them in future years.

HOW TO AVOID LITIGATION OVER DISPUTED BILLS

Billing disputes can involve not $20, but thousands of dollars. When large amounts are at stake, lawsuits are often the result. However, going to court is usually an inefficient way to handle a disputed bill. The costs in time and effort—not to mention legal fees—are normally not worth it for amounts under $5,000. It is normally far more efficient to settle the problem by other means.

Why You Should Avoid a Lawsuit

Despite what your lawyer may tell you, lawsuits seldom produce clear-cut winners. No matter what happens during litigation, you will spend from twenty to several hundred hours that is time not spent in your business. Not only will you not get paid for this time, but you will be distracted from running your business, which will harm your livelihood in the long run.

The best way to avoid litigation over disputed bills is to negotiate with the dissatisfied customers yourself. If you can arrive at an arrangement with a customer over the bill, you may be able to retain that person as a customer in the future. If you go to court, the person will never be your customer again.

SUGGESTING ARBITRATION OF DISPUTED CLAIMS

One solution for billing disputes is to suggest arbitration, which is a means of settling disputes using a neutral party to hear both sides. In effect, the neutral party, called the arbitrator, will be acting as a judge in deciding the issues. If both sides agree to the use of an arbitrator, the dispute can be handled efficiently and you will have the matter settled for better or worse.

If done carefully, a customer might not be angry after losing an arbitration hearing and may continue as your customer. Since the arbitrator makes the decision, the customer may blame the arbitrator for the result, or may see that your position was not as wrong as initially suspected. Arbitration is far less costly and much quicker than going to court over a disputed bill. In some areas, the local court system or the Chamber of Commerce maintains lists of arbitrators who will work for a low fee in resolving small disputes.

Mediation

Another alternative dispute resolution technique is mediation. Mediation is conducted with the help of a mediator—a neutral party who is not affiliated with either party to the dispute. Mediation differs from arbitration in that the mediator does not act as a judge. Unlike an arbitrator, the mediator has no power to impose a solution.

The mediator's role is to listen to both sides and to suggest avenues of agreement and compromise. The mediator will assess the strengths and weaknesses of the rival arguments and point these out to the respective sides. Although the mediator has no power to end the dispute, an experienced and skillful mediator can often help parties resolve issues if they indeed want a resolution.

THE FAIR CREDIT BILLING ACT (FCBA)

Sellers need to be aware of the federal Fair Credit Billing Act, which was enacted in 1975. This Act applies when a sale is made on an open-end account, rather than on an installment basis. In other words, if a customer is buying one item and paying in a series of installments, the FCBA does not apply. However, if the buyer has a charge account, the Fair Credit Billing Act will probably apply.

Under the Act, the buyer has 60 additional days to pay once an error is suspected in the account. Once a potential error has been spotted, the consumer does not have to pay the disputed amount, even if there is an obligation to do so by contract. The seller has 30 days to answer the buyer and has 90 days to correct the credit account or to explain to the consumer why no correction is needed.

If the consumer is in error and the charge was correct, the seller is entitled to all finance charges as of the date of the original billing.

If a consumer complains under the Fair Credit Billing Act, and after an investigation the seller maintains that the billing is correct, but the buyer refuses to pay, the seller is under an obligation to inform any credit bureau that the bill is disputed by the consumer. Further, the seller must notify the consumer about which credit bureaus have received information about the nonpayment, and further, if the matter is finally resolved with the consumer, the seller must notify the credit bureau that the matter has been resolved. In addition, the seller is under an obligation to provide an explanation of the FCBA, not only when the matter arises, but every six months thereafter.

CHAPTER PERSPECTIVE

There is almost nothing as irritating to a customer as a billing dispute. There are four basic types of billing disputes. The first type revolves around price: the customer is upset because the bill is higher than expected. This kind of dispute can be avoided by better communication at the outset. The second type of dispute involves quality. Although increased communication can reduce such disputes, it cannot eliminate them.

Disputes over confusing bills or double billing can be eliminated or at least reduced by better control over billing. Bills should be designed to answer any question the customer might have. At a minimum the customer should be able to see the previous balance, current charges, and how any recent payments were applied. If customers are calling with questions about their bills, the bill probably needs to be redesigned. If customers complain about getting double-billed, the bookkeeping system needs review. If customers' accounts are not being credited in a timely fashion, bookkeeping routines may need to be rearranged or more staff hired.

Billing disputes should be taken seriously because they can cost you customers. It is far cheaper to cultivate established customers than to find new ones. You should carefully evaluate your customers' claims. One can hardly overestimate the importance of handling claims promptly and courteously. You should bend over backwards when handling claims by established customers.

Always remember to apply cost/benefit analysis to disputed bills. It makes no sense to spend one hour arguing over a $10 dispute. When any dispute is under $20, you should find in favor of the customer and get on with your business. When large amounts of money are at stake, you can't just write off the amounts, but you need to resolve the disputes efficiently. Going to court is normally an inefficient means of settling problems. You should suggest arbitration or mediation of larger disputed claims.

Finally, all managers should be familiar with the provisions of the federal Fair Credit Billing Act (FCBA). The business may be subject to a fine if it fails to comply with the billing dispute provisions of this federal law.

Factoring Accounts Receivable

INTRODUCTION AND MAIN POINTS

"Understanding Accounts Receivable" (Chapter 8) examined the importance and operation of accounts receivable—debts owed to the business by customers. This chapter discusses factoring—the sale of accounts receivable to raise cash and avoid credit risk. Although factoring was once limited to certain industries, commercial factors now purchase receivables from a variety of businesses, large and small. Factoring should be viewed as an alternative source of short-term financing.

This chapter covers the following
- The close relationship between accounts receivable and cash
- How you can raise cash through factoring accounts receivable
- Which accounts are most easily factored
- How a typical factoring transaction is structured
- The consequences of a debtor's default on factored accounts
- Techniques used by factors to limit their own risks
- The advantages of using a financing subsidiary

ACCOUNTS RECEIVABLE AS A SOURCE OF CASH

Managers and business owners should always keep in mind the close relationship between accounts receivable and cash. The basic relationship can be seen from the illustration of the operating cycle of a business. An operating cycle includes the transactions by which a company turns cash into cash. The cycle starts with the firm's using its cash to buy inventory. The inventory is sold and produces accounts receivable. Finally the receivables are collected as cash.

Operating Cycle:
    Cash → Inventory → Accounts Receivable → Cash

When a credit sale is made and a bill sent to the customer, the selling firm records the sale as accounts receivable in its books. When the bill is paid, the selling firm eliminates the item from accounts receivable and records cash. Although inventory should be seen as a source of cash, it needs to be sold to a customer before it can be turned into cash. Accounts receivable are just one step away from cash. The exact moment of realization of the cash depends on how quickly the receivable is collected. The speed with which receivables are collected is largely a function of your collection policy. Chapter 10, "Establishing a Collections Policy," details the importance of prompt collections and also suggests techniques to speed collections and realization of cash.

RAISING CASH THROUGH FACTORING ACCOUNTS

For businesses in certain industries, factoring accounts receivable can be a good way to raise cash. When you factor accounts receivable, you essentially sell them for cash to a party called a *factor*. Factoring has traditionally been used in industries such as the fashion industry, but other types of businesses are increasingly turning to factors to raise cash. Factors have been reaching out to other types of businesses that have not used them in the past. Many businesses—both large and small—can use factors as an alternative to short-term bank loans to raise working capital.

How the Factor Operates

Essentially, a factor buys an account receivable for cash. Although the seller may take the cash immediately, it is not uncommon for the factor to hold the cash until it is needed. Typically the factor will buy accounts receivable from a manufacturer. The factor makes money on the transaction, because it does not *pay* the full face amount of the debt, but *collects* the entire amount. Typically, a factor will charge 1 percent to 2 percent of the amount of accounts receivable.

The debtor, typically a retailer, is notified that it must pay the factor directly. For example, assume that Manhattan is manufacturing dresses and other apparel for Rochester, a retailer. Manhattan knows that it will need cash before Rochester makes its payment. Manhattan approaches Federated, a factor. Federated buys the accounts receivable, paying approximately 98 percent of face value. Manhattan takes 25 percent of the cash at the time of the transaction and later draws on the remaining amount held by Federated. Rochester, the retailer, is instructed to pay its debt directly to Federated on the due date. In this transaction, Federated has essentially acted as a financier. Manhattan does not receive the full amount of its receivable, but it has access to cash early. Federated has made a profit on the transaction, and Rochester pays the same billed amount, sending a check to Federated instead of Manhattan.

Variations

In some cases, the factor sends money to the manufacturer right away. In other cases, the factor will hold the cash—or a portion of it—until the manufacturer requests it. Factors, then, are essentially financiers who shoulder a good deal of risk.

For example, assume that Manhattan, our dress manufacturer, sold $20,000 of dresses to a large retail chain, and later factored the accounts receivable to Federated. The retailer would typically pay the factor directly, and the factor in turn might pay the manufacturer over a period of months. In essence, the factor uses its skill and knowledge of the industry to insure payment of the receivable to the manufacturer.

The factor's expertise lies in its experience in evaluating retailers' ability to pay. Because of the factor's expertise, the manufacturer does not have to maintain a sophisticated credit-checking operation. The factor does the credit checking and stands behind the payment. Indeed, the factor nearly always shoulders the risk of nonpayment. For the service, the factor takes one to two percent of the sales transaction.

How the Factor Limits Risk

Not surprisingly, factors need to check carefully the creditworthiness of the debtors. This is why factors tend to specialize in a certain industry. The factor becomes personally acquainted with specific businesses and knows each firm's financial condition. In fact, factors are typically the best-informed commercial participants.

If a factor plans on buying some of your accounts receivable, the factor needs to know the same kind of information that you had when you advanced credit. In other words, the factor needs to know all about the finances and operations of the customer before it will be willing to put up cash for the receivable. The factor will also remember if a particular customer is a slow payer or has a history of default.

WHICH ACCOUNTS ARE MOST EASILY FACTORED?

Generally, factors are more willing to finance accounts receivable of a business with which they are familiar. If you have a receivable from a large established retailer, the factor is going to be more willing to buy it. Factors would be reluctant to risk cash on accounts receivable from an unknown entity.

During the last few years, larger companies have taken over factoring firms and have encouraged the factors to buy accounts receivable outside their normal circle of clients, from firms in a variety of industries. Likewise, financial officers in larger manufacturing firms have turned to factors as a source of short-term capital.

Factoring Transaction Example

In a typical factoring arrangement, a manufacturer will enter into a relationship with a factor before selling to a particular retailer. For example, let's assume that Classy Clothes is a manufacturer of women's clothing. Because Classy does not want its own credit and collection operation, it relies on a factor to purchase its accounts receivable. In effect, the factor will be performing both the credit and collection function for Classy Clothes. Additionally, since it will be shouldering the risk of nonpayment, the factor is also providing insurance for Classy that it will receive cash for merchandise as agreed.

Classy Clothes has been approached by a retailer, The Sixteen Shop, which wants to make a large purchase of women's clothes on credit. Before the transaction is undertaken, Classy Clothes will require credit information from the retailer, The Sixteen Shop, and it will forward this information to the factor. The factor will probably want quite a bit of information from the credit application before making a determination about buying the accounts receivable. The paperwork will be returned to the manufacturer, and the factor will either accept or reject the order.

Of course, the manufacturer can go forward with the transaction even if the factor does not want to buy the receivable. The factor is under no obligation to buy the receivable, and the manufacturer will then be responsible for collecting the receivable.

On the other hand, if the factor has agreed to accept the order, Classy Clothes will have to provide an *assignment* of the accounts receivable along with a copy of the invoice and shipping order that it sent to the retailer. An *assignment* means that the manufacturer has legally agreed that the payment should go to the factor.

Before the invoices are sent to the retailer, a letter or other document will instruct the retailer to pay the amounts due directly to the factor. Once the invoice has been sent, the factor will immediately credit the manufacturer's account for the amount of the receivable, making the funds available to the manufacturer as soon as the manufacturer wants funds withdrawn. (Of course, this will be minus the one or two percent commission that is charged by the factor.)

A factor physically stamps the invoices sent to customers, directing them to make payments directly to the factor. Occasionally, a factor will direct that the payments be made to a particular post office box or lock box at a bank. When this is done, the customer will not know that the account has been factored. In some cases, a factor will buy accounts receivable with recourse. In that case, if the credit customers fail to pay the factor, the company that factored its accounts will be responsible for paying the factor. In a typical transaction that is with recourse, a factor will lend only 60 percent to 80 percent of the firm's high-quality accounts receivable.

Cash Availability

Although the manufacturer can draw on the funds of the factor immediately, the funds often sit with the factor for a period of time. Typically the factor will insist on receiving interest from the manufacturer during the period between the invoice date and the actual payment by the retailer.

Determining whether to take the money is based on the working capital needs of the manufacturer. For example, if additional funds are needed to buy more fabric, the manufacturer will be happy to pay the interest to obtain more working capital. On the other hand, if the manufacturer doesn't need the cash right away, return on the sales transaction can be maximized by not drawing on the full amount. The manufacturer will receive interest on amounts left with the factor, who in effect is financing the transaction.

Typically, a factor will be buying accounts from numerous customers of a single manufacturer. For example, Classy Clothes may be selling its clothes to 50 or even 100 different retailers. The factor may be buying all or most of these accounts, and not surprisingly, the sales can be made at different times and some of the collections may be quick and some of them may be slow.

Because some accounts will be paid promptly while others tend to be slow, the factor will have to send the manufacturer a monthly statement, itemizing the accounts that have been accepted, the amount of the commission charged, the amount of interest payable to the manufacturer, and the progress on collecting the various accounts.

CONSEQUENCES OF DEBTOR'S DEFAULT ON FACTORED ACCOUNTS

The consequences of a debtor's default on a factored account depends on how the factor accepted the accounts receivable. If the factor bought the accounts receivable on a "nonrecourse" basis, then the factor will be liable for any losses through default or bankruptcy. This is the typical situation. In fact, this is one of the reasons for factors: they have special expertise in checking the financial background and stability of customers and should be expert at determining this type of risk.

On the other hand, factors occasionally will accept an accounts receivable on a "recourse" basis. This means that if the debtor does not pay, the factor can reclaim funds that have been disbursed to the manufacturer. In other words, if the factor is not paid by the retailer, the factor can seek return of the cash that it previously paid the manufacturer. Again, this is an unusual arrangement.

Recent Risk Reduction Devices

In recent years, factors have found ways other than recourse basis factoring to limit their risk. For example, factors now will typically guarantee only a part of a manufacturer's accounts receivable. A factor might limit the amount of its nonrecourse participation up to $10,000 per account.

For example, if a manufacturer sold orders of $5,000, $10,000, $15,000, and $20,000 to four retailers, the factor might determine that it would guarantee only the first $10,000 of each of those accounts, or perhaps just 60 or 80 percent of the value of those accounts. In that way, the factor and the manufacturer would share the risk, thus reducing the factor's overall exposure. The great advantage to a manufacturer or a supplier is that the factor provides instant access to cash and assumes the major risk.

Because of concentration in the factoring business, factors have become a lot more powerful in financing in certain industries. For example, because of great reliance on factors in the apparel industry, factors very often control the flow of credit sales to retailers. Assume for a moment that a dozen factors control most of the accounts receivable financing for apparel manufacturers. If a department store slows its paying of bills, the factors who represent most of the store's suppliers will have a lot to say about how fast the store should be paying. If the store fails to make prompt payment, the factors could withdraw their financing and essentially stop the flow of goods into the retail store.

EVALUATING FACTORING COMPARED TO BANK LOANS

Businesses can finance their accounts receivable either through a factor or through a bank. Commercial banks will typically extend loans if a business puts up its accounts receivable as collateral. Naturally, the quality of the accounts receivable will have a direct bearing on the ability of the business to use them as collateral. A bank will typically require that the firm behind the accounts receivable have a high rating from a credit rating agency. Typically, a business shouldn't expect to get more than 80 percent of the face value of its accounts receivable when borrowing from a bank.

Formerly, factoring was seen as an alternative only for companies that couldn't go to the bank, but many more businesses, large and small, are using factors today.

Most factoring arrangements are on a nonrecourse basis. In other words, the factor pays the business for its accounts receivable and the factor bears any risk that the accounts receivable will not ultimately be paid. For this reason, the factor typically will analyze the customer and collection of payment. In many ways, the factor takes over the credit and collection function of the firm. Generally, the factor will try to pick and choose among the receivables and will generally be comfortable only with lending on those most likely to be paid.

Nonrecourse Factoring

The biggest difference between bank financing and using a factor is that the factor shoulders the burden of risk if the debtor defaults. In other words, when you raise cash by factoring your accounts, you get to keep the money even if your customer never pays the factor. This is an important advantage of factoring.

Because the factor shoulders a good deal of risk, the cost of factoring will be much higher than raising funds through more conventional means. However, the factor also provides services in analyzing the accounts receivable and the strength of the buyers.

If payments on receivables are slow, the factor will compensate for the slowness by charging a premium fee. This is fair, since the longer an account receivable is overdue, the less likely the factor will be able to collect it. Additionally, the factor has to get the funds from somewhere and may have to borrow the money. Accordingly, the factor has to build potential borrowing costs into the factoring charge.

DISADVANTAGES OF FACTORING

There are a few disadvantages to factoring accounts receivable. First, factors are reluctant to factor marginal accounts. Since factors will accept only accounts receivable from firms that they can investigate, many smaller firms—although financially strong—might be deemed unacceptable. Second, factors' fees are relatively high. The factor typically receives not only interest on amounts advanced, but also a commission. This commission compensates the factor for running its credit-checking department.

A third disadvantage relates to the transaction itself. If you rely on factoring to raise working capital, your available capital will rise and fall based on your credit sales. If your credit sales drop, your accounts receivable total will drop and the factor will not be willing to advance as much cash. This can create difficulties during a period when you are short of cash.

Factors sometimes do not advance the full amount of the receivables. It is not unusual for a factor to "hold back" an amount to provide for bad debts, because the factor will know that a certain number of the receivables will not be paid.

Finally, although factoring agreements typically last for one year, the factor can pull out of the arrangement after giving appropriate notice.

FINANCING ACCOUNTS RECEIVABLE DISTINGUISHED

Commercial finance companies also purchase accounts receivable, but this transaction differs from the factoring described earlier in this chapter. When a finance company finances accounts receivable, it is lending money and taking the receivables as collateral. Since the finance company is lending based on the value of the receivables, the finance company is a "secured lender."

A factor, on the other hand, actually purchases the accounts receivable on a nonrecourse basis and shoulders the risks if the debtor never pays. Because the finance company is not buying the receivables but is merely using them as collateral, the finance company bears no risk of nonpayment. If the debtor does not pay the accounts receivable, the borrower is still liable to repay the finance company from other sources.

From a practical standpoint, the essential difference between financing accounts receivable and factoring them is who bears the risk in the event of a default by the original debtor. If the debtor pays, the transactions achieve the same result. Both the finance company and the factor are compensated for their services and the party who put up the receivables has access to the cash early, although at a price.

Consequences of a Default

In the event of default the difference between a financing arrangement and factoring become very apparent. Assume that Classic Clothes is a manufacturer who sells an order to Gibbs, a retailer. Classic Clothes chooses to finance its accounts receivable with Friendly Finance, making the receivable its collateral. Unfortunately Gibbs declares bankruptcy and does not pay. In this case Classic Clothes bears the loss. Friendly Finance's collateral is presumably worthless but Classic Clothes can be sued for collection of the debt.

Assume the same facts as in the example just discussed, except that Classic Clothes factored its receivable with Fairfield Factors. Since in a factoring arrangement the factor actually purchases the receivable, if Gibbs declares bankruptcy and defaults on its receivable, the loss falls on Fairfield Factors. Classic Clothes, who has already received the cash, is not obligated to the factor. If the factor has not advanced the full cash amount to Classic Clothes, it remains under an obligation to do so. Its obligation is not discharged by the bankruptcy of Gibbs. Because of this potential liability, factors are very careful to check the credit of retailers such as Gibbs.

ADVANTAGES OF USING A FINANCING SUBSIDIARY

When a company gets to be a certain size, there may be advantages to forming a financing subsidiary. In fact, many larger companies, such as General Motors, Ford, and Sears, have found that the profits from a financing subsidiary can easily outstrip the performance of their core business. Although at one time, financing was typically done by banks and other lenders, sellers have found that they can reap substantial profits by getting access to the interest on financed sales. A very effective means of doing this is through the use of a formal financing subsidiary.

SELLING TRADE ACCEPTANCES

Generally, it makes sense to form a financing subsidiary only if a business is large and engages in a fair number of credit transactions. Generally, a credit subsidiary will make sense only if the business is already operating in corporate form. For example, it is not unusual for an incorporated retailer to form a credit subsidiary that purchases the accounts receivable of the parent corporation customers. In turn, the financing subsidiary will sell these promises to pay at a discount as unrated commercial paper often called "acceptances." Such investments, while somewhat risky, typically carry a favorable interest rate that makes them attractive to many investors. On the other hand, the parent company immediately realizes cash from the financing subsidiary.

CHAPTER PERSPECTIVE

Managers should recognize that accounts receivable are a company's primary source of cash. An increasingly attractive method of raising cash is through the factoring of accounts receivable. In a factoring transaction the factor essentially buys the receivable, paying the seller before the buyer's payment is received.

Accounts from larger companies are generally the easiest to factor. Although at one time factors tended to specialize in only a few industries, the current trend is to extend factoring to more diverse fields.

Normally a factor will purchase receivables on a nonrecourse basis. This means that in the event of the debtor's default, the factor would bear the risk. In some cases, the factor explicitly declines this risk by taking the receivables on a "recourse" basis. Factors have recently developed other risk reduction devices.

Many larger companies have discovered that financing subsidiaries can be used to raise cash from their accounts receivable. Smaller companies are also starting to take advantage of this technique. The financing subsidiary allows a company to sell its receivables to the public in the form of trade acceptances. This gives the company access to cash while providing a good—if risky—return to investors.

Using Promissory Notes and Other Commercial Paper

INTRODUCTION AND MAIN POINTS

This chapter examines another legal area: the operation of commercial paper. Commercial paper includes checks, drafts, and promissory notes. If you have a checking account or have taken or given a promissory note, you have already dealt with commercial paper. A number of concepts and techniques in this area affect any business granting credit to its customers. A knowledge of commercial paper is also essential in evaluating your collection options.

After studying the material in this chapter you will know the following

- How a promissory note reduces risk
- When to request a promissory note
- How to distinguish negotiable from nonnegotiable promissory notes
- How to go about enforcing a promissory note
- The importance of holder-in-due-course status
- When the Federal Trade Commission holder-in-due-course rule applies
- How to distinguish sight and time drafts
- How trade acceptances work
- The operation of drafts and letters of credit
- The rights and liabilities of cosigners

HOW A PROMISSORY NOTE REDUCES RISK

In most credit sale transactions, the customer will be buying on "open account." This means that the credit transaction is based on the good faith of the parties without any special legal documentation of the debt. As we saw in Chapter 8, "Understanding Accounts Receivable," a sale on open account (as in a charge account) is still an enforceable debt; however, the use of a promissory note can reduce the risk of nonpayment by the customer.

A promissory note is merely a more formal IOU—written evidence that a specified amount is owed by the buyer to the seller. Naturally, this will eliminate any problems if the buyer claims that the goods were never shipped, or the services were never rendered, or that the amount was never owed at all, or if the buyer claims that the price was left for further negotiation and the price charged is too high considering the goods or services rendered. In other words, the promissory note documents a fixed dollar amount of the debt.

Advantages of Notes

Promissory notes have other distinct advantages. The promissory note typically sets a due date, after which the note is overdue. In many cases, when sales are made on "open account," it is not entirely clear when the amount is due. By stating a payment date, a promissory note eliminates this possible ambiguity. Promissory notes also provide for interest and sometimes for attorney fees if payment is not made by the due date. In fact, promissory notes are typically seen as a financing device.

For example, the Holiday Novelty Company is selling goods to the West Side Toy Store. West Side needs a large order of goods but does not currently have the cash to pay for it. If the goods are sold on "open account," West Side will probably pay Holiday Novelty when there are sufficient funds.

Holiday might want to formalize this transaction by requiring West Side to sign a promissory note. The note would state the amount due and set a specific time on which payment must be made. Preprinted and customized notes typically designate an interest rate and also monthly installments in many cases.

In this case, West Side could specify that the outstanding balance is to be charged one percent per month until the amount is paid. They may also want to specify precise monthly installment payments. In effect, the seller, Holiday Novelty, would be acting as a lender in the transaction by financing the credit transaction. Additionally, the seller would be receiving 12 percent interest, which may be a good return on the investment. The seller will not only be making a profit on the transaction, but will also be making a handsome profit on the financing. Large retailers such as Sears have found that financing transactions can be even more profitable than selling.

Using a promissory note has an additional advantage that

reduces a seller's risk. In court, it is procedurally more advantageous to sue on an unpaid promissory note than on a contract. Having the written promise to pay will make collection efforts far easier than if no note is used.

WHEN TO REQUEST A PROMISSORY NOTE

A business should request a promissory note in two situations.

1. When selling to a customer who has past payment problems
2. When selling a large order to a new customer who may not pay

Promissory notes should be seen as insurance devices to reduce the risk of default. For example, you may have a customer who has been slow in paying in the past. These sales may still be profitable even though they may be more difficult to collect. The manager must make a determination whether the potential profit from the sale overcomes the risk of nonpayment. One way to reduce this risk is to insist on a promissory note.

If the customer balks at signing a promissory note, you should probably demand cash on delivery. Customers will know in advance that you are concerned about payments if they have failed to repay in the past. If they are reluctant now to obligate themselves legally to pay, the prospects for future payments are bad.

Occasionally, a seller may be able to arrange a sale with a questionable buyer. The buyer may have a bad reputation for payment, or more likely, the seller may be aware that the buyer is in financial difficulty.

For example, the seller may learn from newspaper business pages that a company is in financial difficulty. If a business has been in a number of lawsuits, it may be in a precarious financial position as well. In these circumstances, or when dealing with a company for the first time on a relatively large order, a seller may want to insist on a promissory note. This is especially true if you are unsure of the reputation of a buyer in a distant location.

NEGOTIABLE PROMISSORY NOTES: REQUIREMENTS

Promissory notes are of two types:

1. Negotiable
2. Nonnegotiable

A negotiable promissory note is one that can be negotiated, or sold, to a third party such as a bank or a financing company. Although any promissory note that meets the necessary legal requirements is negotiable, in practical terms only promissory notes of larger companies can be negotiated for cash. However, the sale of a promissory note allows a seller to raise cash while still making a credit sale.

Selling (Discounting) a Note

Assume that Johnson Company wants to sell goods to Cramer Company. Because the transaction is large and the companies have not dealt with one another, Johnson requires Cramer Company to execute a promissory note for the purchase. Cramer's president signs the note on behalf of the company, promising to repay the balance due in six months along with 12 percent annual interest.

In this case, if Johnson, the seller, holds the note until maturity, there will not only be a profit on the sale, but also a prorated 12 percent return on the outstanding balance during the six-month period until the note falls due. However, Johnson may decide to sell the note to a lender or a financing company to raise current cash.

In this transaction, assume that Johnson has proposed to sell a $100,000 promissory note due in six months carrying an annual interest rate of 12 percent to the XYZ Financing Company. After doing a credit check on Cramer, XYZ agrees to purchase the note. XYZ will discount the note depending on the risk involved in the transaction. In other words, XYZ will pay Johnson less than the full face amount of the note today and will receive repayment with interest from Cramer in six months. In calculating the discount on the note, XYZ will consider forgoing potential interest on the funds that it advances to Johnson and also will factor in the risk of nonpayment by Cramer.

When a seller sells a note to a lender or other finance company, the seller normally retains liability on the obligation. In other words, if the maker of the note—the debtor—fails to pay when the note falls due, the seller of the note will have to make good on the obligation.

ENFORCEMENT OF PROMISSORY NOTES

The law provides special protection for purchasers of negotiable promissory notes. However, not all promissory notes are negotiable. There are four requirements for a promissory note to be negotiable:

1. The maker's signature on the note
2. An unconditional promise to pay a "certain sum" in money and no other promises in the note

3. Provision for payment on demand or at a definite time
4. Specification for payment to the order of a named payee or to bearer

There are normally two parties to a note, the *maker* and the *payee*. The maker is the debtor and the payee is normally the creditor, although a creditor could conceivably ask a debtor to pay money to someone else. When a note is negotiated or sold, the debtor pays the money to the buyer of the note.

For example, if West Side obtains a note from Cramer with West Side being the creditor and Cramer being the debtor, and West Side negotiates the note to XYZ Finance for cash, Cramer is the maker, and West Side would be the payee. However, once the note is sold, the debtor will have to pay the new owner of the note.

Liability on the Note

The way a person signs a note is of crucial significance because it determines who will have to pay the note. Although the law requires a note to be signed, it can also be signed with a stamp or any other mark that will identify the debtor. In other words, the name may be typed and no handwriting is needed. In some cases, questions may arise when a note is signed by an officer of a corporation.

For example, assume that James Jones owns 100 percent of JJ Corporation, and Jones signs a promissory note for his corporation. If Jones signs the note, "James Jones" and leaves it at that, he has signed individually and obligated himself, but not the corporation.

If, on the other hand, James Jones signs the note, "James Jones, President JJ Corporation," he has obligated the corporation, but not himself, because he has signed in a representative capacity. If, however, Jones signs the note, "James Jones, President, JJ Corp." and on the next line, signs "James Jones," then he is liable on the note and so is the corporation.

Other Problems

To be negotiable, the note must contain an unconditional promise to pay. If the note is conditional in any respect, then the note will not be negotiable. For example, if the note reads that the corporation will pay if nondefective goods are delivered, this would not be an unconditional promise to pay. Similarly, there may be problems if the note promises to make payments out of a particular fund or bank account. Note that these restrictions do not make the note uncollectible, but merely nonnegotiable. In other words, it cannot be sold to another person.

The note must also mention a certain sum of money, in other words, an exact amount. However, notes can bear interest and they can provide for attorney fees in the event of a default. Generally, if the interest rate cannot be determined from the face of the note, the note will probably not be negotiable. For example, if the stated interest rate is two percent above prime rate, the amount of the note may not be determined from the face of the instrument itself.

Notes are either payable on demand or at a definite time. A note that is payable on demand is called a *demand note*. A note that is payable in the future is called a *time note*. With the demand note, the amount stated in the note will be due and payable whenever the creditor decides to make a demand of the debtor. This is at the creditor's option. When a definite time is stated, the note will not be due until that stated date.

Payable to the Order of or to Bearer

A note must be payable to order of a named payee or to bearer. A note payable to the order of a specific person or to a specific business is called *order paper*. A note payable to bearer or to cash is unusual; this would be *bearer paper*. A note may be payable to more than one person either jointly or to one or the other. In other words, a note could be payable to XYZ *and* ABC Company or to XYZ *or* ABC Company. In the first instance, both payees would have to be present for payment whereas in the alternative, either party could demand payment.

A promissory note is procedurally advantageous to its holder, because it can be readily enforced in court. Procedures for enforcing a note are 1) demand payment from the debtor, 2) send a letter to the debtor, informing that the note is overdue and that legal action will be taken if the amount owed in interest is not paid promptly, 3) sue to enforce the note.

Enforcement of a promissory note is easier than enforcement of a contract because the note fixes the amount of the debtor's obligation and also determines the time in which the obligation is due.

In the absence of a note, the debtor may be able to argue about both the value of the goods or services delivered and the time for payment.

HOLDER-IN-DUE-COURSE STATUS

A holder in due course is a holder who has paid value for the note, in good faith, without any notice that the note was overdue or had been dishonored or was subject to any other defense. A holder in due course gets special enforcement rights under the law. If a holder of a note is a "holder in due course," the holder may have even greater rights than the original creditor.

For example, assume that Taylor Company has sold goods to Baxter Company. Although Baxter has signed an interest-bearing promissory note in favor of Taylor, when the time for payment falls due, Baxter refuses to pay, arguing that the goods it received from Taylor were defective. Baxter may have a good defense against Taylor's enforcement of the note.

Now, assume that Taylor has received the note from Baxter, but has negotiated the note to XYZ Corporation for cash. When the note falls due, XYZ makes a demand on Baxter to pay the note. Again, Baxter tenders the defense that the goods it received from Taylor were defective, and accordingly, it should not have to pay XYZ on the note. However, if XYZ is a holder in due course (HDC), then XYZ will be able to enforce the note even though there was a problem with the underlying sales obligation.

Defenses to a Holder in Due Course

Generally, a holder in due course can enforce a note even when there are problems with the underlying obligation. However, there are certain exceptions when a note cannot be enforced. For example, a note cannot be enforced if the debtor can show

1. The debtor was a minor;
2. The debtor was subject to duress (threats);
3. The underlying transaction was illegal;
4. The legal effect of the note was misrepresented;
5. The debtor is in bankruptcy;
6. There has been forgery or alteration of the note.

FTC HOLDER-IN-DUE-COURSE RULE

When a consumer rather than a business makes out a note as a debtor, there is a Federal Trade Commission regulation that basically abolishes the holder-in-due-course status for a consumer credit transaction. In other words, the rule just discussed does not apply when an individual purchases goods or services for personal family or household use. However, if an individual purchases goods or services for a business, or purchases real estate or securities, then the holder-in-due-course rule still applies to any note.

Also, the FTC rule does not apply if a consumer gets a loan and then uses the money to buy goods in a different transaction. This is in contrast to when the seller finances the transaction and takes back a note for goods or services.

DRAFTS

Although promissory notes are the most common type of negotiable instrument used by smaller businesses, there are other types of commercial paper that may also be used to reduce a seller's risk of nonpayment. One of the most common alternatives is called a draft. A draft is quite similar to a check but in function is more similar to a note. A draft is a written order drawn up by one person, usually a seller, directing the other person to pay to the order of the person indicated in the draft.

For example, if Johnson Company wanted to sell goods to West Side and wanted to use a draft rather than a note, Johnson could make up a draft ordering West Side to pay money to the order of the person named in the draft—normally the seller, in this case, Johnson. However, a draft could be made out with an alternate payee, which makes the use of a draft somewhat more flexible.

Of course, a piece of paper does not obligate anyone until it is signed. As in the case of a note, a draft must be signed by the party or parties who will ultimately pay it. In the case of a draft, this signature is known as an "acceptance" of the draft. You may have heard of a bank draft, and insurance companies typically pay using drafts rather than checks.

Like notes, drafts can be negotiated, that is, sold for cash. Similarly, if a holder pays value without any notices of defenses and takes the draft in good faith, the holder of a draft could also be a holder in due course and will have the same protection against a number of defenses as a holder of a negotiable promissory note.

TRADE ACCEPTANCE

Another type of instrument is known as a *trade acceptance*, which is merely a draft that has been drawn up by a seller directing the buyer to pay and that has been *accepted* by the buyer. A variation of this is a *banker's acceptance*, which is a draft that has been drawn on a bank and that has been *accepted* by that bank for payment when it becomes due.

OTHER COMMERCIAL PAPER

There are some other types of commercial paper and other documents that can also reduce a credit seller's risk. One device is the postdated check. In some cases, a seller may ask a buyer to submit one or a number of postdated checks for payment of goods. The checks could be used as a substitute for a note or a draft.

For example, assume a buyer has bought $10,000 of goods from a seller on credit, and the buyer has agreed to make a series of ten weekly payments to the seller. In lieu of requiring a promissory note, the seller could request ten postdated checks. The buyer would complete the checks but date them for one in each of the following ten weeks. For example, if the payments are made starting in September, there would be four checks valid for September, four for October, and two for November. As the installments become due, the seller would deposit the applicable amounts.

Using postdated checks has all the advantages of using a note—the amount of the debt is documented on paper and the date of the payment is clear. However, by using a series of postdated checks, the seller does not have to nag the buyer for the funds, because the checks are on hand. Naturally if the checks are returned for insufficient funds (NSF), this advantage is undone.

Personal Guarantee

Another risk reduction technique is to request a personal guarantee from the owner of a business. As we discussed in relation to promissory notes, liability depends very much on the manner of signing. (See page 151.)

Additionally, a seller may want to have an owner execute a separate document labeled "guarantee" in which the owner or another party explicitly engages to pay a business's debt if the business fails to do so.

Letter of Credit

A last type of document that limits risk is a letter of credit. A letter of credit is a surety device in which a bank or other party obligates itself to pay an amount should the primary debtor fail to pay. In fact, the letter of credit operates in a manner similar to a performance bond. If the primary debtor fails to *perform*, the letter of credit is there for security.

Although letters of credit can reduce risk, credit sellers should be aware that letters of credit are generally revocable unless they are clearly marked "irrevocable."

COSIGNERS

Inside or outside of bankruptcy, the liability of cosigners is complicated. In analyzing the rights and duties of cosigners the first step is to determine if the cosigners wished to obligate themselves directly or merely wished to act as a surety or backup—in other words, to pay only if the primary party did not. For example, if two brothers join together to buy an apartment building as an investment and they both cosign on a promissory note, there is no surety arrangement because both are considered principal or primary debtors.

On the other hand, the cosigner may have been merely promising to pay another party's debt. For example, if a teenager buys a car, signing a note for the unpaid balance, the car dealer would normally request a parent or other responsible adult to cosign on the note. In this case, parents are not incurring their own debt but guaranteeing the debt of another.

If a cosigner on a debt is clearly acting as a backup, the cosigner may be either a *surety* or a *guarantor*. A cosigner acts as a surety when a promise is made directly to the creditor. Normally a creditor can seek payment directly from the surety without suing and executing a judgment against the debtor. Surety agreements do not normally have to be in writing.

If the cosigner is acting as a guarantor, the cosigner is secondarily liable and will have to pay only after the creditor tries unsuccessfully to get the funds from the debtor. The guarantor's promise must normally be in writing to be enforceable.

Cosigner's Defenses

Cosigners can normally assert the debtor's defenses against the creditor. For example, assume that Jones has guaranteed Travis Furniture's note to Pine Manufacturing, its supplier. If the facts permit, Jones can assert any of Travis's defenses, including fraud or breach of contract on the part of Pine.

An individual or an agent of a business who signs as a cosigner on a negotiable note or check or draft becomes liable along with the original debtor.

Cosigners are not protected in bankruptcy unless an individual debtor has elected Chapter 13 protection. In other bankruptcy chapters, creditors can proceed directly against the cosigners when the original debtor declares bankruptcy. (See pages 229–230 of Chapter 19, "Dealing with Debtors in Bankruptcy.") Outside bankruptcy, cosigners may also guarantee payment by signing a promissory note as an accommodation endorser. If the endorser merely signs "collection guaranteed," the creditor must execute the judgment in court and have it returned uncontested before proceeding against the endorser. Alternatively, if an accommodation endorser has "guaranteed payment," the creditor can proceed directly against the endorser rather than proceeding first against the debtor and getting an unsatisfied judgment.

CHAPTER PERSPECTIVE

A basic knowledge of commercial paper is essential in evaluating your collection options. There are a number of important commercial paper concepts that affect any business granting credit to its customers.

Credit sellers can often reduce their risks by asking for a promissory note. You should request a promissory note whenever sending an order to a untrustworthy old customer or when sending a large order to a new customer. The note reduces risk because it fixes both the dollar amount of the debt and the time for payment.

There are two types of promissory notes: negotiable and nonnegotiable. Negotiable promissory notes can be discounted (sold) to a lender to raise cash. A holder in due course can generally enforce a note even when the buyer has defenses that would be good against the seller. However, if the buyer is a consumer, the federal FTC Holder-In-Due-Course Rule changes this result.

Other types of commercial paper used in credit and collections include drafts, trade acceptances, and letters of credit. Business owners and managers also need to be aware of the rights and liabilities of cosigners in the credit and collections cycle.

Arranging Workouts

INTRODUCTION AND MAIN POINTS

Prior chapters covered debt collections. They examined how to set up in-house debt collection procedures and how to use third parties efficiently to help collect your overdue accounts.

This chapter focuses on workouts—arrangements that let a debtor pay all or a portion of a debt over a long period of time. In some cases, collection efforts may be unsuccessful because the debtor lacks the cash flow to pay the debt. In this case, a workout may be appropriate. The seller will arrange a plan under which the debtor will be able to handle the payments. This chapter also discusses some alternatives to workouts, including compositions, assignments for the benefit of creditors, and bankruptcy.

After studying the material in this chapter you will know the following

- The definition of a workout
- When a workout is preferable
- How to predict which debtors will follow through
- The value of lengthening payment schedules
- When bankruptcy would be a better alternative
- How a composition works
- What is an assignment for the benefit of creditors
- When the appointment of a receiver would be appropriate
- The disadvantages of informal arrangements

WHAT IS A WORKOUT?

A workout is an out-of-court arrangement in which a debtor and creditor agree on one of these alternatives:

1. the debtor will pay less than the full amount of the debt
2. the debtor will have additional time to pay the debt
3. the debtor will pay a reduced amount of debt over a longer period of time.

The workouts described in this chapter are not part of the bankruptcy system. Indeed, they should be viewed as an alternative to a bankruptcy for a debtor that cannot currently pay bills. Sometimes a Chapter 11 or Chapter 13 bankruptcy will be referred to as a "workout." For purposes of this chapter we will confine the use of that term to out-of-court solutions between a debtor and a creditor. Please refer to Chapter 19, "Dealing with Debtors in Bankruptcy," for more details about the operation of the bankruptcy system.

Typical Workout

A workout may involve only one debtor and creditor or it may involve one debtor with a number of creditors. Obviously, it will be easier to structure a workout when only two parties are involved; the more parties, the more potential for conflicting interests.

There is no standard format for a workout, and the interested parties are basically free to tailor an arrangement that will be mutually beneficial to both of them. Typically the creditor will agree to accept somewhat less than originally expected over a longer period of time, and the debtor will agree to make the actual payments. Normally, there is no in-court procedure; rather, the parties bind themselves by an enforceable contract to the new arrangement.

WHEN SHOULD YOU SUGGEST A WORKOUT?

A workout should be seen as a contractual rearrangement of a debtor-creditor relationship. A workout can be preferable to both a debtor and a creditor. If a debtor lacks the funds to pay, a creditor may sometimes force the debtor into bankruptcy. A creditor may get very little under the bankruptcy system. For example, if the debtor is an individual, much of the debtor's property may be "exempt assets" that cannot be reached by the creditor.

Normally, banks and other lenders with collateral do well in bankruptcy, but unsecured creditors may get very little or nothing. A workout may be preferable for unpaid creditors without collateral.

PRIVACY CONCERNS

The workout is arranged privately rather than publicly. When a debtor is sued in court or files for bankruptcy, the papers are filed at the courthouse and become part of the public record. Anyone—including reporters—can request to see the court papers. If either the debtor or the creditor has done something that may prove embarrassing if made public, then a workout may be preferable to a bankruptcy or other legal action. In some cases, a debtor's or creditor's action may have bad consequences once a bankruptcy is entered.

For example, assume that Cole Hardware is in financial distress and owes money to several suppliers. The owner of Cole Hardware transferred several business assets to members of the Cole family in an effort to mislead the company's creditors. If this matter went to bankruptcy court, the transfer would at best be unraveled and the property would have to be returned to the business. At worst, the transfer may be considered a "fraudulent conveyance" to cheat creditors, with possible criminal penalties. If the matter is settled as a workout, there will probably be little or no damaging consequence to Cole.

WHICH DEBTORS WILL FOLLOW THROUGH?

It is important to know which debtors will probably follow through with a workout. In many cases, if a debtor will not follow through, the creditor would have been better off to force involuntary bankruptcy initially to have the debtor declared insolvent by the court. Generally, a debtor that is in merely temporary financial distress is the most likely to follow through with the workout arrangement. Likewise, a business or debtor that is suffering unexpected distress for one reason or another is likely to follow through with the workout plan.

On the other hand, it makes little sense to suggest a workout if the debtor appears to be insolvent with little hope of improving its financial condition in the near term. A workout will involve time, and if you are not going to be paid, it would be better to face up to reality at the start than to spend fruitless efforts trying to collect from an insolvent debtor.

Similarly, do not suggest a workout if the debtor is dishonest. If the debtor has lied to you about the debt in the past, there is no reason to trust new-found sincerity about making installment payments in a workout. With a dishonest debtor you should proceed with ordinary collection procedures, including suing or petitioning for involuntary bankruptcy if the debt is large enough to make this a cost-efficient strategy.

LENGTHENING PAYMENT SCHEDULES

A common method of arranging a workout is merely to lengthen the time over which payments must be made. The debtor will be repaying the same amount, but will be making a greater number of smaller payments. In fact, because interest is normally included, this type of arrangement can ultimately be more profitable for the creditor.

For example, assume that Brown has bought furniture on credit from a furniture store. Brown has been laid off by his employer when his office was relocated to another region of the country. Brown is now unable to meet his payments on the loan. The furniture store has several alternatives: repossess the furniture and try to resell it; try to throw Brown into bankruptcy; try to arrange a workout with Brown.

With a workout, the furniture store could suggest that Brown pay the entire amount of this debt, but over a two-year rather than a one-year period. Although the furniture store is more at risk because of the longer payment period, if the arrangement carries an interest rate, there actually may be profit in lengthening the payment period from what was originally anticipated.

On the other hand, many workouts will only be successful if a debtor pays less than the full amount of the debt. In our example, if Brown is unable to find other employment at or near his former salary, it may be totally unrealistic to expect him to pay the full amount. The furniture store may be better off trying to get 50 cents on the dollar rather than repossessing the furniture and selling it at a fraction of its original cost or trying to throw Brown into bankruptcy. In fact, the store may find that the furniture is exempt property in a bankruptcy. The store may be better off with 50 cents on the dollar than nothing at all.

In practice, many workouts involve a combination of lengthened payment schedules and reduced payments. It makes no sense to structure a workout that is beyond the financial capacity of the debtor. This will just result in frustration and wasted time and effort for both the debtor and the creditor. Creditors should keep in mind that repossessing goods or bankruptcy will not normally result in a full repayment either. Accordingly, creditors should be ready to accept a workout that produces less than the full amount of the debt. A creditor may still be far ahead because there will be fewer attorney fees and other costs involved.

USE OF DEBT CONSOLIDATION LOANS

Alternately, the debtor may be able to arrange a debt consolidation loan. Although a debt consolidation loan does not eliminate any of the debt, it may have a longer maturity and carry a lower interest rate than the individual debts. Large creditors, such as banks and retailers, have formed the Consumer Credit Counselling service (CCC), a nonprofit organization that attempts to assist individuals in structuring workouts with their creditors. The fees for the service are usually nominal. CCC offices are located in most major cities.

ALTERNATIVES: BANKRUPTCY

One alternative to a workout is a bankruptcy. A bankruptcy should be seen as a creditor's remedy in which the creditor or creditors will force the debtor into a court action that will mandate the liquidation of the debtor's property. Refer to Chapter 19, "Dealing with Debtors in Bankruptcy," for a more complete description of the bankruptcy system.

Bankruptcies are somewhat less advantageous for small creditors, because bankruptcy law provides a number of protections for debtors. As discussed before, bankruptcy law allows debtors to keep a certain amount of "exempt property"—that is, property that cannot be seized by creditors for nonpayment of debts.

Also, bankruptcy tends to be a poor choice of remedy for small businesses because unsecured creditors—those without collateral—tend to receive very little in a bankruptcy. For these reasons, bankruptcy is not always a good alternative to a workout.

Workouts within Bankruptcies

Even though a debtor has filed for bankruptcy it might not be too late to suggest a workout, because a debtor and creditors already involved in a bankruptcy action may still initiate a workout in an effort to preserve the assets of the debtor, to save time, or to avoid further litigation with its attendant delays. The bankruptcy court has authority to suspend actions in a bankruptcy case on petition of one or both of the parties.

For example, assume that Wood Corp. is in the midst of setting up a Chapter 11 Reorganization Plan in the bankruptcy court. The creditors may realize that under the reorganization plan it will take years to recoup their losses and the attendant legal costs would dissipate the debtor's assets. To avoid the possibility of years of delay, the creditors may determine that they could do better with a settlement with Wood outside the bankruptcy court. The Bankruptcy Code allows suspension of the court proceeding on petition of the parties while the creditors try to set up an informal workout with Wood.

ALTERNATIVES: COMPOSITIONS

Compositions and assignments for the benefit of creditors are state law alternatives for insolvent debtors. Each of these remedies allows the debtor to pay less than the full amount owed, and that payment will be considered full satisfaction of the debt to the creditors. A fuller discussion of bankruptcy alternatives can be found in Barron's *Keys to Bankruptcy*.

Less than Full Payment

Normally, state law provides that part payment of a debt does not extinguish the full amount of the debt. In fact, if a creditor agrees—orally or in writing—to accept less than the full amount as satisfaction of a debt, the agreement is normally not enforceable against the creditor.

For example, assume a business hires a painter to paint its offices. The painter presents the business with a bill for $5,000 on completion of the job. Also assume that there is no dispute as to the quality of the work or the amount charged, but for financial reasons the business finds itself unable to pay. The painter later agrees to accept $2,500 in full satisfaction of the debt.

In most states such an agreement will be unenforceable. The result would be different if the business gave something in return (termed legal "consideration") for the painter's agreeing to accept less than the full amount—for example, if the business agreed to act as a reference for the painter.

However, if the underlying transaction involved the sale of goods rather than the sale of an intangible or of services, a special rule applies. If the debt arose from a transaction involving the sale of goods, an agreement to accept a lesser amount in full satisfaction of the debt would be enforceable in most states.

"Goods" is simply a term for tangible objects of value that can be moved around; excluded are money, commercial paper, and real estate. Furniture, equipment, and cars are classified as "goods." For example, if a business bought equipment on credit and there is no dispute as to the amount owed, but the business was later unable to pay the bill when presented, an agreement by the seller to accept less than the full amount of the debt as payment in full would be enforceable.

Accord and Satisfaction

A special exception applies when there is a genuine dispute over the amount of a bill. The law terms this an "unliquidated debt" because the parties do not agree on the amount due. For example, assume that a business has hired a contractor to build a new roof on a warehouse, and the parties agree that the price for the work will be $10,000. When the work is finished the business objects to the level of workmanship, believing the work to be worth only $5,000. This is an unliquidated debt because of the dispute about the amount owed.

If the business in our example mails the painter a $5,000 check clearly marked "payment in full," and the painter cashes the check, this would amount to an *accord and satisfaction* that would discharge the debt. A payment-in-full check discharges a debt larger than the value of the check only when there is a genuine dispute. Normally, payment of less than the full amount of a debt will not extinguish a debt.

Composition Rules

A composition is an agreement between creditors and the debtor that provides an exemption to this general rule. In a composition, the debtor and creditors agree that the creditors will take less than the full amount of the debts and/or agree to provide an extension of time in which the debtor may pay the debt.

Although a composition agreement may be enforced against the parties that agreed to it, there is no way that a creditor can be forced to become part of the composition plan. A creditor that fails to join can continue collection activities and need not accept less than full repayment of the amount owed. Similarly, a nonparticipating creditor may also seek to throw the debtor into involuntary bankruptcy.

ALTERNATIVES: ASSIGNMENT FOR THE BENEFIT OF CREDITORS

An assignment for the benefit of creditors is similar to a composition agreement but is normally a more formal procedure. In an assignment for the benefit of creditors, title to the debtor's property will be assigned to a trustee who will then normally sell the property for the benefit of the creditors.

For example, assume that a business has seven unsecured creditors, the debtor has a history of nonpayment, and the creditors suspect dishonesty. Although the creditors may be able to force the debtor into involuntary bankruptcy, as a practical matter the legal fees may exhaust the debtor's assets, which would leave a smaller pool of assets to distribute. However, the creditors are uncomfortable with leaving the debtor in control of the assets they would claim for repayment. An assignment for the benefit of creditors will transfer the assets to a disinterested party while at the same time allowing flexibility and reduced costs for the creditors.

Advantages of Assignment over Compositions
An assignment for the benefit of creditors also has the advantage over a composition in that a nonparticipating creditor may not be able to attach the property once it is in the hands of the trustee. As in a composition, a creditor may not be forced into participating in an assignment for the benefit of creditors. Additionally, a creditor may still be able to throw a debtor into involuntary bankruptcy despite the operation of the assignment.

ALTERNATIVES: APPOINTMENT OF A RECEIVER
The appointment of a receiver is a remedy that is available under state law as an alternative to bankruptcy. A receiver is an officer appointed by the court who is delegated to identify, protect, and often liquidate the debtor's assets. There are businesses that specialize in acting as receivers. For example, there are businesses that specialize in running insolvent hotels and resorts. A judge may appoint an attorney or a CPA or a businessperson with wide business experience to act as receiver.

There are two kinds of receivers:
1. general receivers
2. special receivers

A general receiver normally has broad powers to run a debtor's affairs. For example, a general receiver may be appointed to run a debtor's business for the benefit of creditors. If a business owner has proven either irresponsible or unable to manage the fiscal affairs of the business, the creditors may be able to petition a state court for the appointment of a general receiver to protect their interests. The receiver would be appointed to run the business—or perhaps liquidate it if it cannot be run profitably—for the benefit of the creditors.

A special receiver typically acts on behalf of one creditor or a group of creditors. For example, a receiver may be appointed to protect a bank's interest in a specific piece of real estate in which the bank carries a mortgage. For example, assume that a real estate business is insolvent and one of its properties is a resort hotel. A bank holding a mortgage on the hotel could petition the court for the appointment of a special receiver who would not run all of the debtor's property but merely the resort, which would be operated for the benefit of the bank.

DISADVANTAGES OF INFORMAL ARRANGEMENTS

There are a number of disadvantages to informal arrangements such as workouts, compositions, assignments for the benefit of creditors, and the appointment of a receiver. Generally all the disadvantages have to do with lack of enforcement.

Generally, workouts and other informal arrangements work best when all parties have both the will and the capacity to stay with the arrangement. If the debtor lacks either the will or the capacity, the informal arrangement is almost sure to fail.

For example, assume that Ames is a debtor who owes a number of creditors for goods sold on credit. The creditors approach Ames with a proposed workout arrangement whereby Ames would pay 80 percent of the amount owed over a two-year period. Although Ames is potentially able to pay the amount over the lengthened time period, Ames has no real intention to do so. After three months, Ames again falls behind in making payments. In this case the creditors are little better off than they were before, and they may have given up certain procedural rights against Ames. In fact, Ames may have dissipated many assets during the three months, or may have converted some of the assets into "exempt property" that cannot be touched by creditors in or outside of bankruptcy.

Role of Bankruptcy

Another disadvantage to informal workouts is that creditors cannot be forced into the process. For example, assume that certain creditors agree to either a workout or another informal arrangement such as a composition or an assignment for the benefit of creditors or the appointment of a receiver. If a large creditor disagrees with the arrangement, that large creditor can often throw the debtor into bankruptcy anyway.

Once the debtor is thrown into bankruptcy, the informal arrangement—such as a workout—has to cease, and all legal activity against the debtor must be moved to the bankruptcy court. This threat of bankruptcy either by a large creditor or by the debtor taints the effectiveness of informal arrangements. Once the bankruptcy is declared, the prior work on the informal arrangement has all gone to waste. (Note that workouts are still possible after filing for bankruptcy but before bankruptcy is declared. See page 163.)

CHAPTER PERSPECTIVE

A workout is an out-of-court arrangement in which a debtor and creditor agree that the debtor will pay less than the full amount of the debt, will have additional time to pay the debt, or will pay a reduced amount of debt over a longer period of time.

A workout should be seen as a contractual rearrangement of a debtor-creditor relationship. A workout can be preferable to both a debtor and a creditor if a debtor lacks the funds to pay. A workout would generally be preferable to forcing an involuntary bankruptcy when the creditor is unsecured (has no collateral to attach). On the other hand, a workout is unlikely to be effective if the debtor has no prospects of financial recovery or is dishonest.

Generally, a debtor that is in merely temporary financial distress is the most likely to follow through with the workout arrangement. Likewise, a business or debtor that is suffering unexpected distress for one reason or another is also likely to follow through with the workout plan.

Workouts typically involve lengthening repayment schedules. The creditor will be receiving the same amount but over a longer time and in smaller payments. Because these installment payments are normally interest bearing, the longer payments can actually be more profitable for the creditor while still allowing the debtor more breathing room. Many workouts are fashioned with a reduction in the amount owed. Creditors should not reject such solutions offhand, because creditors are unlikely to recover full payment if other remedies are pursued instead of the workout. Another variation includes a workout that involves a debt consolidation loan.

There are a number of alternatives to negotiated workouts. One alternative is to force a debtor into involuntary bankruptcy. However, some creditors receive very little in a bankruptcy, so care should be used before selecting this option. Another alternative is a state law "composition." In a composition, a creditor or creditors agree to accept less than the full amount of the debt in satisfaction of the debtor's obligation. The result is similar to a bankruptcy although with fewer legal costs. Also, unsecured debtors may receive more in a composition than they would in a bankruptcy. An assignment for the benefit of creditors is another state law remedy. This remedy, normally used with a business debtor, is more extreme than a composition because it requires the transfer of the debtor's assets to a neutral third party—the trustee—for the benefit of the creditors. The trustee will either operate the debtor's business or sell the debtor's assets for the benefit of the creditors.

Another state law alternative is the appointment of a receiver. A receiver is an officer appointed by the court who is delegated the duty of identifying, protecting, and often liquidating the debtor's assets. There are businesses that specialize in being receivers. There are generally two kinds of receivers: general receivers and special receivers. A general receiver normally has broad powers to run a debtor's affairs. For example, a general receiver may be appointed to run a debtor's business for the benefit of all creditors. A special receiver typically acts on behalf of one creditor or a group of creditors and may be appointed to deal with only one property, such as a piece of real estate.

Workouts and the other informal arrangements should all be viewed as alternatives to a bankruptcy. However, there is one major disadvantage to any of these informal arrangements: no creditor can be forced to join in. Accordingly, a major creditor can still force a debtor into bankruptcy. A bankruptcy filing will generally defeat the purpose of any of the informal arrangements.

Using Third-Party Debt Collectors

INTRODUCTION AND MAIN POINTS

This chapter deals with using collection agencies and collection attorneys to help collect your slow-moving accounts. Experience has shown that the older the bill, the less likely it is to be paid. In fact, bills over six months old seldom get paid. Experienced businesses hand overdue accounts to third parties for collection.

Before you use a collection agency or a collections attorney, you should understand the nature of the process and how these third parties operate. Once you understand the process you will be able to use their services more effectively.

After studying the material in this chapter you will understand the following

- Your debt collection alternatives
- How debt collection agencies operate
- How the debt collection agency industry is organized
- The advantages of referring an account to a collection agency
- How to determine which accounts should be referred to an agency
- The steps in "tracing skips"
- How collection agencies set their fees
- Why the Fair Debt Collection Practices Act was passed to address collectors' abuses

COLLECTION ALTERNATIVES

When an account falls seriously overdue, it is generally a good business practice to refer the account to a third party for collection. This referral should generally be made after your own collection efforts have proven unsuccessful. Experience suggests that the referral should be done promptly because even professional bill collectors will have difficulty turning an old bill into cash. Generally any account that is several months overdue is a prime candidate for referral to a third party for collection. Some credit and collection authorities recommend referral for accounts that are one to two month's overdue, especially if the credit profile is weak.

Professional collectors can often get collection results when all efforts by the seller have failed. Once you understand how these third parties operate, you will be able to use their services more effectively.

It is important to understand your alternatives when you have an account that should be referred to a third party. Generally, there are three third-party alternatives:

1. A letter-writing service
2. A collection agency
3. A collection lawyer

Letter-Writing Services

For a fee, you can hire the services of a company that will send form letters to your customers who have not paid their bills. Generally, you will supply the letter-writing service with your letterhead; the service will compose and send out letters that look as if they came directly from your business.

You can arrange for one letter to be sent, or you can arrange for the letters to go out on a regular basis, for example, every two weeks or even every week. The advantage of a letter-writing service is that it will remove this burden from your own staff. Since the letters are standardized, the letter-writing company's fee will be rather modest, compared to the real cost of using one of your employees to do the chore.

Collection Agencies

The next alternative is to use a collection agency. A collection agency is a for-profit company that nags slow payers into paying their bills. Although some agencies have an unsavory reputation, slow payers have nothing to be proud of either. If you buy something on credit promising to pay for it, you should at least make some effort to repay.

As you may know, there are local collection agencies and large national agencies that operate in many states. Although a local firm may provide more personal service, the national agency is likely to be better capitalized and better able to deal with complicated matters, perhaps debtors who have moved out of state. Collection agencies will generally get better results than a letter-writing service because in addition to sending letters they will also telephone the debtors suggesting that they pay up. Personal contacts often get a better response than form letters. Collection agency fees can range as high as 50 percent of what is collected.

Collection Attorneys

The third alternative is to use a law firm or a local attorney to collect the debts. Generally, it will cost you more money to use an attorney, but in some cases, this may be offset if the attorney is more successful than an agency. Generally attorneys will not charge if they are unsuccessful in collecting the bill. Attorneys tend to accept only larger amounts for collection.

Cost/Benefit Analysis

Because your collection efforts are supposed to produce cash, you must determine to whom you should refer an overdue account on a cost/benefit basis. In other words, you need to determine which is the most effective means of collecting your overdue accounts. The letter-writing service will usually charge a modest fee for writing the letter whether they are successful or not. Both the attorney and the collection agency will typically bill a percentage of the recovery. Fees will be discussed more fully later in this chapter.

ORGANIZATION OF THE DEBT COLLECTION INDUSTRY

Collection agencies may be local firms or national firms. The local firm will often give more personal attention to your problem. However the national firm may have more clout because of its size, resources, and reputation. If you do business mainly in one city or locality, a local collection agency may work just fine. On the other hand, if you sell to customers in a number of different states, you probably should use a large commercial collection agency for your bad debt collections.

Usually, when you use a larger company, you don't have to worry about either their tactics or their solvency. You can rely on their working within the laws and on their avoiding tactics that you might find distasteful. Also, you don't have to worry that they may lose your money once they have collected it. Typically a collection agency will collect money directly from your debtor. The agency will then take its fee out of the proceeds before returning the "net" amount to you. Because the collection agency will be receiving the payments from the customer, you need to be concerned about the financial stability and reputation of the collection agency itself. In a number of instances, smaller local collection agencies have liquidated without distributing money owed to clients.

Assume that you have retained a collection agency that you found in the Yellow Pages of the telephone directory. You don't ask for any local references and also you fail to ask for any bank or financial reference. The collection agency is actually quite successful in using strong-arm and abusive tactics against several of your customers. Unfortunately for you, although the customers paid their delinquent accounts, the fact that this disreputable firm was working on your behalf damages your reputation in the local business community. Additionally, although you get the first payment from the agency, soon payments start coming more slowly, and then you learn that the collection agency itself is in financial difficulty as they have been sued because of their abusive tactics.

In fact, some collection agencies do go out of business and some firms who retained such agencies never receive the amounts that have been collected from their own customers. Of course, if the agency collects your bill, the customer no longer owes you money. The mere fact that you never received any cash does not reestablish the debt to you from the customer. For example, if the agency has collected $1,000 from one of your customers, and then the collection agency itself goes out of business, you cannot recover another $1,000 from the customer. The customer has already paid and the debt has been satisfied by payment in full. Your recourse is against the now-insolvent collection agency.

ADVANTAGES OF REFERRING AN ACCOUNT TO A COLLECTION AGENCY

One of the real advantages of referring an overdue account to a collection agency is that the agency will work on the matter promptly to ensure collection. Very often, in-house collections are unable to deal with customers who just refuse to pay their bill. Trying to hound recalcitrant debtors can be a time-consuming process. Collection agencies are good at what they do because they specialize in collections full-time. They know techniques that work, and they can devote their full resources to the matter.

Typically, in the small business, the person doing the collection work will also have other responsibilities, and trying to collect the debt from one or two debtors will distract from other duties. More likely, the difficult collections will be ignored until the accounts are truly uncollectible. By referring a difficult account out to a third party for collection, you will liberate staff time to work on other accounts, and the referred account will get prompt, professional attention by the third-party collector.

Another advantage of referring collections to an agency is that if you use a contingent fee arrangement, you will not be out any cash if the agency fails to collect the bill. On the other hand, if the collection agency is able to collect the overdue amount and charges a fee, the referral was an efficient step.

WHICH ACCOUNTS SHOULD BE REFERRED FOR COLLECTION?

One of the most important things to determine is which accounts should be referred to a third party such as a collection agency or a collection attorney. Generally, if an account is more than 90 days overdue and in-house collection activity has been ineffective, the account should be considered for professional third-party collection. Any account that is more than six months old is certainly a candidate for referral.

However, a business should not be too hasty in referring accounts for collection. Some customers may have misplaced your bill or may only be temporarily short of funds. Referring such accounts to third parties is a good way to lose customers. Referral to third parties should be used when a customer has lied to you or if there is a history of serious problems with the account. This topic is discussed in more detail in Chapter 7, "How to Get Paid."

TRACING SKIPS

One of the best services that a collection agency can provide is called "skip tracing," which is finding missing debtors. It is very difficult for a small business to locate individuals or businesses who have moved and don't want to be found. A "skip" is a credit customer who has disappeared, leaving no forwarding address on purpose. Skip tracing involves a good deal of specialized work.

Very often, the trail can start with information provided in the credit report and the credit application that you constructed. This is one of the reasons it is important to elicit a lot of information in the credit application. (See Chapter 4, "Analyzing Business Credit Applications.") National collection agencies have the resources to locate skips in distant cities and businesses that have assumed new names. Accordingly, if an account requires skip tracing, the account should probably be referred to one of these national firms.

FEES

Third parties use a variety of fee arrangements. Generally, a letter-writing service will provide services for a fixed fee. Depending on the frequency of the dunning letters, however, the charges are relatively minor, because the letters that are sent are standardized and will go out on your own letterhead.

Collection Agency Fee Scale

The fees charged by collection agencies are generally on a contingent basis. In other words, the collection agency will typically charge a fee only when it has success in collecting the overdue debt. However, fees can be as high as 50 percent of the amount collected. It is very unusual for an agency to offer a flat hourly rate, although this may be possible in some cases.

Generally, a collection agency will have a flexible scale for its collection fees. In other words, the agency will charge a higher rate for the first $300 to $500 that they collect, a lower rate for up to $2,000, and a lower rate still on amounts over $2,000. In other words, the collection agency will charge you more to collect small bills or the first part of the collection because there are certain procedures that have to be accomplished whether the collection is a large amount or a small amount. This higher percentage covers the initiation costs for collecting the small fee. However, you can benefit when a larger amount is being collected, because collecting a large amount is often not very much harder than collecting a small amount.

Attorney Fees

When you use an attorney, the attorney may ask for an hourly fee, but you should also ask the attorney to use the more usual contingent fee. Attorneys typically use the same types of arrangement in collections work and have a sliding fee arrangement that varies with the amount of the debt they collect. Again, if the collection attorney fails to collect anything, no fee will be charged.

Additional Charges

Note carefully that while your fee is calculated on the basis of the amount collected, there may also be some additional charges that are set by either an attorney or a collection agency. Generally, neither a collection agency nor an attorney will assume any costs involved in filing a lawsuit. In fact, it is considered unethical for an attorney to pay or even front the court filing fee. The idea is that the attorney is not supposed to be financing the lawsuit. Although the attorney can agree to take a fee only out of any possible winning, the attorney is not the one who is supposed to be bringing the lawsuit and filing papers. Also, if there are additional fees for process serving and garnishment, those fees will be an addition to the amount of the contingent fee.

Occasionally, a collection agency will refer an account to a collection attorney for action. For example, assume that you have used a collection agency to collect a $2,000 overdue account. After a number of attempts, the collection agency has been unable to persuade the debtor to pay, so the agency refers the matter to an attorney with whom they have a working arrangement. The attorney files suit in local court against the debtor. In this case, the attorney's fees will typically be paid by the collection agency itself. You will not normally need to pay a double contingent fee to both the collection agency and the attorney. If you hire the attorney, you will be paying the attorney directly. When the collection agency hires the attorney, the amount of your recovery will be reduced by the agency's initial fee. The agency will use part of their fee to pay the attorney for the legal action.

Hourly Rates

In some cases, an attorney or even a collection agency may ask for an hourly rate. For a small company, the hourly arrangement could be a problem if no cash is produced by the third party's activities. When an attorney or a collection agency asks you to pay the more usual "contingent fee," the fee is contingent upon the third party's success, which enhances the agency's incentive to recover the debt.

A Caution about Fees

When using a third party to collect a debt, you should discuss the fee at the outset. If the third party suggests an hourly fee, you should inquire whether a contingent fee arrangement is possible. Although an hourly fee may work out wonderfully if the debtor rolls over and pays after receiving an attorney's letter, more often the hourly fee will equal the contingent fee. An hourly fee is payable whether or not the third party has any success. On the other hand, a contingent fee is due only when the third party is successful. If the collector is only partially successful, the fee will be decreased accordingly.

For example, assume that a firm is owed $20,000 by a debtor. After several unsuccessful collection attempts, the matter is handed over to a third party who accepts the collection on a contingent fee basis; the collector is to receive 33 percent of any retrieved money. Even the professional collector is able to recoup only $9,000, instead of the full $20,000. In this case the third party would get a fee of $3,000 ($9,000 × 33%). A fully successful collector would have realized $6,600 ($20,000 × 33%).

Once you have reached agreement on a fee arrangement, you should insist that this be documented in an engagement letter. This engagement letter—which is really a contract between you and the third party—should clearly state four things:

1.   What services will be provided
2.   Who specifically will be providing the services
3.   When the services will be rendered
4.   The details of the fee arrangement

Typically a reputable third party will suggest that you sign an engagement letter detailing these points; if not, you should suggest it. If the third party is unwilling to commit these details to writing, look elsewhere. Fee disputes often arise when there is no engagement letter. A simple precaution of getting it in writing can save a lot of headaches later.

COLLECTION AGENCY ABUSES

Collection agencies have a bad reputation because of their many abuses against debtors. Although most collection agencies behave ethically, a number of firms have adopted such outrageous tactics that the entire industry has always worked under a cloud of suspicion. Because of these abuses, businesses that refer accounts to collection agencies are sometimes criticized for having the audacity to refer the accounts in the first place. Debtors sometimes feel embarrassed that a collection agency is reminding them to pay their bills, yet without the collection agency's efforts, many of these same debtors feel little or no embarrassment that they have received goods or services for free.

Although some of your customers may resent the fact that you refer past due accounts to a collection agency, such referrals may work to your advantage. If your customers fear professional collectors, they may decide to pay your bill first, even if other bills go unpaid.

Types of Abuses

In the past, employees of collection agencies were known to call individuals both at home and at work and to use threatening and obscene language. For example, a collector might call a person at work and ask to talk to "that deadbeat Joe Smith." Similarly, collectors would call people in the middle of the night, often repeatedly. At one time it was not unusual for some collectors to argue, shout, and even scream at debtors. It was also not unusual for collectors to show up at people's homes or to follow them down the street, screaming about some overdue account.

In some cases, collectors were known to introduce themselves as attorneys, or even government agents. In other cases, collectors would falsely tell debtors that they could be thrown into jail for not paying their debts. In still other cases, collectors threatened to harm or to beat up debtors. Collectors often assembled "deadbeat lists" that they sent to family, friends, and business associates of the debtor.

Although people should pay their debts, these kinds of activities created such a backlash against collectors that the federal government finally stepped in and passed federal legislation in this area.

FAIR DEBT COLLECTION PRACTICES ACT

The federal Fair Debt Collection Practices Act (FDCPA) establishes basic guidelines for collectors. Because this is a federal law, it applies equally in all states. Anyone who does collection activities should be aware of how this law works. Whenever you collect a debt for another person, you must comply with this law, even if you are not a professional collector.

For example, if one of your customers owes money to another business and you agree to try to collect the bill for the other business as you collect your bill, you are working as a professional bill collector at that point and probably need to comply with the Fair Debt Collection Practices Act. You may have liability under the Act if you fail to live up to the statutory provisions.

Avoiding FDCPA Liability

It is important to understand the provisions of the Fair Debt Collection Practices Act to avoid potential liability. This federal law governs activities by debt collectors when they are dealing with consumers. Generally, it applies only to collection agencies rather than to businesses who are trying to collect debts from their own customers.

The FDCPA imposes certain restrictions on a collector's contact with a debtor:

1. Contact only during reasonable hours
2. No contact with the debtor at the place of work if the employer prohibits personal calls
3. No contact with the debtor once the debtor has asked the collector in writing to stop contact

Additionally, when a debtor has an attorney, and the collector learns it, the collector may talk only to the attorney and not to the debtor. In fact, even when the debtor has no attorney, if the debtor denies owing any money, the collection agency may not contact the debtor again for 30 days. After that, the agency may resume contact only after sending to the debtor some proof of the debt.

Additionally, if the collection agency is tracing the debtor's whereabouts or talking to a third party about the debtor, the agency may not mention that a debt is involved.

As you might expect, the use of abusive tactics as described is prohibited by the statute. Additionally, collection lawsuits may not be filed in a court in a distant state, hoping for procedural advantage. Any collection lawsuits must be filed either where an underlying contract was signed or where the debtor lives so the debtor can defend the suit.

Finally, debtors have the right to sue collection agencies for damages for violation of this statute. For example, if a debtor ended up losing a job because of the tactics of a collection agency, the debtor could sue for a substantial amount of money.

CHAPTER PERSPECTIVE

When an account falls seriously overdue, it is generally a good business practice to refer the account to a third party for collection. Once you understand how these third parties operate you will be able to use their services more effectively.

When an account is overdue, you can either refer the account to a debt collection agency or a collection attorney for collection. Generally attorneys handle larger and more complicated claims. At times collection agencies engage their own attorneys to help them collect an overdue account. The debt collection industry includes both local firms and national firms.

Referring an account for collection has some advantages. The account will get more professional attention from a specialist who may get better results. The referral will also liberate your staff's time, which they can use to help collect less troublesome accounts. Finally, the third party will give prompt attention to the collection. Professional collectors know that if they are to get paid they need to collect the debt as soon as possible.

Generally, accounts more than 90 days overdue that have been resistant to in-house collection efforts should be referred to an agency or a collections attorney. Certainly any accounts over 6 months overdue should be considered for referral. One of the more valuable services that larger collection agencies provide is tracing skips—finding debtors who have disappeared.

Although collection agencies and collection attorneys normally take contingent fees based on results, they may also suggest a flat hourly fee. It is in your favor to use a contingent fee arrangement. The fee arrangement, once agreed upon, should be documented in an engagement letter that also details what services the third party will provide.

For many years collection agencies engaged in outrageous tactics. To curb these abuses the federal government passed the Fair Debt Collection Practices Act, which provides stiff penalties for violators. Although the Act applies mainly to professional collection firms, sellers must also take care to avoid liability under this law.

Enforcing Debts in Court

INTRODUCTION AND MAIN POINTS

Chapter 14 explored when and how to arrange informal work-outs with debtors. This chapter will look at the opposite extreme—when you should take a debtor to court. In this chapter you will learn when it is in your interest to go to court and when it can backfire. There is guidance for selecting an attorney and how to use small claims court against nonpaying debtors.

After studying the material in this chapter you will know the following
- When to enforce a debt in court
- The importance of assessing the debtor's real reason for nonpayment
- When you should not go to court
- The main reasons for choosing the legal route
- How to go about selecting an appropriate attorney
- The importance of selecting the appropriate court
- How to collect your debts in small claims court
- What you need to show the judge when you get to court
- The effect of a bankruptcy filing

WHEN TO ENFORCE A DEBT IN COURT

It is important for a business owner or manager to know when to enforce a debt in court. Generally, going to court to enforce a debt is a bad idea. First, it is a rather inefficient way to collect your debts. Second, once you go to court, you will never deal with that customer or client again. Once sued in court, a customer will always be distressed with you and will probably never again deal with your firm. This might not happen when you use other approaches to collect your overdue bill.

For example, when you send a number of "dunning letters" to a customer who hasn't paid, or even if you hand the matter over to a collection agency, it may be possible to maintain a profitable relationship with the customer in the future. The result may depend on the reason the customer has failed to pay.

Bad Apples
Although some customers never intended to pay, there are usually reasons the customer has not paid your bill. Some of these reasons are beyond the customer's control, and the customer is not dishonest, but only unreliable. Such customers may prove profitable to you in the future, and you need to cultivate them and keep them as potential customers.

When Does Suing Make Sense?
Although there are reasons you should not sue a customer to enforce a debt, there are a number of instances when suing makes sense.

1. When you determine the customer never had any intention of paying the bill right from the start.
2. When it is clear you will no longer do any business with the customer.
3. When the unpaid bill is so large that it threatens the financial health of your company.
4. When the collection agency exhausts normal collection procedures.

These four situations point out that when it is senseless to deal with the customer anymore or when the overdue bill is so large that it could threaten the financial health of your company, you should go to the courthouse. Until that time, other collection strategies will probably be more productive in the long run. You should have a goal not only of collecting but of preserving the debtor as a potential customer. Remember, it is far easier to make a sale to a current customer than to advertise and try to find a new one or take a customer away from someone else.

What You Need to Show in Court
Generally, when you go to court, you will have to show the judge that a bona fide debt exists, that the debt has not been paid, that the amount is overdue, and that the legal time limit for collections (called the statute of limitations) has not expired. Additionally you will have to answer any defenses that the debtor may bring up; in other words, reasons they don't need to pay.

Even if you can show all of these, you still might not get paid. Even if the court finds in your favor and awards you a judgment, you still have to "execute" against the debtor's assets. The court will give you a piece of paper deciding that you are in the right and are owed the money. However, that is all a judgment entails. You still need to take legal action to find and seize the debtor's assets. In many cases the debtor will be not only uncooperative, but may actively try to hinder this process.

ASSESSING THE REASON FOR NONPAYMENT

Since your goal should be to go to court when it is highly unlikely that the debtor will pay without a court order, it is important to be able to assess the reason for nonpayment. You need to know if the debtor is being dishonest or is unable to pay for other reasons.

For example, some companies order goods or services with no intention of paying the bill, or with no intention of paying the full amount. This is common with service contracts or construction contracts, where some people will accept a bid and pay the first few installments but not the last installments. In effect, they try to get a discount for quality work.

In some cases, the debtor may feel that the service provider will probably not sue for a small amount. For example, assume that a carpenter has extended credit to a customer and has arranged to finance a home addition by providing for six payments over a period of one year. The homeowner makes the initial payments until the work is approximately 90 percent completed and 50 percent paid for, at which time the homeowner tenders an additional 20 percent with a check marked "Payment in full." The carpenter must decide whether to accept 70 percent payment or to fight for the full agreed amount.

FULL PAYMENT CHECKS

Legally, if the contractor cashes the check marked "Payment in full," and the amount is disputed, the homeowner may be off the hook for the balance of the bill. This is known in law as an "accord and satisfaction." When there is a dispute over a bill, cashing the check satisfies the debt in full.

Dealing with Customers' Cash Flow Shortages

A customer may not pay because of unexpected financial difficulties. For example, a customer may have ordered goods or services from you on credit, anticipating receipt of payments from a third party. If your customer fails to get paid, a cash flow shortage may prevent payment to you.

Very few business people will volunteer that they have a cash flow shortage for a particular reason. However, when dealing with a business, it is vital to know why payments are not being made. Is there a dispute about the amount or is the business merely having a cash flow shortage?

Whether the cash flow shortage is completely unexpected and due to the wrongful actions of the third party or whether it is due to the mismanagement of the customer really isn't relevant to collecting your debt. What is relevant is whether the cash flow shortage is going to be permanent or temporary.

For example, assume that a printing company has done a job for a local business and sold the printing on credit. Here it would make very little sense to repossess the printing work, because it can't be used by anyone else. If the company is unable to pay the printer right away, the printer should determine the reason. It may be an unexpected shortfall in revenues; it could be a lawsuit, or any number of other reasons.

If the explanation seems reasonable and the company expects to return to profitability and have enough cash in the future, the printer should strive to work out an arrangement with the customer that could be mutually beneficial.

Suggesting Installment Payments

A customer may be willing to pay even a bit more in interest if you agree to extend the payment schedule for an additional six months or even a year. You may have better luck collecting if you arrange the payments in a series of monthly installments rather than presenting a large bill. For example, if someone owes a $20,000 bill, it may be far better to send ten $2,000 bills than one overwhelming $20,000 bill. Many people would send no money at all if they didn't have the entire $20,000. To counteract this, you should give them the option of an initial partial payment with an incentive to pay more by offering a discount for making payment in full.

BUILDING CUSTOMER LOYALTY

Showing compassion and understanding of your customer's business problems may make a customer very loyal in the future. Many businesses will continue to be loyal to suppliers and professionals who have helped them in their early years. Merchants may be eager to return a favor in the future if you show them some consideration now.

On the other hand, you may determine that although the cash flow shortage is not the fault of your client's mismanagement, the cash flow shortage is probably going to be permanent rather than temporary. Then you probably should consider going directly to court for the money. Remember, you are running a business, not a charitable organization, and your employees and their families are relying on the continuation of the business. Although it is nice to be loyal to customers, you have loyalty to your business and your employees as well, and that makes for hard choices sometimes.

WHEN NOT TO GO TO COURT

You should never go to court when
1. the amount is trivial,
2. the costs of going to court exceed potential benefits,
3. you merely want to get even with the customer,
4. you want to embarrass the customer,
5. the customer is one of your better clients.

One thing business owners and managers often forget when determining when to sue is the amount of time and effort the lawsuit takes. Although the matter may seem straightforward to you, when there is nonpayment of a debt, there are often two sides to the story. Additionally, if the other side wants to contest the matter, there can be a number of added complications.

In court not only the facts count, but procedure as well. Not infrequently lawsuits involve procedural posturing that can be costly to the clients on both sides, although financially profitable to their attorneys. Normally, litigation is not the most efficient means of resolving disputes.

REASONS FOR LITIGATION

There are a number of reasons for choosing to file a lawsuit, however:
1. There is a lot at stake.
2. You want vindication of your side of the story.
3. The other side wants to avoid going to court because facts exposed could be embarrassing.
4. The other side needs to avoid publicity for one reason or another.
5. You want to send a message to other customers.
6. You are big and the costs involved don't scare you.

Unavoidable Litigation

There are two situations where litigation is probably unavoidable—first, when there is a bona fide debt that the debtor acknowledges, but merely refuses to pay. For example, suppose you provide services on credit to a business, and after sending several bills, the owner acknowledges the amount due, but merely says, "I don't feel like paying; go ahead and sue me if you want."

Generally, collection efforts are futile with a customer like this. You certainly don't want to deal with this person in the future, and if you want to collect the bill and the amount is worth it, probably the only course is to go to court. If you can get an admission of liability, it will be easier to proceed once you get to court. However, as we discussed earlier, although you get a judgment, in some cases it is still hard to find assets to claim.

The second situation in which you will probably have to go to court is when the factual situation is extremely complex and what went on and who owes the money will be unclear to anyone but a judge. This is especially true when you don't have full access to records held by the other company or client.

For example, suppose a company hires a computer programmer to work on a customized computer software program. The terms of the agreement provide for a cash payment up front of $2,000 and then the remainder to be paid in two installments—one when the documentation is delivered, and the second installment when the client agrees that the program is up and running as promised.

Assume that during the course of the engagement, the programmer has problems and makes some proposals to change the fee arrangement to which the client agrees orally. Additionally, the client asks for several changes to be made during the course of the work. Because of certain misunderstandings, the program doesn't work as expected, and there is disagreement whether the programmer has completed the assignment as agreed. As a result, the second two payments for the contract are never made.

This is an example of the kind of disagreement that probably belongs in court because of the complexity of the case and the amount of money involved.

Also assume that much of the documentation for the program is now in the hands of the company, which has refused to turn over copies to the programmer. Note that in a lawsuit, both sides will have equal access to the relevant evidence. This equality of evidence can sometimes speed settlement negotiations.

SELECTING AN APPROPRIATE ATTORNEY

If you do decide to go to court, it is important to select the right attorney. The attorney will help you to determine whether going to court is a cost-effective idea. Remember this should be a business decision rather than an emotional one. It doesn't make any sense to go to court to sue a customer unless you think that it will be worth it from a financial standpoint. Even if you aren't out any money in legal fees because the attorney has taken the matter on a contingency fee basis, you are still out some time and effort.

You wouldn't want to hire a divorce attorney to do your collection work, although you don't always need a special collections attorney either. If you have a fairly uncomplicated collection case, most attorneys who practice general business law will be competent to handle the matter.

If you have a more complex case or a matter that involves a large dollar amount, you would probably be wise to retain an attorney who is experienced in collection matters. Many such attorneys belong to an organization called the Commercial Law League of America, and they are normally experienced in credit and collection matters. If you have an important case, that would be a good place to look for an attorney. Collection attorneys' names can be obtained from the Commercial Law League, whose number is (312) 431-1305. Bankers and accountants are typically good sources of advice on which attorneys to consult for a particular matter. You may ask other people in businesses similar to yours for their advice in selecting an attorney.

You can also check the Yellow Pages in your locality; however, the attorneys that list collections as an area of expertise may be experienced or merely seeking work in collections. Some state bar associations and local bar associations also have attorney referral services, and they may be able to put you in touch with a local attorney to handle your problem.

Attorney Fees

You should be very frank with the attorney about fees. First, determine whether the attorney charges a fee for an initial consultation. If the attorney decides not to handle the case or that there is no case, you may not want to pay for that kind of advice. Many attorneys do not charge for the initial 15 minutes or half hour. Other attorneys will waive their initial fee if you so request and if you explain you just want 15 minutes of their time to ask whether they would like to take a case. If you want to save some money it never hurts to ask.

You should also ask about the fee arrangement in the lawsuit. Attorneys generally charge based on four different methods.

1. Flat fee
2. Hourly fee
3. Contingent fee
4. Retainer

When attorneys accept a matter on a flat-fee basis, they agree to handle the matter for a specified amount. This is like getting an estimate from a plumber, carpenter, or electrician about the price to do a particular job at your house. Normally, attorneys are reluctant to charge a flat fee except for routine work, such as drawing up a will or performing a no-fault divorce. It is difficult for the attorney to know how long the collection matter will take and the result could be that you will either be undercharged or overcharged for the amount of work that is actually done.

The second arrangement is the hourly fee for each hour of work. For example, if an attorney charges $100 per hour and works for 10 hours on the case, the bill would be $1,000 (10 hours × $100 = $1,000). Obviously the attorney has little incentive to keep the charges low except to the extent that the attorney thinks you may not pay if the bill becomes too high. However, an hourly rate can work to a consumer's advantage if a small amount of work provides a large recovery.

The third type of arrangement is known as a contingent fee. In this arrangement, the attorney gets a percentage of the recovery, although the client must pay any court filing fees. For example, assume an attorney has taken on a collections case that will probably proceed to court and agrees that if the matter is settled before going to court, the attorney will get 25 percent of the recovery; if the matter proceeds to court, the attorney will get 33 percent of any recovery; and if the matter is won on appeal, then the attorney will get 50 percent of any recovery. Although the client must pay the court costs and certain filing fees with the court, win or lose, if the attorney fails to win any money, the client will not have to pay any attorney's fee. On the other hand, if the attorney gets a very large judgment, then the attorney may get a windfall. Contingent fees have the advantage of being efficient, especially for small businesses who don't have enough money to retain an attorney on an hourly basis or on a retainer fee.

A fourth way of hiring an attorney is on a retainer basis. In this arrangement a client pays an attorney a monthly fee, and the client will receive either a fixed number of hours, or more typically an unlimited number of hours for a flat fee. For example, a business may pay a law firm $5,000 per month with the understanding that the attorney will handle any volume of business that the client brings in, whether it is no cases, one case, or 20 cases.

Retainer fees are appropriate only for people that have lots of legal business—for example, a larger retailer selling on credit who has a lot of collections matters. A retainer basis may be more cost effective for both of them. From the attorney's point of view, the retainer eliminates the need for a lot of bookkeeping and billing, which allows the attorney to charge a lower overall retainer fee to the client.

SELECTING AN APPROPRIATE COURT

Your attorney will help you select an appropriate court in which to bring your claims. Generally, most contracts are state law matters and are filed in state court rather than federal court. However, if the matter involves a federal claim, it may be brought to federal court, and certain claims over $50,000 may also be brought in federal court. If the matter involves a party who is in bankruptcy, the claim must be heard in the federal bankruptcy court. Refer to Chapter 19, "Dealing with Debtors in Bankruptcy."

Selecting the right court can be complicated. First, there are sometimes jurisdictional limitations normally based on the dollar amount of the claim. For example, in some states, claims under a certain dollar amount, say $5,000, must be brought in one court, while larger cases must be brought in a different court.

In other areas, claims under a certain amount will be referred to an arbitration panel. In other words, even if you bring a claim in court for a matter under the dollar threshold, it would be immediately referred to an arbitrator rather than a judge, because all small claims in that jurisdiction are required to go to arbitration rather than to have a full trial.

Also, if the claim involves a buyer and seller in two different states, the selection of the proper court may be more complicated. Your attorney will be the best judge of which state court to choose.

SMALL CLAIMS COURT

In some cases, you can go to court yourself by bringing a case to small claims court. Usually small claims courts are set up for citizens and small businesses to settle disputes before a judge without using lawyers or juries. The jurisdictional limitation varies state by state. Typically, the claims must be relatively uncomplicated and must be under a specified dollar amount, typically from $500 to $2,000.

As mentioned, small claims courts run without lawyers. In fact, in most states lawyers are not permitted in the small claims courtroom, because the goal is to arrive at solutions rather than to provide every available legal procedure.

In a typical case, a complaint must be filed, for example, alleging that a debtor owes a certain amount of money, and service of process must be made on the debtor. Typically, there is a filing fee and an additional fee to have the court papers served on the defendant.

What Happens at Trial

When the day of trial arrives, both sides, if they are both present, will give their versions of the dispute to the judge, who will then decide the matter either wholly for one side or the other or perhaps may reach a compromise decision. Generally, if only one party appears for the trial, a default judgment can result, which means that the party who came to court will automatically win.

In some states, a small claims decision can be appealed, but in other states, the decision will be final. You will have to call the clerk at the local small claims court to determine the following:

1. The jurisdictional dollar limit of the court
2. Whether your type of claim can be heard by the court
3. How to start the process
4. The filing fees required to go to court

Using a Paralegal

Many small debts are collected by businesses in small claims court. In some cases, a paralegal in an attorney's office can file in small claims court to assist you with a collection if you don't want to do it yourself. A paralegal is a nonlawyer who works in an attorney's office and performs many legal functions, such as filing court papers and performing research. This can also be a cost-effective route for people who don't want to take the time off to go to court.

Keep in mind that when you go to court, you are going to lose at least half a day away from your business and your clients, merely to try to collect a debt that may never be paid at all. As with the regular court system, although you may get a judgment in small claims court, you will still need to "execute" the judgment—you will need to get the judgment issued by the court turned into cash or property.

What You Need to Show the Judge

When you go to a small claims court, you need to be prepared. If you are collecting a debt, you need to show the following:

1. Written or oral evidence of the debt
2. Proof of the amount of the debt outstanding
3. Any evidence from the debtor admitting the existence of the debt

On the other hand, if you are the debtor in small claims court, you need to be prepared to show why the debt need not be paid. For example, you might need to show that work was never done or the goods were never delivered, or alternately the work was done in a slipshod way or the goods were not as promised and were subsequently returned.

Keep It Short and Simple

Generally, the more documentation and evidence you can bring, the better. Remember, you will have only a short period of time in which to tell the judge your story. If the judge can't understand the facts, the judge will not decide in your favor. Rehearse your presentation with another party and work to express the matter simply and understandably. The judge will be looking for justice, not legal technicalities. If justice is on your side, you should prevail in small claims court.

EFFECT OF A BANKRUPTCY FILING

If a debtor has already filed for bankruptcy, you must file a "proof of claim" in federal bankruptcy court if you want to collect anything at all. Once a bankruptcy has been filed, then all other court efforts to collect must come to a halt.

Even if you are involved in a lawsuit with a debtor or creditor, once the other side has filed for bankruptcy, your claim will be either suspended or transferred to the bankruptcy court. Generally, it will be to your advantage to have the claim determined by the bankruptcy court, because the bankruptcy court will be overseeing the distribution of the debtor's assets. If you are not involved, you may miss out on a distribution of any available assets.

Individuals involved in a bankruptcy get to retain certain "exempt" property. This is property that cannot be taken by creditors. However, creditors can reach the nonexempt property of the debtor. If you don't participate in a bankruptcy process and receive a portion of the nonexempt property, the debtor may have only exempt property after bankruptcy. In practical terms, if you don't participate, you may receive nothing at all. See Chapter 19, "Dealing with Debtors in Bankruptcy," for a more detailed discussion of this topic.

CHAPTER PERSPECTIVE

This chapter stressed the practical reasons for going to court. Managers and business owners need to know when to enforce a debt in court and when to avoid this. It is vital to assess the debtor's reason for nonpayment. If nonpayment is due to a temporary cash shortage, it may be better to avoid court to try to preserve the debtor as a customer. However, there are also a number of valid reasons for choosing the legal route.

Once the decision has been made to proceed to court, the next step is to select an appropriate attorney. The attorney will help select the right court in which to bring the claim. Business owners can bring smaller claims themselves in small claims court. The key to success in small claims court is good organization. If the debtor has filed for bankruptcy, you must bring your claim in the federal bankruptcy court.

Understanding Liens and Garnishments

INTRODUCTION AND MAIN POINTS

The previous chapter detailed how to enforce debts in court, including how to select an attorney to pursue your claim, how to select an appropriate court, and what you need to show the judge to win.

This chapter describes what you need to do to enforce your claims. The chapter describes the operation of liens—claims against property of the debtor—and garnishments—a legal process of attaching the debtor's property such as bank accounts and wages to satisfy your claim. Garnishments are typically used after you've won in court and need to reach the debtor's assets.

After studying the material in this chapter you will understand the following

- What a lien is
- Some common types of liens
- The operation of the rules governing lien priorities
- Certain government liens
- What happens in a garnishment
- The steps required to garnish a bank account
- How to carry out a wage garnishment
- The federal restrictions on wage garnishments

WHAT IS A LIEN?

A lien is a legal claim that comes into effect by operation of the law. A lien attaches to property and can create serious legal consequences. In many cases, a creditor who holds a lien can have property sold to satisfy the lien. For example, if you fail to pay your property taxes on real estate you own, the local taxing authority can place a lien on the property. If the taxes are not paid within a statutory period, the taxing authority can list the property for sale and have it sold. The proceeds from the sale will go first to paying the overdue taxes.

Governments are not the only parties to hold liens; in fact, private liens are probably more common. For example, a mortgage on a piece of real estate creates a lien. When a person borrows money from a lender for a mortgage, typically the purchased property is the lender's security for the debt. In other words, if the borrower fails to repay the loan as promised, the lender can use legal process to foreclose the property and have it sold to satisfy the debt. The mortgage creates a lien—or claim—on the property.

Consequences of Liens

A lien is merely a claim until it is enforced. In other words, it takes the positive action of the lien holder to make things happen. However, the mere presence of a lien can have serious consequences. For example, the presence of a lien attached to real estate will normally make the property unsalable until the lien is removed. This is because the lien attaches to the property itself, not to its owner. For example, if a lien attaches to real estate and the real estate is sold, the lien would survive the sale: the buyer would end up purchasing property with a lien attached to it. Buyers normally want to avoid this result. For this reason, a title insurance company will not insure the legal title of a parcel with an outstanding lien. In other words, the lien must be paid off before the property can be sold.

For example, assume Jones owns a piece of property. Smith is able to legally attach the property with a lien. At this point, Jones cannot sell the property because the title is clouded by the lien. If he wants to sell the property, he will have to have the lien removed, most often by paying it off.

Execution

If the owner did not pay off the lien, the creditor can force the matter by *executing* the lien and having the property sold. In some cases, the imposition of a lien can aid in recovering amounts due. Although filing a lien is complicated, it is generally less complicated than going to court and suing. Additionally, those who have liens imposed on their property often choose to pay them off rather than fight. For these reasons, the use of liens can be quite effective. Because filing procedures vary depending on the state in which you live, the requirements for filing specific liens will not be detailed in this chapter. You should consult a local attorney for help in enforcing a lien.

COMMON TYPES OF LIENS

There are a number of common types of liens.

1. Property tax liens
2. Income tax liens
3. Mechanic's liens
4. Artisan's liens
5. Judgment liens

Tax Liens

Property tax liens are imposed by taxing authorities, including the authority that assesses local property tax. Additionally, the state and federal governments often attach tax liens when income or business taxes go unpaid. These liens must normally be paid before the property can be sold. The government can also execute against the property to have it sold after a statutory period of time.

Mechanic's and Artisan's Liens

In most states, a party who has rendered services or material to improve real property and has not been paid can normally attach a mechanic's or artisan's lien on a property. Generally, a mechanic's lien can be imposed only on the property that is benefited by the materials or services. Although mechanic's lien statutes differ state by state, in many states the lien attaches when the materials and supplies are delivered, not when the lien is actually filed. The date of the lien has practical application because these liens are paid off in the order of attachment. (See pages 199–200.)

Assume a party hires a carpenter to remodel a small retail store. The price of the remodeling is to be $20,000, payable in four $5,000 installments. The storeowner makes the first and second payments as agreed, but after disagreements about the work arise, the owner refuses to make the final two payments until the disagreement is cleared up either in or out of court. At this point the law provides some help for the tradesperson. The carpenter can attach a lien on the store and on the land under it unless payment is made for labor and material. The storeowner may ultimately prove to be correct and may not have to pay, but the mechanic's lien does give the tradesperson a procedural advantage.

Artisan's Liens

Strictly speaking, an artisan's lien is one that is imposed on personal property. Personal property is property other than real estate or things attached to it. Raw land is real property, as are buildings. On the other hand, furniture, most equipment, and vehicles are considered personal property. Artisan's liens are imposed because of nonpayment for materials or services that benefit personal property.

For example, assume a business has two copying machines that need servicing. A service company sends a technician to the place of business and performs a major overhaul on both machines. After the owners receive the bill, they refuse to pay. In this case, the service repair business can assert an artisan's lien against the two copying machines themselves.

Like mechanic's liens, artisan's liens are designed to protect workers who render services and cannot easily recapture the value of their services. When a store sells a refrigerator on credit and is not paid, normally the refrigerator is collateral and can be repossessed if the bill is not paid. When a service provider renders services, neither the services nor the value of time can be recovered. Hence the law has provided these liens to help workers protect their rights in a credit transaction.

Judgment Liens

A judgment lien is one that comes into effect after a party has won a lawsuit. For example, assume that a seller sells goods to a buyer on credit, taking back a promissory note. After the buyer fails to pay, the seller proceeds to court with the unpaid note and wins a judgment for $20,000 against the buyer. If the buyer is unable to pay the $20,000, the seller may get a judgment lien, which can be attached to the buyer's property. However, the lien does not arise automatically; the winner must take affirmative steps for the lien to attach.

Generally you will need the services of a lawyer to properly record a judgment lien. The lien can be recorded in the real estate records of the county—or counties—in which the buyer owns the property. This will prevent sale of the property. As discussed before, when real estate is involved, title insurance companies will not insure property with liens attached, and banks will not grant mortgages to buyers of such property. In practical terms, imposing a lien places a cloud on the title that will prevent sale of the property. To remove the cloud the property owner needs to pay off the lien.

Forcing a Sale

The holder of a lien can enforce the lien and ultimately have the property sold. The proceeds of the sale would go first to pay the expenses of the sale and then to satisfy the outstanding debt. If the sale yields more than the amount of the debt, this surplus would be returned to the property owner. If there is a deficit—if the sale proceeds fell below the amount of the lien—the debtor normally would still be liable for the unpaid balance of the debt. Mere execution and sale of the property will not by itself extinguish a legal debt.

LIEN PRIORITIES

Sometimes there is more than one lien attached to property. This frequently happens when a debtor is in financial distress. In such a case, for example, a manufacturing business may have a first and a second mortgage on its plant. If it has not paid its real estate taxes, the local tax district may have imposed a property tax lien on the plant. Additionally the state revenue department and the IRS may have also filed liens if the company has been delinquent in sending payments for income and payroll taxes. Finally tradespeople and creditors may also have filed liens against the company. If there are ten or twenty liens against a property, how does this all get sorted out? Who will get paid, and how much will they receive?

This is the area covered by lien priorities. It can be messy, but it becomes more complicated if you need to find out if the debtor will be paying your bill. It is important to understand—at least generally—how lien priority rules operate.

Reconciling Competing Claims

Because there can be dozens of conflicting claims, the law provides a set of rules to impose some order in this process. Some liens have priority over other liens. Generally, the rule about priorities is "first in time, first in right." In other words, generally, the first lien to be filed takes priority over the others.

For example, assume that a business has bought various items and services on credit. After failing to pay a number of suppliers, the suppliers individually go to court, win judgments, and get judgment liens that are attached to the buyer's property. If the property is sold, the proceeds of the sale will go to fully satisfy each lien in the order that it was recorded. The creditors do not each take a percentage of the proceeds.

Assume in the example that there are four creditors who are each owed $25,000. Also assume that none of the creditors has any collateral to attach. Each is granted a judgment lien for $25,000. One lien was recorded in May, the next in June, one in July, and the last in August. Let's assume that the debtor has only $80,000 of property. You might assume that the four creditors would share the property and each would get $20,000 ($80,000/4 = $20,000), but this is not how the priority rules operate. The creditors do not share the property equally. Here, the first three creditors would get paid in full but the last creditor would get only $5,000. Out of the $80,000, the first three creditors took $75,000 ($25,000 each), leaving only $5,000 for the unlucky fourth and last creditor. The lesson to be learned from this is that the law protects the rights of those who act promptly! When liens are concerned, if you sit idly by, you may get left out when the debtor's bills are finally paid off.

Special Priorities

Note that certain types of liens get higher priority: in some states, mechanic's and artisan's liens relate back to the start of work, rather than the time the liens were actually filed. This allows the mechanic's liens to go to the front of the line for payment.

For example, assume that a plumber has installed plumbing at a business. The plumber did the work in February. After four months, when still unpaid, the plumber asserted a mechanic's lien against the property. The lien was filed on June 1st. The effective date of the lien is February 1st, rather than June 1st, in many states. In these states, the effective date of the lien is not when the paperwork is filed, but when the actual work commenced.

This special priority rule can be a great advantage to the tradesperson if other liens have been filed after the start of work. For example, assuming the same anecdotal facts, in a state that does not recognize that mechanic's liens date back to the beginning of work, liens filed by other creditors between February 1st and June 1st would have priority over the plumber's lien. In that case, the plumber's potential recovery might be greatly reduced.

Effect of a Bankruptcy Filing

The lien priority rules operate even after a debtor has filed for bankruptcy. In other words, even in bankruptcy the lien with most seniority will be entitled to recovery first. Note that liens also compete with UCC security interests. A security interest is an interest in personal property when personal property is put up as collateral. For example, when a car is purchased on credit the car is typically collateral for the loan. The party financing the car loan has a "security interest" in the car until the loan is paid off. UCC security interests are more fully described in Chapter 5, "Using Collateral."

For example, assume that a mechanic has serviced a large machine and has not been paid. The mechanic files an artisan's lien against the equipment. However, if the property was previously financed by a lender who created a UCC security interest in the equipment, the lender will probably have priority to any sales proceeds under the "first in time, first in right" rule. The lender probably took the machine as collateral when financing the sale. If the property is ultimately sold, the artisan's lien will be second in line to the lender's, if the lender's security interest was filed at the time of the financing.

GOVERNMENT LIENS

The most important type of government lien is a tax lien. Tax liens are imposed by various levels of government. Property tax liens are imposed by local taxing authorities, including cities, towns, and counties. Tax liens are also imposed by the state and federal government when income or business or payroll taxes go unpaid. Government liens are also imposed in connection with worker's compensation claims. Government liens generally enjoy no special priority and must compete against private liens when the two conflict. The general priority rule discussed before—first in time, first in right—applies to government as well as private liens.

COMPETING INTERESTS

Liens and security interests compete against one another when they coexist. For example, a retailer has a security interest in a wall oven sold to a customer who has not paid. Suppose the customer also hired a contractor to remodel his kitchen. The contractor installed the oven in a custom cabinet that was in turn installed in the customer's residence. Now let's assume that the customer has defaulted on both agreements and neither the retailer nor the contractor has been paid. Let's also assume that the contractor has filed a mechanic's or artisan's lien that covers all the work done in the kitchen, including installation of the oven.

The resolution of this problem will hinge on the priority of the security interest versus the lien. Generally, if the security interest has priority, the retailer can repossess the oven despite the lien. On the other hand, if the lien takes priority, the contractor can repossess the oven.

Necessity of Filing

Although a valid written security agreement creates a security interest in property of the buyer, a security agreement establishes the interest in the property only between the two parties and not to a third party. In order to establish priority to collateral, a seller on credit must take a step in addition to obtaining a security agreement from the buyer. The seller must also "perfect" a security interest in order to protect the collateral against the claims of other parties.

A security interest is normally "perfected" by filing a document with the state called a *financing statement*. This is sometimes called "UCC Form 2," and the security agreement is sometimes referred as "UCC Form 1." Once the UCC Form 2 is filed with the government—usually at the state capital—the seller will have priority to the collateral over competing claims by other creditors or the government.

However, when consumer goods are sold there is "automatic perfection" without the need to file a financing statement. Consumer goods are goods valued at under $2,500 that will be used for personal, family, or household use. When consumer goods are sold, a security interest will be considered to be perfected at the date of sale. Accordingly, the security interest's relative priority will be determined by the sale date.

WHAT IS GARNISHMENT?

A garnishment is a legal process in which a creditor attaches either wages or a bank account from a debtor once a debt has been established. To protect the public, there are a number of legal restrictions involving wage garnishment.

GARNISHING WAGES

When wages are garnished, a creditor gets a court order that orders an employer to pay a portion of an employee's wages directly to the creditor.

For example, assume that Carter, an individual, hires Ames to do some consulting for the Carter business. After Ames has supplied $20,000 of services on credit, Carter defaults. In fact, Carter leaves the business and takes a salaried position with a large corporation. Ames goes to court and gets a judgment against Carter. Carter, however, seems to have no assets against which a lien can be imposed. Instead, Ames, the creditor, seeks a court order for a garnishment against Carter's salary. Carter's employer will be legally compelled to pay a portion of the debtor's wages directly to Ames until the debt is repaid.

Obviously wage garnishments are effective only when a debtor is an employed individual. When a business debtor is involved, a wage garnishment will be ineffective. This is also true with a sole proprietorship. Here the owner-operator will be taking profits out of the business but may not have a salary or wages that can be garnished. Another disadvantage of wage garnishments is that they are limited in amount by law.

FEDERAL RESTRICTIONS ON WAGE GARNISHMENTS

Because of the obvious hardship imposed on debtors, the federal Consumer Credit Protection Act has established certain limits on how garnishments operate and also limits the amount of wages that may be garnished. Because this is a federal law, the law applies in all 50 states and the District of Columbia. Generally, the amount of wage garnishment may not exceed the lower of either of the following:

1. 25 percent of take-home pay
2. The amount by which the employee's weekly pay exceeds 30 times the highest current minimum hourly wage

An employer may not fire an employee whose wages are garnished. The Act also prohibits employers from discriminating against employees who have had their wages garnished. In fact, there may be a $1,000 penalty if an employer violates this rule.

GARNISHING BANK ACCOUNTS

A creditor with a judgment needs to execute against the debtor's assets. This is not always simple if the debtor wants to protect the assets. Additionally, much of the debtor's property may already be encumbered by liens. For example, assume that Johnson wins a judgment against Carter for $3,000. After winning in court, Johnson still needs to reach Carter's property to satisfy the judgment. Carter has a house, but it is already encumbered by a home mortgage. Carter also owns a car, but it is encumbered by a car loan. Although these assets could theoretically be sold to satisfy Johnson's lien, the legal costs involved may argue against this course. Additionally, because the assets are already encumbered by debts, the senior creditors will receive any proceeds from a sale of the assets ahead of Johnson.

Another alternative is to garnish Carter's bank account. If Carter has a bank account of any kind, Johnson can use legal process to attach the account. After reviewing the underlying judgment, a court will issue a writ of garnishment ordering the bank to remove funds from Carter's account to pay the judgment debt.

Although this may sound easy, it may be hard to locate the account. For this reason, creditors should always keep a copy of a buyer's first check. The check will have the buyer's name and address on it and will also have the name and address of the buyer's bank and the all-important account number. Armed with this information, the garnishment will go much smoother for the creditor. The creditor should instruct the accounts receivable staff person always to note when a customer uses a new account, so the check on the new account can be photocopied and kept in a special file if needed.

Even if you do not have a check, it is still possible to locate a bank account. Possibly the easiest way is to actually trail the debtor to a bank. You may then call the bank and verify that the debtor does have an account there. At that point you can start the garnishment proceedings.

Occasionally a sophisticated debtor will make garnishment impossible. A skilled debtor who loses a lawsuit will quickly change banks, emptying out old accounts, and will use cash machines in supermarkets to make deposits and withdrawals to keep the bank identity secret. Some debtors are even able to avoid banks completely by running businesses on a strictly cash basis, demanding cash payments or cashier's checks from customers and paying bills (if paying them at all) using cash. It may be impossible to use garnishment against this type of a debtor.

CHAPTER PERSPECTIVE

A lien is a legal claim that comes into effect by operation of the law. A lien attaches to property and can create serious legal consequences. In many cases, a creditor who holds a lien can have property sold to satisfy the lien. Common types of liens include:

property tax liens, income tax liens, mechanic's liens, artisan's liens, and judgment liens. Property tax liens are claims against a debtor's property imposed by a local taxing district for the nonpayment of property taxes. Income tax liens can be imposed by either a state department of revenue or the IRS for the nonpayment of income taxes by either an individual or a business. Tax liens may also be imposed if a company fails to make required payroll tax deposits on behalf of its employees.

Because there may be more than one lien attached to property, the law has a system of lien priority rules. Generally, creditors who have collateral get to claim the collateral before any other liens are satisfied. After that, the general priority rule is: first in time, first in right. The creditor with the first lien filed typically has priority to any property. Junior liens—those filed after the senior lien—follow in order. The mere repossession of property does not ordinarily extinguish a debt if the property is worth less than the debt.

Garnishment is a legal process in which a creditor seizes either wages or a bank account from a debtor. Because of the obvious hardship imposed on debtors, the Federal Consumer Credit Protection Act has established certain limits on how garnishments operate and also limits the amount of wages that may be garnished. Generally, the amount of wage garnishment cannot exceed the lower of 25 percent of take-home pay, or the amount by which the employee's weekly pay exceeds 30 times the highest current minimum hourly wage.

Repossessing Collateral

INTRODUCTION AND MAIN POINTS

The previous chapter detailed the operation of liens and garnishments. These are claims against property authorized by law. This chapter will detail the repossession of collateral by a seller or lender. The process is similar to enforcement of a lien because the seller reaches property that can be sold to satisfy an unpaid debt. Yet repossessing collateral also differs conceptually from a lien because the debtor has agreed beforehand that the collateral could be retrieved and forfeited in the event of nonpayment.

Although the concept of repossession is simple, the procedures are anything but simple. Any seller taking back collateral needs to be aware of the rules.

After studying the material in this chapter you will know the following

- What collateral is
- When collateral may be repossessed
- How collateral is repossessed
- What the disabling option is
- Your legal options after a foreclosure
- When the Federal Trade Commission Consumer Goods Rule applies
- How to give notice of sale to the debtor and creditors
- The requirements for the conduct of the collateral's sale

WHAT IS COLLATERAL?

Collateral is specific property that a creditor may attach if a debtor does not pay a debt. (See Chapter 5, "Using Collateral," for a more detailed explanation of the different categories of collateral.) Generally, although many kinds of property may be used as collateral, including real and personal property, there is another way of classifying collateral. Generally, collateral fits into two categories.

1. Collateral under the control of the creditor
2. Collateral possessed by the debtor

In most cases, collateral is held by the debtor. For example, when a finance company finances an automobile, the car owner has possession and use of the collateral. In other cases, the creditor actually has possession of the collateral. For example, a creditor may demand that the debtor leave stock certificates with the creditor as collateral.

When a party leaves property with a pawnbroker they are creating a "pledge." The pawnbroker makes a loan to the debtor, and can claim the property as collateral. When the debtor pays off the loan (and interest) the pawnbroker returns possession of the collateral to the debtor. If the debtor fails to return to pay off the loan, the pawnbroker will have the right to resell the collateral to satisfy the unpaid debt. Pawnbrokers' operations are normally regulated by law in the state in which they operate.

As you may guess, a creditor who has physical possession of the collateral is in better shape. If the debtor defaults, the creditor has the collateral and can have it sold to satisfy the debt. The creditor will not have to go through the trouble of locating the collateral and physically repossessing it. This advantage should not be overlooked. If the debtor tries to hide the collateral this can create problems for the creditor. Also, the creditor will normally take good care of the collateral that will be claimed in the event of the debtor's default.

When the debtor is in possession of the collateral, there can be practical difficulties in reaching the collateral. In most cases the debtor will continue to have physical possession of the collateral. For example, a party who purchases an auto or truck will normally possess and use the vehicle that is collateral for the loan. If the debtor defaults on the loan, the creditor must find a way to gain possession of the collateral. Normally the creditor must either convince the debtor to relinquish the property or the creditor must take active steps to retrieve it.

WHEN MAY COLLATERAL BE REPOSSESSED?

As a rule, collateral may be repossessed after a default. Generally, defaults are not defined in state law, but rather in the contract between the debtor and the creditor. There is no strict rule that defines what period of nonpayment establishes default. If a contract for sale of goods provides that the goods themselves are to be collateral, the contract will typically specify what constitutes default.

For example, the contract may specify that once the installment payments are 30 days past due, the seller has the right to declare a default and repossess the collateral. Many preprinted installment sale contracts utilizing collateral have a default clause similar to this. Since the seller has the right to declare the default, the default does not happen automatically. The seller has the option to declare a default or to wait and see what happens. The debtor might pay later, or the debtor might suggest that the parties work out a different payment arrangement.

Once the seller has declared a default and notified the buyer, the seller generally has the right to repossess the collateral.

After the Default

When personal property (not real estate) is involved, the law permits so-called "self-help remedies," in other words, a private repossession. When real estate is repossessed, which is called "foreclosure," the foreclosure is typically done by a sheriff rather than by the creditor. In the case of personal property, however, such as automobiles and other goods, the repossession will be done by private parties rather than by a government official. This is one of the substantial differences between real estate and personal property foreclosures.

Self-Help Remedies

Private repossessions are a rather unusual provision in the law. At one time the law had many self-help remedies, but these have fallen by the historical wayside. Today, most legal remedies involve getting the court system or the police or sheriff to help enforce your rights. Repossession is one area where the law has moved in the opposite direction. Repossessions of personal property (anything other than real estate) are carried out by private individuals.

Actually repossessions are normally carried out by businesses hired by lenders and retailers that specialize in carrying out seizure of collateral. Although repossessions are supposed to be accomplished with no breach of the peace, a repossession of someone's property can incite trouble.

When you hire a separate business to carry out your repossessions, you generally won't be liable if their actions lead to a lawsuit. However, a few courts have imposed liability on lenders when they have employed a third party to carry out their repossession work. You should carefully investigate the reputation of any firm that you engage to perform your repossessions.

HOW COLLATERAL IS REPOSSESSED

Collateral can be repossessed in two ways.

1. The creditor can convince the debtor to return the collateral
2. The creditor can take the collateral when the debtor isn't paying attention

For example, once the seller declares a default, the seller could ask the debtor to return the collateral if it is in the debtor's possession. Notice that if the collateral is retained by the creditor, there is no need to take further action. The property only has to be sold to satisfy the unpaid debt.

If the debtor agrees to return the collateral and does so, the process is greatly simplified. However, if the debtor does not cooperate and resists returning the collateral, the creditor has to take further action.

Repossessions

Generally, a creditor can repossess collateral as long as there is no "breach of the peace"—that is, no physical altercation.

For example, if a business has bought an auto on credit, and a default is declared, the finance company may break into the auto if it is parked on the street, "hot wire" the ignition, and start the car. Although they may need to pry a door open or break a window, this could all be done legally. In most cases, the creditor will merely have the car towed away.

Similarly, the creditor may have the car towed from a public parking lot without notifying the debtor. For example, assume that a finance company has notified a debtor of default on a car loan. One evening a short time later, the debtor drives to a movie theater and parks the auto in a public lot. The debtor returns to the lot after the movie only to find the car missing and reports the "theft" to the police. In fact, the car has been repossessed; the creditor had the car towed away without giving any notice. This was all within the law. In fact, most cars are repossessed during the day while debtors are at work.

Breach of the Peace

It is against the law for a repossession to involve a commission of a crime. For example, a repossession may not be accomplished during a physical trespass at an individual's home or an individual's business. If a company has fallen behind with payments on a copy machine, sales representatives may not barge into the business and seize the machine if the business owner asks them to leave or not to enter the place of business.

Although creditors have a right to retrieve the property, they may not commit a breach of the peace. For example, if the debtor defends the property or refuses to surrender it, the repossession may not involve physical violence.

THE DISABLING OPTION

Another alternative to foreclosure is the disabling option. Disabling is an alternative to physical repossession of the property. This works with items that cannot easily be resold or are too large to move easily.

For example, if a sign company sells a sign to a motel on credit, there is very little reason to repossess the sign, because it could not be sold to another motel. However, the sign company would have the right to take a light bulb out of the sign or to turn the sign so it faces away from the street to render it useless.

Similarly, heavy equipment dealers have been known to disable large machinery by removing a critical part, such as a steering wheel or brake lever; this renders the equipment unusable and often a nuisance where it is parked. One computer software vendor called up a nonpaying customer's computer and instructed its software to turn itself off. Disabling the computer program effectively shut down the client's business. In some cases, disabling collateral can be as effective as actual repossession.

OPTIONS AFTER REPOSSESSION

Generally a creditor who has repossessed goods has three options:
1. Conduct a public sale
2. Conduct a private sale
3. Retain the collateral

When the creditor holds a sale the goal will be to produce enough funds to satisfy the outstanding debt. If the proceeds of the sale exceed the amount of the debt, the surplus goes back to the debtor. If on the other hand, the sale does not produce enough money to pay off the debt, the debtor will continue to owe the balance to the creditor. The creditor will need to get a deficiency judgment and proceed against assets other than the collateral. A deficiency judgment is a court order stating that the debtor still owes money on a debt despite a repossession of collateral.

For example, assume that a creditor is owed $14,000 and has a security interest in collateral that is equipment used in the debtor's business. The creditor repossesses the collateral and it is sold at a public sale. The sale proceeds, after expenses of the sale, are $9,000. This $9,000 will go to pay the debtor's debt to the creditor. However, the debtor continues to owe the creditor the $5,000 outstanding balance ($14,000 minus $9,000). The creditor will need to go to court to get a deficiency judgment against the debtor. With the judgment in hand the creditor can then go after the debtor's other property (see Chapter 17, "Understanding Liens and Garnishments").

Strict Foreclosure

Occasionally a creditor will take the third option—seizing the collateral but not selling it (strict forclosure). This might happen when the creditor doesn't expect the collateral to bring a good price at the sale and wishes to avoid the trouble of conducting a sale.

However, there is a steep price to the creditor in selecting this option. When a creditor repossesses collateral and does not resell it, the creditor is not entitled to a deficiency judgment. In other words, if the creditor retains the collateral, the collateral acts as full satisfaction of the debt.

For example, assume again that a creditor is owed $14,000 and has a security interest in collateral that is equipment used in the debtor's business. The creditor repossesses the collateral but decides to retain it rather than resell it. In this case, the debt will be satisfied in full by the collateral. If the collateral would yield only $9,000, the debtor would get a windfall of sorts. The debtor owed $14,000, but the creditor got property that might bring in $9,000 and no right to sue the debtor for the balance. It appears that the creditor is worse off by $5,000 and the debtor better off by the same amount.

However, note that the creditor also gets to keep the collateral. Let's change the numbers in the example and see how the results could vary. Now let's assume again that a creditor is owed $14,000 and has a security interest in collateral that is equipment used in the debtor's business. The creditor repossesses the collateral but decides to retain the collateral rather than resell it.

In this example, let's assume that the collateral is worth $100,000 and that the debtor has already paid $86,000 of the purchase price, but has run into temporary difficulty making payments. Here the creditor ends up with a $100,000 piece of equipment to collect a debt of only $14,000. In this example there was a real windfall for the creditor on the repossession.

Because of the potential for injustice, strict foreclosure is not always available. The repossessing creditor must send the debtor notice explaining the creditor's intent to keep the property. Likewise, if other secured creditors have informed the creditor in writing of their potential interest in the collateral, the repossessing creditor must also provide them with notice of the strict foreclosure. If either the debtor or the secured creditors object, the collateral must be sold. However, if none of them objects, the repossessing creditor may retain the collateral in full satisfaction of the debt, be it large or small.

The use of strict foreclosure is further limited when consumer goods are involved. This limitation is discussed in the next section.

CONSUMER GOODS RULE

The procedure just discussed—strict foreclosure—where the creditor repossesses property but does not resell it, may not always be used. The law provides that strict foreclosure is not available if the collateral is a consumer good (for personal, family, or household use) and either of the following is the case:

1. the debtor has paid at least 60 percent of the debt; *or,*
2. the debtor refuses to sign a statement giving up the right to bar the strict foreclosure, thus forcing a sale.

For example, assume that a consumer has defaulted on an installment contract after paying 75 percent of the debt. The seller repossesses the item and sends the consumer notice of its intent to pursue a strict foreclosure rather than a sale. The seller must also send the debtor a statement in which the debtor renounces the right to bar the strict foreclosure. If the consumer does sign the statement giving up the right to bar the strict foreclosure, the creditor may pursue the strict foreclosure and retain the collateral in full satisfaction of the debt. On the other hand, if the consumer refuses to sign the statement, the creditor will have to conduct either a private or public sale of the item. The debtor will get notice of the sale and participate as one of the bidders.

If the creditor fails to sell the goods within 90 days, the creditor may be liable to the debtor for the full value of the goods. Because of this rule, sales need to be scheduled promptly after repossessions.

NOTICE OF SALE TO THE DEBTOR

Before collateral can be sold, specific notice must be given to the debtor. Generally, the debtor must be given the right to buy the collateral back at the sale. In other words, the repossession also puts the debtor to the test: the debtor may have to refinance the obligation in order to buy back the collateral if desired.

For example, assume that a business has bought a computer system on credit and now has defaulted on an installment plan with the seller. The seller has repossessed the collateral and plans to sell it. The debtor can recover the collateral by paying the outstanding debt at any time prior to the sale. In practical terms, the debtor may have to refinance the purchase price with another lender in order to pay off the first lender at the sale.

NOTICE OF SALE TO CREDITORS

In addition to providing notice to the debtor, the party that repossesses and sells collateral must provide notice of the sale to other creditors. This allows the other creditors to protect their interest at the sale and also allows them to bid on the collateral.

For example, assume that a manufacturer has a large machine that it uses in its metal fabrication business. A number of years ago, the business obtained a bank loan and pledged the machine as collateral. More recently, the business obtained a second and much larger loan from a different bank and again put up the same equipment as collateral. The second bank accepted the collateral with knowledge of the first loan, because the fair market value of the equipment far exceeded the balance of the two loans.

If the manufacturer defaults on the larger loan and the second bank repossesses and sells the equipment at a sale, the second bank must give notice to the first bank, the other creditor, about the sale. The other bank will also get proceeds from the sale and must be present to be able to protect its interest.

CONDUCT OF THE SALE

When collateral is repossessed, it may be sold at either a public or a private sale. A public sale is open to the public, whereas a private sale is one with invited bidders. A private sale would be appropriate when there is specialized equipment and when only a few potential bidders would be involved. For example, if a specific kind of ship were repossessed, there would most likely be only a limited number of parties who might be interested in buying at the sale.

Commercially Reasonable Manner

If either a public or a private sale is held, the sale must be conducted in a commercially reasonable manner. This means that

1. The sale must be advertised sufficiently.
2. The sale must be conducted during normal working hours.
3. There must be no surprise conditions.
4. The terms of the sale must be in accord with normal commercial practice.

In other words, the sale must not be rigged to favor certain buyers. If a sale of a consumer good such as a car is not advertised to the public or to other potential bidders, a friend of the creditor could easily come to the sale, bid a low amount, and receive a bargain purchase. The goal of the sale is to produce as much money as possible to pay off the debt. If the sale is not opened to enough bidders, this would defeat the purpose of the sale.

For example, assume a retailer has repossessed several rooms of furniture that it had sold on credit. The average grouping would be worth about $1,000 to $2,000 if brand new. When the store had about $10,000 of repossessed furniture in inventory, it advertised the sale in the used furniture section of the classified ads in the local paper. The ad cost $100. The store also posted a notice of the sale in its lunchroom.

The sale was held at the store's showroom at 8 A.M. on Saturday morning, two hours before the store normally opened. Four outsiders were present and two employees. The sale was conducted as an auction, but the auctioneer announced that there was no "floor" on the bids, and all bids would be accepted. Additionally, only cash or cashier's checks would be accepted. If the highest bidder did not have cash or a cashier's check, the next lower bid would be accepted. The outsiders at the sale had not brought enough cash or cashier's checks because this requirement had not been noted in the classified ad announcing the sale. All the furniture was sold to employees of the store for nominal prices. A typical room set sold for about $100. The retailer did not get much at the sale, so it still had the right to get a deficiency judgment against the nonpaying customers.

This sale was not commercially reasonable because of the surprise cash requirement. Other tricks include holding the sale at unusual hours or in unusual places. In the past, some sellers advertised the sale only within their own premises, which limited bidders to employees and other official creditors. If a sale is held to be less than commercially reasonable, the debtor can have the results set aside.

Application of Proceeds

The proceeds of the sale will go to satisfy the outstanding debt. If the sale produces a surplus, the surplus will be returned to the debtor. On the other hand, if there is a deficiency, the remaining amount of the debt is still outstanding between the debtor and the creditor.

For example, assume that a company has bought a printing press and defaulted on the purchase price to the seller who financed the transaction. Assume that the amount owed is $80,000. If the sale produces a net of $90,000 beyond the expenses of the sale, the $80,000 will be applied to satisfy the debt, and the remaining $10,000 would be returned to the debtor, who would have a windfall. On the other hand, if the sale produces only $70,000 net, the $70,000 would be applied against the debt, and the debtor would continue to owe the remaining amount (here $10,000) to the creditor, who has not been fully paid.

Note that when there is more than one creditor, the creditors will share the proceeds, not proportionately, but in order of priority. Generally the "senior" creditor will get to tap the proceeds of the sale first. The senior creditor is normally the first creditor within a class to establish its legal interest. The priority of creditors is discussed more fully in Chapter 5, "Using Collateral."

CHAPTER PERSPECTIVE

The rules surrounding the repossession of collateral are complex, and managers and business owners who take collateral need to understand these rules so that they can take action and also protect their rights. Generally, anything of value can be used as collateral. When real estate is used as collateral, the interest is called a mortgage. When personal property (things other than real estate) is used, the interest is called a security interest.

Collateral may be repossessed after a default. The law does not stipulate a specific number of days after nonpayment for a default. Rather, this time period will be established in the contract between the debtor and the creditor. Once a default has been declared, the creditor has the legal right to repossess the collateral.

Collateral can be repossessed by convincing the debtor to relinquish the property voluntarily. Alternately, the creditor must locate the property and seize it without committing a breach of the peace. Another alternative is to disable the collateral.

The creditor has a few different options after foreclosure. Instead of reselling the collateral at a public or private sale, the creditor may choose to retain it. However, if the collateral is consumer goods, retention of the collateral is not an option if the consumer has paid at least 60 percent of the debt or objects to the creditor's actions.

When repossessed collateral is to be sold, the repossessing creditor must provide notice of the sale to both the defaulting debtor and to other creditors. Both the debtor and other creditors may then come to the sale to protect their interests. They might do this by bidding on the collateral. In practical terms, they may be able to obtain the collateral at a bargain price.

When collateral is sold at a private or public sale, the sale must be conducted in a "commercially reasonable manner." This normally requires that the sale be advertised sufficiently, and that the sale be conducted during normal working hours. Also, there must be no surprise conditions and the terms of the sale must be in accord with normal commercial practice.

Dealing with Debtors in Bankruptcy

INTRODUCTION AND MAIN POINTS

Although bankruptcy was once viewed solely as a creditor's remedy, a bankruptcy filing can often work to a debtor's advantage, and not all creditors will be treated well in a bankruptcy. While some creditors will find their positions improved by the customer's bankruptcy, other creditors will find that they recover little or nothing at all. However, businesses can often protect themselves—either before or after a bankruptcy filing—if they know how the bankruptcy rules operate. Accordingly, managers and business owners both need a good working knowledge of the bankruptcy system.

After studying the material in this chapter, you will know the following

- The basics of the bankruptcy system
- Which kinds of debts may be discharged in a bankruptcy proceeding
- The effect of bankruptcy filing on different types of creditors
- The requirements for voluntary and involuntary bankruptcy filings
- How a bankruptcy is commenced
- Why it is vital for a creditor to file a proof of claim promptly
- The effect of a bankruptcy filing on collection and repossession activities
- A seller's limited right to reclaim delivered goods after the bankruptcy filing
- The right of the bankruptcy trustee to reclaim past payments
- The effect of a bankruptcy filing on cosigners

BANKRUPTCY BASICS

A working knowledge of bankruptcy law will enable you to make the right managerial decisions when confronted with a customer's bankruptcy. More importantly, understanding how the bankruptcy system works may cause you to rethink your credit policy with a view toward limiting your losses should a customer unexpectedly file for bankruptcy.

The Risks of Bankruptcy

The availability of bankruptcy poses a real risk for a company that extends credit to its customers. For example, assume that a small business, Prestige Supply, that sells office supplies lands a major contract with a large local company, the Jackson Corporation. Over time, the orders grow and this client represents over half of Prestige's revenues. Although the customer has always paid promptly, during the winter Jackson Corporation's payments start coming in slower, and occasionally only a partial payment is received.

Because Jackson's orders represent more than half of this office supply business, Prestige's owner is reluctant to discuss the billing and collection problems and hopes for the best. In late spring, the customer submits a large order for $80,000 of supplies. After the order is shipped, the client's total open account stands at $110,000. Two weeks later, Prestige's owner reads in the newspaper that Jackson Corporation has filed for Chapter 7 bankruptcy and is unlikely to pay its creditors more than five cents on the dollar. Not only has Prestige lost more than half its sales, but also is out about $100,000; this loss may be material to Prestige's financial health.

The prospect of bankruptcy adds a high degree of risk to the credit and collections cycle. When a small business has one or two major customers, a bankruptcy can lead to a devastating loss.

Sometimes the bankruptcy filing is expected, sometimes it is not; but a bankruptcy filing always has immediate consequences not only for the party filing for bankruptcy, but also for other parties who will be affected either directly or indirectly.

Who Might Go Bankrupt?

A small business will be adversely affected by the bankruptcy of any of the following:

1. an important customer
2. important suppliers
3. a lender or financier
4. the owner

The consequences of a customer's bankruptcy were described already. Bankruptcy of a supplier can be just as disruptive. For example, assume that Prestige Office Supplies gets its inventory from various suppliers. By custom, Prestige must make a 25 percent down payment for the goods and pay the remainder in thirty days. If one of Prestige's suppliers goes bankrupt, Prestige could lose a sizable down payment (although if it acts quickly it may be able to recover this money).

The bankruptcy of a lender or an individual who helps finance the business can also have a disastrous effect. This type of problem will immediately cause a cash shortage. Cash shortages are one of the leading causes of small business failures.

Bankruptcy of an Owner
The personal bankruptcy of one of the company's owners will have different consequences, depending on the legal form of the business. If the business is a sole proprietorship, the bankruptcy will normally close the business. In most states, the bankruptcy of a partner will cause a dissolution of a partnership. Although corporations are legal entities distinct from their owners, an individual bankruptcy filing can have an effect on a business even if that business is conducted as a corporation.

Because most loans to family businesses must also be cosigned by the owners of a business, the individual bankruptcy of one of the owners, with its resulting destruction of the individual's credit rating, may imperil the company's access to bank loans or other financing. The result may be a cash shortage that may in turn imperil the fiscal health of the business itself. The ultimate result may be the bankruptcy of the business.

Goals of Bankruptcy
Although the best-known feature of the bankruptcy system is the discharge of debts, our federal bankruptcy system also has the important goal of the orderly payment of creditors. Some businesses will inevitably fail in a competitive economy, and the bankruptcy system is designed to minimize the social costs that result from such business failures.

Bankruptcy Chapters
Although all bankruptcy filings are normally referred to as "bankruptcies," the federal bankruptcy code actually provides for five distinct types of filings:
1. Chapter 7 liquidations
2. Chapter 9 municipal bankruptcies
3. Chapter 11 reorganizations

4. Chapter 12 adjustments of debts of family farmers
5. Chapter 13 adjustments of debts of individuals with regular income

Each of these proceedings varies not only in detail, but in their goals. Municipal bankruptcies and Chapter 12 proceedings are limited to cities and farmers respectively and are beyond the scope of this chapter.

Liquidations and Reorganizations

In a Chapter 7 liquidation, an individual will be discharging debts and getting a "fresh start." A business involved in a liquidation normally distributes property to creditors and disappears. In a Chapter 11 reorganization, a business will normally continue operations but will be immune from creditors' claims during the pendency of the bankruptcy proceedings.

Any person, including an individual, partnership, or corporation, may file a voluntary bankruptcy petition under the Chapter 7 liquidation rules of the Bankruptcy Code. In a liquidation, the bankruptcy trustee will take possession of all of the debtor's nonexempt property, which will be sold for the benefit of the debtor's creditors. Individuals or businesses may also file for a Chapter 11 reorganization.

An individual debtor may also petition for a Chapter 13 adjustment of the debts of an individual with regular income. However, businesses cannot seek protection under Chapter 13, which is reserved for individual debtors. In a Chapter 11 or Chapter 13 proceeding, the bankruptcy trustee does not normally take possession of the debtor's property. This is where the phrase "debtor in possession" comes into play. The debtor remains in possession and control of the business.

The Federal Bankruptcy System

All bankruptcy actions must be brought in special federal bankruptcy courts rather than in state courts. There are bankruptcy courts in all major cities. Although procedures may vary depending on the court's local rules, a citizen who files for bankruptcy will generally get the same type of treatment in a bankruptcy court in any locality. This uniformity of treatment is an important feature of the bankruptcy system and facilitates recoveries of debts by out-of-state lenders and businesses.

When an individual or business is in bankruptcy, all claims must be brought in the bankruptcy court. In other words, if a business is being sued by three parties in three separate lawsuits, all these matters will be transferred to the bankruptcy court once a bankruptcy is filed. The bankruptcy courts and judges have surprisingly broad powers, including the right to determine a debtor's federal tax liability to the government.

Discharge of Debts

Even though a debt is legally valid, it may be discharged without full payment if the debtor files for bankruptcy. In the event the debtor has property, but not enough to pay all the debts in full, the creditors will recoup a percentage of their debts.

For example, assume that Acorn Products has liabilities (debts) of $100,000 and assets of only $40,000 after the administrative expenses of the bankruptcy have been deducted. If all the creditors are "unsecured" (have no collateral to claim), they will probably each receive 40 percent of their debts. (Here the assets were 40 percent of the debts—$40,000/$100,000.)

In many cases, creditors other than banks get nothing or next to nothing in a bankruptcy. Once an individual's debt is "discharged," it legally disappears and the debtor is under no legal obligation to pay it. At one time debtors could legally "revive" debts, but this can only happen today if they do it before the bankruptcy court—a very unlikely occurrence. However, some debtors will pay a legally unenforceable debt out of a moral obligation. It never hurts to suggest this course if your debt has been discharged.

When Debts Are Not Discharged

Occasionally, a debt will not be discharged in bankruptcy. Accordingly, the creditor will be able to commence collection efforts after the debt survives bankruptcy, for two general reasons:

1. The law provides that certain kinds of debts are never dischargeable in bankruptcy proceedings.
2. The debtor's own actions have made the debts nondischargeable.

These debts include certain customs duties and taxes such as Social Security taxes, debts created where fraud was involved, debts that the debtor failed to list on a schedule filed to the bankruptcy court, alimony and maintenance, child support, fiduciary obligations, any amounts owed for willful or malicious injury to persons or property, fines, penalties, and forfeitures. Finally, most education loans are normally not dischargeable.

General Effect on Creditors

The effect of a bankruptcy on a creditor normally depends on whether the creditor is a "secured" creditor or an "unsecured" creditor. Generally, secured creditors do well in bankruptcy, while unsecured creditors often get very little or nothing at all.

Secured versus Unsecured Creditors

A secured creditor is one who can claim specific collateral for repayment of a debt. Secured creditors do quite well in bankruptcy, because they can generally reach collateral that they can resell to satisfy the debt. For example, assume a credit seller has sold a piece of equipment and can claim that equipment in the event of the buyer's default. Even if the buyer goes bankrupt, the seller can normally recover the equipment, which can be sold to satisfy the debt.

However, even secured creditors can have problems in a bankruptcy. A secured creditor is secured only to the extent of the remaining value of outstanding debt. For example, if a car dealer has an automobile as collateral and the car is worth $10,000 but the remaining loan balance is merely $7,000, the creditor is "secured" to the extent of $7,000 and is an "unsecured" creditor for the $3,000 balance.

Typically, the bankruptcy trustee will ask creditors to take their collateral in lieu of other actions. This is a good course, especially where the fair market value of the collateral has dropped below the balance of the outstanding debt. In practice, the secured creditor would get little beyond the value of the actual collateral.

Fraudulent and Preferential Transfers

It is illegal for persons or corporations both inside and outside of bankruptcy to make a transfer to defraud creditors. In most states, this is a felony. Creditors may petition a court to set aside a fraudulent transfer of property. Even in the absence of evidence of actual fraud, creditors may be able to persuade a court that a conveyance was fraudulent when the debtor did not receive fair market value for the property. A gift of property, for example, may be characterized as a fraudulent conveyance when the effect is to deny creditors full payment of valid debts. However, when a good-faith purchaser receives property, the creditors may be without a remedy. Likewise, the transfer of exempt property is not normally a fraudulent conveyance.

How a Bankruptcy is Commenced

Bankruptcy proceedings are initiated by the debtor's filing a voluntary petition with the bankruptcy court asking for relief under Chapter 7 liquidation rules, Chapter 11 reorganization proceedings, or Chapter 13 individual debt adjustment arrangement. Alternately, a debtor's creditors may file an involuntary petition seeking a Chapter 7 liquidation or a Chapter 11 reorganization.

Although bankruptcy may take place only in federal court, there are state alternatives for insolvent debtors.

Voluntary and Involuntary Bankruptcy

There are two types of bankruptcy filings: voluntary and involuntary. A voluntary bankruptcy is started when an individual debtor or a business files with the local bankruptcy court a voluntary bankruptcy petition, a schedule of assets and liabilities, and a statement of affairs. A husband and wife may file a joint voluntary bankruptcy petition.

Voluntary Filings

Although at one time, a debtor had to be insolvent to file for bankruptcy, insolvency (inability to pay debts as they fall due) is no longer a prerequisite to a voluntary bankruptcy filing. A voluntary bankruptcy petition must be accompanied by schedules listing all creditors and the amount of debt, a statement detailing the financial affairs of the debtor, and a listing of the debtor's current income and expenses. The debtor must swear to the accuracy of all the information provided in the voluntary bankruptcy petition and accompanying schedules. Failure to list a debt will render the debt nondischargeable, while supplying false information may result in a denial of a debt discharge.

Involuntary Filings

Although debtors normally file for bankruptcy themselves, under certain circumstances creditors can force a debtor into involuntary bankruptcy. Individuals, businesses operating as partnerships, or corporations may be subject to an involuntary bankruptcy initiated by creditors. However, farmers and ranchers may not be forced into involuntary bankruptcy.

A debtor may be forced into involuntary bankruptcy only if the appropriate number of qualified creditors file a petition. If a debtor has fewer than twelve creditors, any creditor with at least

$500 of unsecured debt may file an involuntary petition. An unsecured debt is one for which there is no collateral. If a debtor has more than eleven creditors, at least three creditors who each have $5,000 of debts above any collateral must file an involuntary bankruptcy petition. For example, a creditor owed $10,000 who may claim collateral worth $4,000 could force a bankruptcy. A creditor owed $10,000 with collateral worth $6,000 could not.

Additionally, the creditors must prove to the court that a debtor is either 1) not paying debts as they become due or 2) has entered into an assignment for the benefit of creditors within the 120 days immediately before the filing of the involuntary bankruptcy petition.

When Should You Force a Debtor into Bankruptcy?

Although you may find that you have the legal ability to force a nonpaying customer into involuntary bankruptcy, you need to consider the consequences. First, if your debt is unsecured you may receive less in a bankruptcy proceeding. Even if your debt is secured you may have problems.

Creditors do not achieve perfect protection of their interests even after an involuntary petition has been filed, because the debtor still has the power to sell off assets for cash until the court provides otherwise. However, you can sometimes petition the court for the appointment of a temporary trustee to protect creditors' interests if there is a chance that the debtor will dissipate the assets of the business.

Additionally, the creditors who file an involuntary bankruptcy petition without cause may be liable for all of the debtor's attorney fees in connection with an involuntary petition that is ultimately dismissed by the bankruptcy court. If a creditor files an involuntary petition in bad faith, for example, merely to harass the debtor or to damage the debtor's business reputation, then the creditor may be forced to pay the debtor compensatory and even punitive damages.

Filing a Proof of Claim

To recover property through the bankruptcy court, creditors must file a timely proof of claim with the court. Failure to file a proof of claim will preclude the creditor from receiving any dividends from the bankruptcy trustee. The bankruptcy trustee has the power to determine whether the proof of claim is valid or invalid.

Effect on Collection and Repossession Activities

A bankruptcy filing has major consequences in your collections activities. When a bankruptcy petition is filed, it operates as an "automatic stay." Generally, all debt collection or repossession activities by creditors must come to an abrupt halt. Likewise, all lawsuits must be held in pendency while the bankruptcy action is before the bankruptcy court. The purpose of the automatic stay is to shift all collection and debtor-creditor matters to the bankruptcy court. For example, creditors may not enforce prior judgments or liens against either the debtor or the property of the estate. However, any criminal actions against the debtor will continue, as will actions for the collection of back alimony or child support payments.

The Automatic Stay

Although the automatic stay suspends a creditor's right to repossess collateral, secured creditors are allowed to petition the bankruptcy court for a relaxation of this rule. This procedure is known as requesting adequate protection. A secured creditor is a creditor who can claim specific property as collateral for repayment of a debt.

When a secured creditor requests adequate protection, the bankruptcy court will try to fashion a remedy so that the collateral is not impaired by the automatic stay, and the secured creditor will be no worse off after the bankruptcy filing. This would be important where the collateral is losing value over time. For example, if the collateral is a car that is being used by the debtor, in most cases the car will be worth less in the future because of wear and tear and because each new model year will reduce the value of the car as collateral for repayment of the debt.

The bankruptcy court might, for example, require the debtor to get a third party as a surety. The court also might require the debtor to start making periodic cash payments to the secured party. In some cases the court will allow the creditor to repossess and sell the collateral if no other alternative seems to protect the creditor's interest.

The automatic stay ends when the case is closed or dismissed or when the debtor receives a discharge of debts. A secured creditor can ask for relief from an automatic stay for cause, including lack of adequate protection of its interests. This essentially ends the automatic stay for that particular creditor.

Limited Right to Claim Goods

Even if your customer has declared bankruptcy, it may be possible to reclaim goods that you have shipped—if you act promptly. For example, suppose you have just sent a $20,000 shipment of goods to Hart Corporation, taking a $4,000 check as down payment. The check has been returned by your bank stamped: NSF, Not sufficient funds. You learn that Hart Corporation has filed for a Chapter 7 bankruptcy liquidation.

Seller's Remedy

Although it might seem that you have lost the $20,000 of goods to the bankruptcy trustee, who will use them in paying off all of Hart's creditors, you may be able to recover the debt if you act promptly.

Buyer's Remedy

On the other hand, if a buyer has partially paid for goods, and the seller files for bankruptcy, the buyer can recover the goods by rendering full payment of balance within ten days after the first installment for the goods was paid.

Right of the Trustee to Reclaim Past Payments

Even if a customer has paid you in full, a bankruptcy filing may upset the transaction. Surprisingly, in some cases the bankruptcy court can order you to return a cash payment that you legally received from one of your customers if the payment is found to be a "preferential transfer."

Preferential Transfers

The goal of bankruptcy is the orderly payment of creditors. Generally, all creditors must share equally in the property in the bankruptcy estate. If one creditor receives more than its proportionate share, this is considered a "preferential transfer." Preferential transfers can be made either with the consent or, at times, without the consent of the debtor. In either case, the bankruptcy trustee has the power to set aside preferential transfers for the benefit of all the creditors.

Generally a preferential transfer is a transfer made to or for the benefit of a creditor on account of an antecedent (prior) debt owed by the debtor to the creditor. Such transfers are made while the debtor is insolvent and within 90 days prior to the commencement of the bankruptcy proceedings, enabling the creditor to obtain a bankruptcy preference, unless paid within the "normal course of business," that is, 45 days. In other words, a preferential transfer to a creditor is for payment of a prior debt that results in that creditor's getting more than the normal share of the bankruptcy estate's property.

Preferential transfers do not include cash sales for new consideration or the payment of debts that occur in the ordinary course of business after the bankruptcy filing, nor do they include payments on loans made during the pendency of the bankruptcy proceeding. In other words, a business can still continue to operate and pay third parties despite the pendency of the bankruptcy action.

Insiders
In the case of insiders, the trustee may set aside transfers made within 90 days of the filing of the bankruptcy petition and for an additional period up to one year before the petition. Insiders are generally family members and close business associates. Besides making outright transfers of property, a debtor may make a preferential transfer by allowing a creditor to take a security interest in certain collateral.

Trustee
The bankruptcy trustee has a number of specific duties in administering a bankruptcy estate for the benefit of creditors. Specifically, the bankruptcy trustee must collect and convert to money all property in the estate, including fraudulent and preferential transfers. The trustee also has the power to set aside so-called "executory contracts," including long-term leases. Finally, the trustee must account for all property received and must make a final report and accounting of the administration of the bankruptcy estate to the federal bankruptcy court.

Effect of a Bankruptcy Filing on Cosigners
Inside or outside of bankruptcy, the liability of cosigners is complicated. In analyzing the rights and duties of cosigners, the first step is to determine if the cosigners wished to obligate themselves directly or merely wished to act as a surety who would pay only if the primary party did not. For example, if two brothers join together to buy an apartment building as an investment and they both cosign on a promissory note, there is no surety arrangement because both are considered principal or primary debtors.

On the other hand, the cosigner may have been merely promising to act as a surety for another party's debt. For example, if a teenager buys a car, signing a note for the unpaid balance, the car dealer would normally request a parent or other responsible adult to cosign the note. The parent is not incurring the debt but guaranteeing the debt of another.

Cosigners are not protected in bankruptcy unless an individual debtor has elected Chapter 13 protection. In other chapters, creditors can proceed directly against the cosigners when the original debtor declares bankruptcy.

CHAPTER PERSPECTIVE

It is vital for managers and business owners to understand the basics of the bankruptcy system, including the difference between Chapter 7 liquidations and Chapter 11 reorganizations. Although most debts can be discharged in a bankruptcy, some can survive and may still be collectible. Creditors need to be prompt in filing a proof of claim with the court to protect their interests in the bankruptcy proceeding.

Bankruptcy is commenced by a filing with the federal bankruptcy court. Although most filings are voluntary, in some cases creditors can force an involuntary bankruptcy filing. Once the bankruptcy is filed, the automatic stay precludes all collection and repossession activities during the pendency of the bankruptcy proceedings.

A bankruptcy filing can alter the relationships of the parties. For example, the bankruptcy trustees may be able to recover preferential transfers, including monies paid to you by the debtor. Buyers and sellers both need to know the rules so they can exercise important rights immediately after a filing.

Glossary

Acceptance also known as a "trade acceptance," a time draft drawn by a seller and accepted by the buyer of goods. Trade acceptances can be sold to raise cash.

Accommodation endorser a second endorser on commercial paper, who signs to guarantee payment of the check or note.

Account receivable money owed on a current account by a debtor; normally arises from the sale of goods or services.

Accounts receivable aging schedule that segregates accounts receivable by age for analysis.

Accrual basis accounting convention whereby income is recognized when earned, not when cash is received. Expenses are matched against the revenues they help produce.

Adjustable rate a loan interest rate that is not fixed, but varies along with some other financial measure or interest rate, such as the prime rate.

After-acquired clause a clause in a security agreement that allows a secured creditor to claim as collateral property that the debtor will obtain after the debt is incurred.

Artisan's lien a lien against property that has been constructed or repaired to force repayment of mechanics and artisans for labor on the property. The lien may have priority in the event of liquidation.

Assignment a unilateral contract right that lets one party transfer the right to performance or the right to payment under a contract.

Assignment for the benefit of creditors state law alternative to bankruptcy in which a debtor's business assets are transferred to a trustee to be liquidated for the benefit of creditors.

Assumption taking upon oneself another's mortgage obligation. Certain mortgages allow a buyer to assume the seller's mortgage.

Attach, attachment process of creating a security interest in property that allows a creditor to claim the property as collateral.

Audit in accounting, the inspection of the accounting records and procedures of a business and the formulation of an opinion about the entity's financial statements by a CPA.

Average collection period the average time required to collect a company's debts.

Bad debts debts owed to the business that have been determined to be uncollectible (also called "uncollectible accounts").

Balance sheet financial statement that lists assets, liabilities, and equity (also called the "Statement of Financial Position").

Banker's acceptance a time draft, drawn on and accepted by a bank. Used extensively to finance foreign sales transactions.

Bankruptcy federal remedy that allows the discharge of debts of individuals and businesses and the orderly payment of creditors.

Bearer party holding commercial paper such as a check.

Bearer paper commercial paper payable "to bearer" or "to cash." When commercial paper such as a check is in bearer form, anyone in possession of the paper has the power to negotiate it.

Cash position the amount of cash held at a given date.

Cash-flow statement financial statement that illustrates a company's sources and uses of cash.

Chapter 7 bankruptcy bankruptcy procedure calling for appointment of a trustee to take title to debtor's nonexempt property for the benefit of creditors. Chapter 7 bankruptcies are called liquidations.

Closed end credit a credit transaction in which the dollar amount is fixed, for example, credit extended to buy a particular asset such as a car.

Collateral property used as security for a loan or extension of credit. Upon nonpayment, a creditor may have collateral sold to satisfy the unpaid debt.

Commercial paper checks, drafts, and notes. Commercial paper also refers to short-term obligations issued by corporations and banks with idle cash.

Commercially reasonable manner accomplished according to normal business procedures without surprise requirements or unfair exclusionary tactics.

Compilation assembly of a client's financial data into financial statements by a Certified Public Accountant. A compilation is a lower level of service than an audit.

Composition a state law alternative to bankruptcy in which creditors agree to accept less than full repayment of a debtor's obligations.

Conveyance transfer, usually by sale, of property.

Cooling-off period period in which a consumer may avoid being obligated on a transaction. The period varies according to the specific law.

Cosigner party that signs a contract or commercial paper, thereby becoming obligated to share responsibility to pay the debt.

Credit application written form provided by a creditor or seller to a borrower or customer to assist the decision on making a loan or granting credit.

Credit bureau for-profit business that investigates a party's credit history and provides information to subscribing lenders and others.

Credit insurance insurance that guarantees the collectibility of accounts receivable.

Credit scoring system a system used in the credit application process that allows a creditor to rate the relative credit strength of a party seeking a loan or credit.

Creditor a business or person who extends credit or makes a loan.

Current assets cash and "near cash" that will be turned into cash within one year or within the operating cycle, whichever is shorter.

Current liabilities debts that will fall due within one year or within the operating cycle, whichever is shorter.

Days sales outstanding average number of days required to collect an account receivable.

Default failure to pay an obligation as promised. After a default a creditor has certain remedies against the debtor. Default is typically defined in a loan or credit agreement.

Deficiency judgment court order allowing a creditor to attach a borrower's or customer's property even though it is not collateral for the obligation.

Demand note a promissory note that is payable on demand—at any time it is presented for payment.

Direct write-off method an accounting method that recognizes bad debt expense when accounts receivable are deemed uncollectible. Although required for tax purposes, the method is not allowed for financial accounting purposes.

Disabling option in lieu of repossessing collateral, a creditor may render the collateral nonoperational.

Discount a reduction in purchase price if prompt payment is made.

Drafts commercial paper in which the drawer obligates the drawee to pay a named payee who is often the drawer. The drawee is not obligated until the draft is accepted for payment.

Endorser party that signs a negotiable instrument, such as a check, to transfer and negotiate it to another party such as a bank.

Equal Credit Opportunity Act (ECOA) federal law prohibiting discrimination in the granting of credit.

Executory contract contract that has not been fully performed.

Exempt property in bankruptcy, property that an individual debtor may retain. Creditors have access only to the debtor's nonexempt property.

Factor party whose business is to collect another firm's accounts receivable for a commission.

Factoring financing transaction in which a factor buys or obtains another firm's accounts receivable. The factor pays less than the face value of the accounts receivable but receives full payment when they fall due, thereby making a profit.

Fair Credit Billing Act (FCBA) federal law regulating correction of billing errors.

Fair Credit Reporting Act (FCRA) federal law regulating credit bureaus and providing consumers with remedies to correct inaccurate credit reports.

Fair Debt Collection Practices Act (FDCPA) federal law regulating collection agencies.

Federal Reserve Board federal board that oversees U.S. banking and monetary policy.

Financing statement form that establishes a secured creditor's rights and priority to collateral.

Fixture personal property that is so affixed to real property that it legally becomes part of the real property.

Fixtures filing a special financing statement used with fixtures.

Foreclosure judicial procedure in which a lender obtains title to a debtor's real property as a remedy for default.

Fraudulent conveyance transfer of property made with the intent to defraud creditors; often a crime.

FTC consumer goods rule federal rule requiring that collateral must be sold after repossession if the consumer has paid 60 percent of its purchase price.

FTC holder-in-due-course rule federal rule barring repossession of a consumer's collateral in specific cases.

GAAP generally accepted accounting principles. Conventions and procedures that accountants normally apply.

Garnishments legal procedure whereby a creditor can attach a party's wages or bank accounts.

Guarantor party that guarantees payment of a debt.

Holder in due course a party who in good faith pays value for a negotiable instrument (commercial paper) without notice of any defect. Such a party is favored by the law.

Implied by law a contract may be presupposed by law even without a written document.

Income statement a financial statement listing a party's income and expenses (also called the profit and loss statement).

Itemization process of listing or detailing.

Letter of credit bank instrument that guarantees the bank's payment of a customer's obligation.

Lien charge against property as security for a debt.

Line of credit a prearrangement whereby a lender agrees to make future cash advances without the need to submit new loan applications.

Liquidations a Chapter 7 bankruptcy proceeding in which the debtor surrenders property to creditors. An individual may retain exempt property and may also discharge debts.

Maker the person who undertakes obligation to pay a promissory note.

Marginal risk a party who may not be creditworthy.

Matching rule an accounting convention that expenses should be matched against the revenues they help to produce.

Mechanic's lien a lien by an artisan on property that has been improved. Such a lien discourages sale of the property, giving the artisan leverage.

Mortgage security device that allows real property to be used as collateral for repayment of the loan. When the property itself is being purchased it is known as a purchase money mortgage.

Negotiable something that can be sold or transferred to another party.

Nondischargeable in bankruptcy, a debt that legally cannot be discharged by the court.

Nonnegotiable something, usually a financial instrument, that cannot be sold or transferred to another party.

Nonrecourse a type of debt on which liability excludes the personal assets of the borrower.

Notice of sale notice to a debtor or others that collateral will be sold.

Open account a relationship between a buyer and seller in which the debt is unsecured by collateral or a note, as in a charge account.

Open-end credit a credit arrangement that is flexible in amount, such as a credit card account.

Operating cycle the time in which it takes to turn cash into inventory and back into cash.

Order paper negotiable paper, such as a check, that is made out to a named payee, rather than "to cash" or "to bearer."

Payee on a negotiable instrument, such as a check or note, the party who is to receive payment.

Pendency the period during which a legal case is proceeding.

Percentage past due the portion of a company's accounts receivable that is overdue.

Perfect to proceed legally to prioritize one creditor's right to collateral over another creditor's right.

Performance bond a surety device that guarantees satisfaction in the event of nonfulfillment of a contract.

Pledge transfer possession of collateral, but not transfer of title to it.

Prepayment payment made in advance of the time due.

Promissory note a written obligation in which a maker accepts obligation to pay a payee. Also called a *note*.

Proof of claim a bankruptcy court form used by a creditor to request that an unpaid bill be paid by the bankruptcy court.

Realizations accounts receivable that are collected.

Receivable account receivable.

Receivables turnover the number of times a firm's average accounts receivable are collected during a year.

Receiver a party appointed by a court to run a business.

Recourse the right to demand payment of a debt not only from the borrower, but also from the endorser or guarantor.

Regulation Z federal regulations containing the Truth in Lending Act.

Repossession physical seizure of collateral by a creditor.

Review assembly of a client's financial data into financial statements by a Certified Public Accountant. A review includes analytical study of the numbers. A review is a lower level of service than an audit, but higher than a compilation.

Secured creditor a creditor who has collateral.

Security interest a creditor's right in collateral.

Service of process process of delivering legal papers to a party involved in a court case.

Sight draft a draft payable on presentation (in contrast to a time draft that is payable in the future).

Skip a defaulting credit customer who moves and leaves no forwarding address.

Strict foreclosure a creditor's seizure of property with no intent to resell.

Super priority having priority higher than other claims and liens.

Surety device a device such as a lien that gives a creditor an advantage, such as recourse to collateral.

Time draft a draft payable at a future date.

Time note a note payable at a future date.

Tracing skips process of locating defaulting customers who have moved and whose whereabouts are unknown.

Trade acceptance a time draft that has been accepted by the seller of goods allowing the acceptance to be sold.

Trade discount a percentage discount allowed to business purchasers.

Trustee in a Chapter 7 bankruptcy, the individual appointed to liquidate the bankruptcy estate for the benefit of creditors.

Truth in Lending Act (TIL) federal law governing credit disclosures including the annual percentage rate and finance charge.

UCC Form 1 a security agreement allowing a creditor to attach specific property as collateral.

UCC Form 2 a financing statement that gives a creditor priority to collateral against other creditors.

Usury law state law setting a maximum interest rate.

Working capital cash and near cash.

Workout an informal procedure allowing a debtor more favorable repayment terms.

Write-off process of removing accounts receivable from the books when they are deemed uncollectible.

Index